Writing Outside the Nation

TRANSLATION | TRANSNATION

SERIES EDITOR   **EMILY APTER**

Writing Outside the Nation BY AZADE SEYHAN

AZADE SEYHAN

Writing Outside the Nation

PRINCETON UNIVERSITY PRESS

PRINCETON AND OXFORD

Copyright © 2001 by Princeton University Press
Published by Princeton University Press, 41 William Street,
Princeton, New Jersey 08540
In the United Kingdom: Princeton University Press,
3 Market Place, Woodstock, Oxfordshire OX20 1SY

Library of Congress Cataloging-in-Publication Data

Seyhan, Azade.
Writing outside the nation / Azade Seyhan.
p.   cm. — (Translation/transnation)
Includes bibliographical references and index.
ISBN 0-691-05098-8 (alk. paper)—ISBN 0-691-05099-6 (pbk. : alk. paper)
1. Literature—Minority authors—History and criticism. 2. Immigrants' writings—
History and criticism. 3. Literature, Modern—20th century—History and criticism.
4. Multiculturalism. I. Title. II. Series.
PN491.5 .S49 2000
809'.8920691—dc21   00-032639

This book has been composed in Minion with Gill Sans display.

The paper used in this publication meets the minimum requirements
of ANSI/NISO Z39.48-1992 (R1997) (*Permanence of Paper*)

www.pup.princeton.edu

Printed in the United States of America

10 9 8 7 6 5 4 3 2 1
10 9 8 7 6 5 4 3 2 1
[pbk]

To my Mother

Hazime Seyhan

Chemist and Alchemist of Tales

CONTENTS

vii

ACKNOWLEDGMENTS

I would like to extend my sincere thanks to my editor Mary Murrell of Princeton University Press for her support of this study and her vision and intelligence. The lives and stories of many women friends and colleagues, Maria Alter, Diana Behler, the late Katrin Burlin, Oliva Cardona, Yeşim Doğan, Alice Donohue, Peggy Hollyday, Anna Kuhn, Catherine Lafarge, Imke Meyer, Kamakshi Murti, Maria Cristina Quintero, Jacquie Ream, and Nona Smith, continue to inspire me, and their support during various stages of this project has been invaluable. The thirty-six Bryn Mawr students from diverse cultural, linguistic, and national backgrounds who took my course Ethnographies of Memory: Women's Narratives on Modern Migrancy, Exile, and Diasporas tested the many ideas of this book and guided me through difficult passages. I am grateful to Mary Patterson McPherson, the former president of Bryn Mawr College, and my many colleagues there for providing an institutional culture where cosmopolitan imaginations and modes of knowledge are cherished.

John and Leslie Alexander, Walter Andrews, Önol Bilkur, Cynthia Bisman, Anne and the late Bob Boyden, Dale and Ruth Hultengren, Francisco LaRubia-Prado, Wolfgang Lorenz, Yüksel and Inci Pazarkaya, Jeffrey Peck, John Pizer, Hinrich Seeba, and Brett Wheeler have provided intellectual and emotional sustenance throughout the years. I am indebted to my fellow Turkish Germanist Ülker Gökberk for her invaluable critical feedback. My brother Selim Seyhan keeps me going with his irrepressible humor and his wisdom. My son Kerim Yasar, my best critic, suggested the title of this book. And Kurt, the family friend who is no longer with us, kept us all sane through difficult times.

This study was partially supported by a National Endowment for the Humanities Summer Stipend (1995). Parts of this manuscript were presented at national and international conferences and symposia. I would like to thank all the organizers for the opportunity they offered me to share my work. Some passages from chapter 4 were previously published in "Geographies of Memory: Protocols of Writing in the Borderlands," in *Multiculturalism in Transit: A German-American Exchange,* edited by Klaus J. Millich and Jeffrey M. Peck (Providence, R.I.: Berghahn, 1998), and an earlier version of the essay on Emine Sevgi Özdamar in chapter 5 was published in modified form in "Lost in Translation: Re-Membering the Mother Tongue in Emine Sevgi Özdamar's *Das Leben ist eine Karawanserei,*" *German Quarterly* 69 (1996). All translations from original German and Turkish texts are mine. Available English translations for these are listed in works cited.

PART ONE

Neither Here/Nor There: The Culture of Exile

> There [in the homeland] nature appears more human and understanding, a dim memory reflects, through the transparent present, sharply outlined images of the world, and so one enjoys through memory a double world, free of all cruelty and violence, a world that is the magical, poetic, fable-like projection of our senses.
>
> Novalis, *Heinrich von Ofterdingen*

> It may be said that writers in my position, exiles or emigrants or expatriates, are haunted by some sense of loss, some urge to reclaim, to look back, even at the risk of being mutated into pillars of salt. But if we do look back, we must also do so in the knowledge—which gives rise to profound uncertainties—that our physical alienation from India almost inevitably means that we will not be capable of reclaiming precisely the thing that was lost; that we will, in short, create fictions, not actual cities or villages, but invisible ones, imaginary homelands, Indias of the mind.
>
> Salman Rushdie, *Imaginary Homelands*

The words of the eighteenth-century German Romantic poet Novalis (Friedrich von Hardenberg) resonate beyond the boundaries of their history and geography and are poignantly rearticulated by a contemporary master of the arts of memory. Salman Rushdie's critical sentiment stands as a testimony to the labor of remembrance that reclaims the lost experience of another time and place in language and imagination. The work of commemoration is often the only means of releasing our (hi)stories from subjugation to official or institutionalized regimes of forgetting. Remembering is an act of lending coherence and integrity to a history interrupted, divided, or compromised by instances of loss. We engage in history not only as agents and actors but also as narrators or storytellers. In narrative, we may be able to redress forcibly forgotten experiences, allow the silences of history to come to word, and imagine alternative scripts of the past.[1] Our understanding of the present is invariably predicated on actual or imagined links to, or ruptures from, a recalled past.

This is a narrative about narratives, more specifically, it is an investigation of stories and histories that recuperate losses incurred in migration, dislocation, and translation, those deeply felt signs and markers of our age. The recent history of forced or voluntary migrations, massive transfers of population, and traveling and transplanted cultures is seen as part and parcel of the postwar, postindustrial, and postcolonial experience. Understandably, narratives that originate at border crossings cannot be bound by national borders, languages, and literary and critical traditions. Born of crisis and change, suffering alternately from amnesia and too much remembering, and precariously positioned at the interstices of different spaces, histories, and languages, they seek to name and configure cultural and literary production in their own terms and to enter novel forms of inter/transcultural dialogue. This is not an easy task, since the heterogeneity of culture is not a given but is predicated on interaction, contestation, and possibly confrontation. In the chaotic dynamics of a world constantly on the move, "Culture . . . shifts from being some sort of inert, local substance to being a rather more volatile form of difference,"[2] and "Intercultural dialogue unleashes the demons of history."[3] Although the contemporary tales of migration, exile, and displacement are often seen as mirroring the fragmented consciousness of postmodern culture itself and certainly participate in many of the aesthetic and literary legacies of the latter, they part company with it in terms of certain historical and geographical boundaries. For if the postmodern is to be defined either as a sociohistorical epoch or a philosophical or aesthetic school of the late-twentieth-century Western world, then it would be impossible to contain the culturally and temporally diverse articulations of diasporic experience in the postmodern syntax.

Emily Apter considers exilic consciousness, in its successive generational articulations, "a deeply engrained constant of the field [comparative literature], shaping its critical paradigms and providing a kind of overarching historical paradigm for the ontology of the discipline." For Apter, postcolonial theory, as an expression of exilic experience, has inherited "the mantle of comparative literature's historical legacy" by politicizing postwar criticism and investing it with a critical idiom synthesized from a host of cultural languages.[4] In reference to Homi Bhabha's turn to fictional texts to articulate such theoretical notions as hybridity and in-betweenness, she correctly observes that "[t]he task of translating nuanced modalities of split, interiorized exilic ontology into a curricular mandate would appear reductive and caricatural at best" (92). Although Bhabha instrumentalizes fictional texts to perform theoretical tasks, he does not always engage them in a genuine dialogue. Notwithstanding the power and ubiquitousness of the image, fictional texts still remain a forceful medium in understanding the turbulent global culture at the end of the millennium. However, when they are abstracted away from the specificity of historical and political contexts to serve as theoretical fictions, their capital of cultural nuance disappears in the haze of totalizing concepts. The idea of hybridity as a constant of all modes of cultural expression and as the "third space" that enables the emergence of multiple positions, for example, forgoes an analysis of actual social spaces where cultures interact and literature as an institution of cultural memory intervenes. Similarly, the highly productive investigation of textual constructions and cultural affiliations that shape the notion of nation and the transformation of the losses incurred in displacement and migration "into the language of metaphor"[5] calls for a more nuanced historical understanding of literary texts. Without a story and actors/characters to flesh out the skeletal abstraction of such statements as, "The perplexity of the living must not be understood as some existential, ethical anguish of the empiricism of everyday life in 'the eternal living present,' that gives liberal discourse a rich social reference in moral and cultural relativism,"[6] theoretical enunciations can lose their footing on conceptual ground and turn into their own parodies. Literary expressions of contemporary sociopolitical formations offer critical insights into the manifold meanings of history and take us to galaxies of experience where no theory has gone before.

Mexican critic and performance artist Guillermo Gómez-Peña defines his role as a border artist in terms of a context-specific hermeneutic practice that supersedes Hans-Georg Gadamer's theory of intersubjective understanding. For Gadamer, understanding takes place in the common ground of language. The world exists not as an impersonal object but as a structure of shared understanding, and the medium that makes this understanding possible is language. Language embodies and enacts the totality of our experience of the world: "[I]n language, the world represents itself."[7]

This experience of the world transcends all temporalities and relationships and envelops us within a horizon of language. We participate in human experience through a dialogue sustained by shared tradition. Gadamer argues against the naïveté of "so-called historicism" (283) that does not reflect on its own historicity, that is, does not recognize in its object (history) its own otherness and, therefore, fails to understand the elemental relation of identity to alterity. Although Gadamer maintains that the desire for understanding originates in the self's experience of its otherness (283), and understanding is always the interpretation of the other, the realization of historical understanding takes place in the fusion of familiarity and foreignness. And this fusion comes very close to consuming the foreign. The ontological ground of understanding in language, the fusion of horizons in interpretation, cannot explain other, vastly different cultures that do not share our histories. By the same token, Emmanuel Lévinas's new ontology, which stresses not the contemplation of being, but being engaged with "the dramatic event of being-in-the-world,"[8] and whose ethical dimension resides in the relation to the other, being face to face with the other, does not relate to the real social situation. Lévinas's ethics of the relation to the other, which makes forgetting, forgiving, sympathy, and love possible, is also predicated on language, on speaking to the other. "To understand a person is already to speak to him," Lévinas writes. "Speech delineates an original relation. The point is to see the function of language not as subordinate to the *consciousness* we have of the presence of the other, or of his proximity, or of our community with him, but as a condition of that conscious realization" (6). By inscribing into the structure of speech the ethical code of opening oneself to the other's experience, Lévinas prevents the assimilation of the other's horizon into one's own. Iain Chambers maintains that the ethical determinant of Lévinas's concept of dialogue acknowledges the impossibility of speaking for the other and urges that we— that I—inscribe that impossibility, that limit, into my discourse and . . . recognise my being not for itself but for being with and for the other. . . . Lévinas proposes the open web of language."[9] The ennobling character of dialogue, however, remains a philosophical abstraction when the content and nuance of dialogue(s) with others are not embodied, witnessed, or recorded in social and political spaces.

To resist the danger of solipsism that threatens the idea of "dialogue" as universal equalizer, Gómez-Peña propogates a brand of border art that focuses on "the need to generate a binational dialogue, the need to create cultural spaces for others."[10] He radically (though not reflectively) politicizes the notion of intercultural dialogue when he defines it as "a two-way, ongoing communication between peoples and communities that enjoy equal negotiating powers." The proof of any real celebration of difference is the right of the other to participate fully in defining the terms of the dialogue. The realization of a dialogue between cultures involves real tasks, such as learning the languages, literatures, histories, and political systems of others. It encourages travels "south and east, with frequency and humility, not as cultural tourists but as civilian ambassadors" (48). By advocating a genuine engagement with the concrete forms of expression of other cultures, Gómez-Peña counters a hermeneutic approach where neither the anatomy nor the economy of a rhetoric of otherness has changed much since romanticism. As cultures collide, unite, and are reconfigured in real and virtual space in unprecedented ways, postcolonial, migrant, and border-crossing theorists and artists fine-tune received critical traditions in order to safeguard historical and cultural specificities. Ultimately, every theory of postcolonial, transnational, or diasporic literature and art is most convincingly articulated and performed by works of literature and art themselves. Literature as an institution and literary fiction as an expression of human experience predate their theoretical articulation, a truism perhaps best exemplified by Aristotle's *Poetics*. Literature as social document resists the erasure of geographical, historical, and cultural differences. Friedrich Nietzsche, Sigmund Freud, and Walter Benjamin's enduring insights into memory, mourning, history, language, and translation gain in critical astuteness through the stories of diasporic and exilic experience. Arjun Appadurai convincingly argues that a cultural study of globalization and "new cosmopolitanisms" requires an understanding of how imagination functions as a major social force in the contemporary world, creating alternative prescriptions for identity, agency, and solidarity.[11] "Like the myths of small-scale society as rendered in the anthropological classics of the past," he writes, "contemporary literary fantasies tell us something about displacement, disorientation, and agency in the contemporary world" (58).

"Two moves amount to a fire," a Turkish saying goes. Multiple migrations end in the loss of our homes, possessions, and memorabilia. When the smoke clears, we are faced with charred pieces of identification, shards of language, burned tongues, and cultural fragments. However, from the site of this fire, the phoenix of a transnational, bi- and multilingual literature has arisen. Some of the best contemporary literary works are published by writers writing in a language not their own. Michael Ondaatje, author of *The English Patient* and Booker Prize recipient, is a Sri Lankan-Dutch resident of Canada. Writers born into Spanish, such as Pulitzer Prize winner Oscar Hijuelos, Rosario Ferré, and Ana Castillo have emerged as brilliant voices of American English. This trend in bilingual poetics is not confined to the English-speaking world. Major European literatures are no longer under the monopoly of monolingual writing. Some of the most innovative artists of the German language are native speakers of Turkish, Arabic, Italian, Spanish, or Czech. Arabic is the mother tongue of many prominent French writers (e.g., Assia Djebar, Abdelkebir Khatibi, Amin Maalouf). And modern Italian literature is enriched by the work of italophone writers from Ethiopia, Morocco, Tunisia, and Senegal.[12] Today's writing erupts at unexpected junctures and represents new linkages of disparate and distant places and identities. Novel constellations of writing flourish, as Cuban writers move to Paris, Jamaican writers to the States, and Japanese writers emerge in Germany. Hélène Cixous, herself a multilingual writer, sees the very position of writing analogous to writing in a foreign country. Writing is a "journey toward strange sources of art that are foreign to us. 'The thing' does not happen here, it happens somewhere else, in a strange and foreign country."[13] Writing between borders and languages, many writers plot complex strategies of translating in an effort to negotiate their loyalties to nation, language, ethnicity, class, and gender.

If language is the single most important determinant of national identity, as many have argued, and narratives (specifically, epics and novels) institute and support national myths and shape national consciousness (e.g., the Finnish epic *Kalevala*), what happens when the domain of national language is occupied by nonnative writers, writers whose native, mother, home, or community language is not the one they write in? Etienne Balibar maintains that the national language unites people of different classes or people who were never in direct communication and connects them up "with an origin which may at any moment be actualized and which has as its content the *common act* of their own exchanges, of their discursive communication, using the instruments of spoken language."[14] This language offers its speakers a framework of reality and identity they can appropriate in their own way. There is no contradiction between the institution of one national language and the practice of other languages, for example, "class languages," in the nation, asserts Balibar, since they are all projected back to "the mother tongue," the idea of a common origin that becomes a metaphor for the loving ties between fellow nationals. Nevertheless, Balibar states that although "the linguistic community induces a terribly constraining ethnic memory," the construction of identity in language "is by definition *open*" (98). The linguistic community as collective memory naturalizes new idioms and glosses over their origins. Thus, " 'the second generation' immigrant . . . inhabits the national language (and through it the nation itself) in a manner as spontaneous, as 'hereditary' and as imperious, so far as affectivity and the imaginary are concerned," as the native (99). Although the national language community appears as if it had always existed, it cannot script the destiny of future generations or assimilate them.

Once we accept the loss of stable communities and the inevitability of exile, then the interdependency of linguistic and cultural experiences both at the local and the global level becomes self-evident. Thus, despite coercively manufactured and enforced national antinomies and fortified borders, history and geography are transfigured in new maps and new types of dialogic links. However, our critical terms for literary study are not adequate for an exploration and explanation of these transfigurations. The emergent literatures of deterritorialized peoples and literary studies beyond the confines of national literature paradigms have as yet have no name or configuration. In fact, as Appadurai has noted, even "postnational formations," that is, contemporary forms of complex nonterritorial and transnational alliances and allegiances, cannot be defined within the lexicon of available political languages.[15] "[N]o idiom has yet emerged," he writes, "to capture the collective interests of many groups in translocal solidarities, cross-border mobilizations, and postnational identities" (166). Descriptions such as *exilic, ethnic, migrant,* or *diasporic* cannot do justice to the nuances of writing between histories, geographies, and cultural practices. Although as critics we do not have the language commensurate with our task, we have the responsibility to reflect, problematize, and preface the terms we employ. In this study, I do not use the terms *exilic, diasporic,* or *ethnic writing* in a strictly technical sense, but as signifiers of texts conceived in and operative between two or more languages and cultural heritages. The subjects of this study speak with varying degrees of accents indicating national, ethnic, geographical, and historical origins and the transitions that have shaped the memory of these origins. The field of investigation of such scholarly journals as *MELUS (Multiethnic Literatures of the United States)* or *Diaspora* is not limited to strictly "ethnic," "migrant," or "diasporic" texts; these descriptive categories are often collapsed. The texts of my investigation are mostly written in a language that is not the writer's own. Their idiomatic status is bi- or multilingual. They are the voices of transplanted and translated subjects. As the bilingual Puerto Rican author Rosario Ferré states, "Only a writer who has experienced the historical fabric, the inventory of felt moral and cultural existence embedded in a given language, can be said to be a bilingual writer."[16] Ferré correctly observes that bilingual writers imagine translation not only as a literary but also as a historical project, as an interpretive task that attempts to explain a complex cultural equation subject to the changing fortunes of time and place.

In spite of the difficulty involved in finding a language to discuss literatures written in a second language or bilingually and literary phenomena that have parted ways with national literature paradigms, I have tried to distinguish between a few strictly technical definitions. Following Appadurai's usage of the term *transnational*, I understand transnational literature as a genre of writing that operates outside the national canon, addresses issues facing deterritorialized cultures, and speaks for those in what I call "paranational" communities and alliances. These are communities that exist within national borders or alongside the citizens of the host country but remain culturally or linguistically distanced from them and, in some instances, are estranged from both the home and the host culture. *Ethnic* is a loaded and contested term. Ethnicity, as understood for the purposes of this discussion, does not refer to a stable ethnic identity but rather to a culturally constructed concept regulated by specific historical conditions. For example, the first-generation Turkish-German writers of Germany, who immigrated to Germany in the sixties and began publishing shortly thereafter, are technically (im)migrant writers. However, since Turks have, in effect, been transformed from a migrant population into an ethnic minority, the second-generation Turkish-German writers, who were born and educated in Germany, can be considered producers of an ethnic culture. Chicano/a writers of the United States who have never had Mexican citizenship would technically be writing ethnic literature. In art and literature, ethnicity is often a self-proclaimed form of cultural identification. In literary texts, ethnicity is recognizable as a linguistic mode, cultural idiom, or discursive practice. Nevertheless, the term *ethnic literature* implies that its signified is not an integral or natural part of a land's literary history. The same is true of immigrant literature. Although many writers of this study such as Eva Hoffman, Rafik Schami, or Emine Sevgi Özdamar have actually *immigrated* to the countries where they now publish and are permanent residents or citizens of the country of immigration, to call their work immigrant writing (the term *MigrantInnenliteratur* [migrants' literature] is routinely used in German), though technically correct, would suggest that this body of cultural production constitutes a transitory tradition in national literary history. Cathy N. Davidson notes that English writers "have rarely been called 'immigrants.' The term needs to be used circumspectly, with an awareness that who or who is not an 'immigrant' often changes with a group's increasing assimilation to dominant cultural norms."[17] Therefore, I prefer the terms *diasporic, exilic* (the stress here is on voluntary not forced), or *transnational* literature, except in the case of texts that represent a conscious ethnic allegiance.

In current usage, the term *diaspora* has moved into a broadly conceived semantic realm. Although it originally designated the forced dispersion of major religious and ethnic groups, such as the Jews and the Armenians, a dispersion "precipitated by a disaster often of a political nature,"[18] in the modern age, greatly diversified exile and ethnic communities, expatriates, refugees, "guest" workers, and other dispossessed groups sharing a common heritage have moved into the semantic domain of the term. In their discussion of the problems concerning the conditions and limits of terminology, Gérard Chaliand and Jean-Pierre Rageau state that although in reference to the Jewish people the term *diaspora* is unequivocal, it gets contested when applied to other religious, ethnic, or minority groups. In an attempt to define the larger context and modern uses of the term, they suggest the following criteria that "constitute the specific fact of a diaspora" (xiv). These are, in addition to forced dispersion from a center to foreign regions, "the role played by *collective memory, which transmits both the historical facts that precipitated the dispersion and a cultural heritage (broadly understood)*—the latter being often religious" (xv) and "*the will to survive as a minority by transmitting a heritage*" (xvi). The final criterion in defining a group as a diaspora is "*the time factor*" (xvii) that bears testimony to the survival and adaptation of a group possessing the above characteristics. In a comprehensive study on global diasporas, Robin Cohen also sets similar criteria and adds that the memory of the single traumatic event that caused the dispersion binds the members of the exiled group together by continuously reminding them of the great historic injustice they suffered. Cohen also asserts that diasporic communities are committed not only to the restoration and maintenance of the homeland but to its very creation. The latter refers to the notion of imagined homelands that only resemble "the original history and geography of the diaspora's natality in the remotest way." In this context Cohen cites Kurds and Sikhs for whom "a homeland is clearly an *ex post facto* construction."[19]

Cohen emphasizes that globalization has radically expanded the scope of the study of modern diasporas. In the contemporary world, diasporas have the historic opportunity to create tolerance for plurality in host countries. Globalization has in many ways created opportunities for diasporas to emerge, survive, and thrive. Since global economic, political, and media powers are located in the major metropolises of the world, where diasporas are concentrated, the latter, by virtue of their own transnationalism, can benefit from the cosmopolitan character of these forces: "Deterritorialized, multilingual and capable of bridging the gap between global and local tendencies, diasporas are able to take advantage of the economic and cultural opportunities on offer."[20] Still other critics, writers, and artists explore the metaphoric designations and implications of the term. In his *First Diasporist Manifesto*, renowned painter R.B. Kitaj visualizes diasporist painting as a vigilant guardian of its memory of origin, a contemplation of passages, "a *Midrash* (exposition, exegesis of non-literal meaning) in paint," and a secular response to the sense of uprootedness, homelessness, and transcience that has our time in its grip.[21] In this sense, all "diasporist" art becomes a link that insures a form of continuity between different times—past, present, and future—rootedness and dispersion, and "rupture and momentum" and negotiates the stresses these transitions deploy (19).

In the broadest sense, then, "diasporic narratives" discussed in this study represent a conscious effort to transmit a linguistic and cultural heritage that is articulated through acts of personal and collective memory. In this way, writers become chroniclers of the histories of the displaced whose stories will otherwise go unrecorded. Literature tends to record what history and public memory often forget. Furthermore, it can narrate both obliquely and allegorically, thereby preserving what can be censored and encouraging interpretation and commentary in the public sphere. Through the lens of personal recollection and interpretation, the specificity of class, ethnic, and gender experiences gains a stature that is often erased, forgotten, or ignored in the larger management of public memory. I believe that paradigms of transnational and multiethnic writing in the American literary landscape provide critical clues for a better understanding of the nature and significance of new cultural identities in contemporary Europe. As Rushdie has correctly observed, "America, a nation of immigrants, has created great literature out of the phenomenon of cultural transplantation, out of examining the ways in which people cope with a new world."[22]

Since the United States and, more recently, Germany have come to represent the destination of choice for large and heterogeneous populations of immigrants, exiles, and transnational subjects, this study focuses mostly on nonnative writers living in these countries and writing in English and German, respectively. In this context, it is important to note that these writers' mastery of their literary languages is not the result of colonial experience but of migration, resettlement, and redefinition of identity. Therefore, the questions that inform the present project differ, to some extent, from the concerns of postcolonial studies. In this case, the diasporic writers and their compatriots do not share with their hosts the kind of historical, cultural, and linguistic intimacy (however problematic) that exists between the colonizer and the colonized. Nevertheless, voices of postcolonial theory are in ample evidence here. There are also distinct differences between writing in the American cultural mosaic and writing in the fairly homogeneous German cultural scene. Partly because of their temporal proximity to their cultures of origin and partly out of a determination to achieve intellectual legitimacy and to legitimize cultural difference, the works of the nonnative writers of Germany tend to be linguistically and historically more nuanced than those of their American counterparts. The German reading public and critics still categorize the work of non-German writers and artists as ethnic and minority literature and art and do not regard it as an integral part of the national culture.

Although the diversity of diasporic writing does not lend itself to abstract categorization, which would effectively erase or neutralize differences, the works discussed here share the common feature of being both creative and experimental and self-reflexive and theoretical. In other words, questions of speech and writing, fiction versus nonfiction, history and story, and official history and communal memory themselves become subjects of "fiction." This metanarrative impulse has taken diasporic and transnational writing to a high level of aesthetic experimentation and critical transformation. As important social documents of the culture(s) of dislocation and exile, literary and critical texts of diasporas serve as condensed archives of national, ethnic, and linguistic memories. In order to balance the specificity of individual accounts of exilic experience with an existential understanding of displacement, expatriation, and marginality, I have tried to discuss selected texts in conceptual frameworks of contiguity that link them to larger issues of identity, exclusion (from real or imagined communities), memory, language politics, translation, and the psychology of loss. The irreducible untranslatability of one's language and cultural idiom marks for many writers the space of exile and defines what I call diasporic pathos.

What are the implications and consequences of writing between national paradigms, "bilingually" or "multilingually"? Transnational writing can potentially redress the ruptures in history and collective memory caused by the unavailability of sources, archives, and recorded narratives. By uncovering obscure poetic traditions, discovering forgotten idioms and grammars, and restoring neglected individual and collective stories to literary history, it introduces the riches of hitherto neglected cultures into modern literary consciousness. In *Culture and Imperialism*, Edward Said suggests that we read the major works of the Western literarary canon and perhaps even all the cultural productions of the Western world "with an effort to draw out, extend, give emphasis and voice to what is silent or marginally present or ideologically represented (I have in mind Kipling's Indian characters) in such works."[23] Imagining and filling in omitted references to cross-cultural contexts and silences of history in the text—for example, the absence of French colonial history in Albert Camus's *L'Etranger* (67)—is an instance of "contrapuntal reading" (66). In an earlier piece on exile, Said writes that an exile's plurality of cultural experience gives rise to an awareness of simultaneous dimensions. Borrowing a phrase from music, Said terms this awareness *contrapuntal.* In Said's view, "for an exile, habits of life, expression, or activity in the new environment inevitably occur against the memory of these things in another environment. Thus both the new and the old environments are vivid, actual, occurring together contrapuntally."[24]

Texts that sensitize the reader to the power of language, its capacity to mark cultural difference, and its responsibility to respond creatively to cultural difference contribute new structures of knowledge to the body of criticism. Furthermore, the participation of the diasporic subject in the cultural life of the host country registers the moment when other literary and artistic forms of expression enter (Western) history. Through this dialectic (in its original sense as dialogue), the distance between the ports of departure and arrival appears to collapse; the migrant, exile, or voyager not only crosses the threshold into another history and geography but also steps into the role of an itinerant cultural visionary. In Salman Rushdie's words,

> The effect of mass migrations has been the creation of radically new types of human being: people who root themselves in ideas rather than places, in memories as much as in material things; people who have been obliged to defend themselves—because they are so defined by others—by their otherness; people in whose deepest selves strange fusions occur, unprecedented unions between what they were and where they find themselves. The migrant suspects reality: having experienced several ways of being, he understands their illusory nature. To see things plainly, you have to cross a frontier.[25]

The literary productions of diasporic communities represent both a celebration and an incisive critique of the different cultural spaces they inhabit. In sharing their experiences of multiple—linguistic, geographical, historical—dislocations, the writers of the modern diaspora invite their readers to see culture not as a fundamental model but in its interaction with other cultures. They ask their readers to experience life "on the hyphen," to use Cuban-American critic Gustavo Pérez Firmat's metaphor.[26] A hyphen simultaneously separates and connects, contests and agrees. It creates new dialect(ic)s, such as Chicano-Spanish, Turkish-German, and Algerian-French. As Rushdie has clearly seen, the human product of mass migrations cannot find a place to call home on any map. Almost all the writers discussed in this study express the sentiment that neither a return to the homeland left behind nor being at home in the host country is an option. They need an alternative space, a third geography. This is the space of memory, of language, of translation. In fact, this alternative geography can now be figured as a terrain (of) writing, as the Greek roots of its two syllables suggest.

The first part of this study establishes the conceptual framework for a critical reading of migrant, transnational, or diasporic literatures of the United States and Germany through an understanding of notions of linguistic and cultural memory and of textual strategies operative in the "nongeneric" genre under discussion. These strategies inhere in the predominantly testimonial nature of the works, their self-presentation as "translated" or "bilingual" texts, and the "collective" authorship that reflects the conflicting interests and politics of the groups they speak for. Social ruptures caused by displacement, migrancy, and exile lead to an impoverishment of communal life and shared cultural histories. This loss requires the restorative work of cultural memory to accord meaning, purpose, and integrity to the past. I use the term *cultural memory* to describe an intentional remembering through actual records and experiences or symbolic interpretations thereof by any community that shares a common "culture." This culture could be linguistic, religious, institutional, migrant, diasporic, ethnic, or some combination of these. However, since "culture" itself is often understood as a diachronic development, as a composite of texts, institutions, superstitions, beliefs, and other intellectual and material products of human expression transmitted in time, it is difficult to clearly demarcate the line between culture and the memory of that culture. Yurij Lotman and B. A. Uspensky, for example define culture as "the *nonhereditary memory of the community,* a memory expressing itself in a system of constraints and prescriptions."[27] The very existence of culture, Lotman and Uspensky argue, presupposes a system for translating experience into text. As the long-term memory of a community, culture houses knowledge in the form of texts. The activity in the memory archive of culture involves both a recoding and rearrangement of these texts, depending on hierarchic evaluations, and also the forgetting and exclusion of certain texts. Although culture is "by its very essence" against forgetting, "[i]t overcomes forgetting, turning it into one of the mechanisms of memory" (216). These insights into the semiotic transformation of culture and memory are worth remembering, since in a world marked by widespread relocations, (symbolic) constructions of cultural memory are subject to political intervention, pedagogical prerogative, ancestral force, community contestation, and, most recently, pressures of global technology.

Insofar as culture is memory, it is embedded in the past and will have to be retrieved in symbolic action. Memory marks a loss. It is always a re-presentation, making present that which once was and no longer is. "Representation as rememoration foregrounds the fact that experience *is* always *other* than it *was*: inevitably and constitutively *historical*," writes Richard Terdiman. "Such a construction situates memory as the most consistent agent of the transformations by which the referential world is made into a universe of signs."[28] Similarly, Lotman and Uspensky argue that culture, as a record of community memory, is intimately tied to "*past* historical experience."[29] Thus, culture and memory share an a posteriori structure. As culture experiences changes, memory is contested, repressed, or reconfigured. During times of social turbulence, we witness "a sharp increase in the degree of semiotic behavior" expressed in the changing of names, regulative metaphors, or societal myths, and "even the fight against the old rituals may itself be ritualized" (212). One of the most devastating forms of social oppression "is the obligatory demand to forget certain aspects of historical experience. Epochs of historical regression (the clearest example is the Nazi state culture in the twentieth century)" impose upon societies and communities "highly mythologized schemes of history" (216–17) and demand that they forget anything that does not conform to this manufactured and manipulated fiction of the collective past. In a moment of possibly intended irony—a censorship-resistant trope—Lotman and Uspensky silently evoke an analogy to the totalitarian Soviet regime that censored any reference to the present oppression at the time they wrote this essay.

Since the existence of a diaspora is so intimately connected to cultural memory, diasporic writing articulates a real or imagined past of a community in all its symbolic transformations. It provides a translation of the semiotic behavior of dislocation and resettlement. Writers of diasporas often employ linguistic forms of loss or dislocation, such as fragments or elliptical recollections of ancestral languages, cross-lingual idioms, and mixed codes to create new definitions of community and community memory in exile. "Society from time to time obligates people not just to reproduce in thought previous events of their lives," writes French social theorist Maurice Halbwachs, "but also to touch them up, to shorten them, or to complete them so that . . . we give them a prestige that reality did not possess."[30] For the displaced populations of our age, parents' biographies, autobiographies—veiled or revealed—autobiographical fictions, testimonies, and memoirs become the restorative institution of personal and group memory. Here memory is an intersection between personal recollection and historical account, and though self-consciously fragmentary, it intimates the virtual existence of a longer collective narrative of a nation, ethnic group, or class. Stories of these collectivities are never automatically available in the currency of memory. They have to be represented in terms of self-portraiture, group dynamics, and community and national history to become memory. However, in the process of recounting, the status of memory itself is often challenged, and its hidden baggage of nostalgia is dismantled and repackaged through irony, parody, and allegory, so as to prevent an uncritical examination of history and to keep alive the challenge of learning through remembrance.

The second part of the book introduces a specific comparative study of contemporary Chicano/a and Turkish-German literary productions as an example of two "minor" cultures operating within the larger "national culture" of the United States and Germany, respectively. However, these works are not analyzed in terms of similarity and contrast. Rather, my reading is predicated on a critical vision that involves what anthropologists George E. Marcus and Michael M. J. Fischer call "multiple-other cultural references." Marcus and Fischer maintain that the expansion of the referential field in ethnographic discourse prevents "the basic dualistic character of ethnographic cultural criticism from becoming overpowered by simplistic better-worse judgments about two cultural situations being exposed." They further contend that, at a very basic level, this form of cultural criticism participates in an enhanced mode of communication.[31] The juxtaposed reading of Chicano/a and Turkish-German forms of cultural expression and intervention allows for a differentiated understanding of the critical linkages between local and global cultures and linguistic transposition, bilingualism, and reimagined nationalisms. I believe that comparative readings of texts of different cultural traditions offer an enhanced appreciation of their respective positions by allowing them to be reflected through one another. This process of reflection and counterreflection also accentuates differences in historical course, critical agendas, and modes of expression. The objective of comparative literary and cultural studies is to investigate the imaginary as a mode of understanding both within a language area and between several linguistic and literary traditions without erasing cultural specificities.

The following chapter summaries offer an overview of the areas of inquiry this study addresses. Chapter 2, "Geographies of Memory," begins with a brief discussion of Gilles Deleuze and Félix Guattari's notion of "minor literature," which focuses on a specific geography (Prague), linguistic history (use of German as a "paper" language by the Jews of Prague before the First World War), and writer (Kafka), to conceptualize the role of linguistic self-alienation in nonterritorial, paranational islands of literature. "Geographies of Memory" draws upon and synthesizes theoretical insights and formulations of Friedrich Nietzsche, Sigmund Freud, Walter Benjamin, Hans-Georg Gadamer, Julia Kristeva, Michel de Certeau, and others to provide a conceptual framework for the complex relationship between cultural displacement, memory, and language, where the nuances and inflections of a community's experience of loss, trauma, and eventual recovery are recorded. These critical views live their "afterlife" (Benjamin) in literary translation. Syrian-German writer Rafik Schami's *Erzähler der Nacht* (Storytellers of the night), told in a narrative frame characteristic of Arab storytelling traditions, reclaims, through the seasoned perspective of exilic memory, a chapter of modern Syrian history deleted from official records by state censorship. Edwidge Danticat's *Breath, Eyes, Memory,* and Rosario Ferré's *The House on the Lagoon,* two novels where memory speaks with a Caribbean accent, illustrate how island cultures, as compact archives of diverse (hi)stories, preserve, accommodate, and perform contesting ideologies and idioms.

Chapter 3, "Autobiographical Voices with an Accent," is a discussion of parents' biographies, autobiographical fictions, and cultural autobiographies by Oscar Hijuelos, Maxine Hong Kingston, Eva Hoffman, and Lubiše Moníková, all of which negotiate or reinvent the boundaries of the "out-law" genre of autobiography.[32] For the displaced peoples of our age, family histories and testimonies as well as community memory offer a means of continuity with their pasts. The autobiographical works discussed in this chapter resonate beyond the protocols of self-representation, for they present the constitution of selfhood as the interlinkage of personal experience and historical process and define culture not as a site of origins and ancestral roots, of birthrights and blood rites, but rather as one of transposition and translation.

When migration is necessitated by the poverty in the homeland, as in the case of Mexican and Turkish labor migrations to the United States and Germany, respectively, writers often show a conscious effort to resist the assimilation of their culture into the instrumentality of the economic life of the hostland. Like Mexico, modern Turkey is the borderland to affluent Western neighbors and supplies them with cheap migrant labor. Chapter 4, "At Different Borders/On Common Grounds," introduces a comparative study of writers representing two "minor" literatures within the national culture of their host countries. Both Turkey and Mexico are heirs to ancient and multiethnic cultures and home to many languages and civilizations. The rich textures of Turkish and Mexican cultures are not visible in the toiling bodies of migrant laborers. It becomes the writer's labor to salvage the cultural fabric from the dust of the fields and the fume of the factories and to repair its net of significations. Although the topos of border originated in an actual topography, at a geographical border, it has since traveled to sites where borders mark passages not only in space, but also in time, history, and memory. Here *borderlands* does not signify a line on the map but a historical condition for new critical form(ul)ations. The border, in Teresa McKenna's words, "is an area that stands geographically, as well as politically and culturally as figure and metaphor for the transition between nations . . . a metaphor that underscores the dialectical tension between cultures."[33] This tension informs the identity of the region, its people and culture. However, McKenna also warns that the metaphor, in inadvertently emphasizing the romance and adventure of crossing borders, could hide the real issues at stake. These real issues—the constant threat of detention and arrest at borders, exploitation of human labor, loss of dignity and money, imprisonment, and even death—are definitely not glossed over in symbolic transfiguration in Chicana writer Gloria Anzaldúa's bilingual account *Borderlands/La Frontera* and Turkish-German actress and writer Emine Sevgi Özdamar's *Mutterzunge* (Mother tongue). In a powerful poetic voice, these works not only portray the trials of border citizens, but also critically engage questions of bilingualism and interlinguality[34] and reflect on the relations of power and language. The steadily growing impact of Chicano/a and Turkish-German literatures shows that the two "majority minorities" of the United States and Germany, respectively, take their role in the "cultural citizenship" (Rosaldo) of their adopted lands seriously. Their literary productions have entered a critically productive stage characterized by multiple voices, allegorical transfiguration, and inscriptions of new identities.

Issues of linguistic and cultural transposition implicitly and explicitly raise another set of questions about writing outside the nation. What happens to the memory of a nation outside (without) the nation? How is national identity transformed in the modern world that exists in a state of perpetual geopolitical shifts? When origins and heritages become recollections and merge into other histories, who guards and guarantees our national histories and the specificity of our pasts? Who claims that past and to what ends? In many Chicano/a works, the translation of the idea of nation into a linguistic and metaphysical idiom becomes an object of intense reflection, since as a quintessentially hybrid identity, the Chicano/a cannot return to a national origin. These works often represent the notion of the lost nation by perceiving Mexicanness as a state of mind and force of ancestral memory. Chapter 5, "Writing Outside the Nation," illustrates how fragments of a displaced national culture are re-membered in another language and idiom in Ana Castillo's *The Mixquiahuala Letters*, Aysel Özakin's *Die blaue Maske* (The blue mask), and Emine Sevgi Özdamar's *Das Leben ist eine Karawanserei* (Life is a caravansary). Though written by writers with very different voices and styles, these novels illustrate in comparable ways the act of writing the nation outside the nation. Castillo and Özakin explore unorthodox versions of a politics of "belonging" in their respective tales of travel and transit, which incorporate elements of the *Bildungsroman* yet transfigure this genre by foregrounding the theme of exile and issues of class and gender. Özdamar's personal and allegorical version of modern Turkish history implicitly argues that the necessary but hastened transition from empire (in this case, the Ottoman Empire), which, by its very nature, was multinational, multiethnic, multilingual, and multireligious, to the modern nation-state (the Republic of Turkey), which for its belated arrival and survival had to propagate an essentialist unity of language, geography, and ethnicity, unhinged age-old loyalties and communities. When exile becomes a condition of critical reflection, its writers find the narrative and cultural coordinates to offer another version of their lands' history, a version free of official doctrine and rhetoric, a history of the actual human cost of transformation and migration.

Modern narratives of migrancy, exile, and displacement have generated new epistemologies of bilingualism, language change, and translation. The afterword, "Pedagogical Gains," is a discussion of the enormous potential of this supplement of imaginative knowledge in the classroom.

To access the many forms of knowledge produced by modern diasporic voices, we need to approach their cultural productions not as token representatives of a ghettoized aesthetics, but as complex signifying systems that demand for their comprehension a cultivated sense of cultural history and an understanding of theories of representation. In the interlinked spaces of language, memory, and imagination, these voices reclaim cultural heritages whose emotional and intellectual force had been suppressed by a monolingual and monocultural parochialism that masqueraded as successful acculturation.

2

Geographies of Memory

> We preserve memories of each epoch of our lives, and
> these are continually reproduced; through them as by a con-
> tinual relationship, a sense of our identity is perpetuated. But
> precisely because these memories are repetitions, because
> they are successively engaged in very different systems of no-
> tions, at different periods of our lives, they have lost the
> form and appearance they once had.

Maurice Halbwachs, *On Collective Memory*

> Through metaphor, the past has the capacity to imagine us,
> and we it.

Cynthia Ozick, *Metaphor and Memory*

From Minor Literature to Transnational/Translingual Writing

How many people today live in a language that is not their own?
Or no longer, or not yet, even know their own and know poorly
the major language that they are forced to serve? This is the
problem of immigrants, and especially of their children, the
problem of minorities, the problem of a minor literature, but
also a problem for all of us: how to tear a minor literature away
from its own language, allowing it to challenge the language and
making it follow a sober revolutionary path? How to become a
nomad and an immigrant and a gypsy in relation to one's own
language? Kafka answers: steal the baby from its crib, walk the
tightrope.[1]

In *Kafka: Toward a Minor Literature*, Gilles Deleuze and Félix Guattari develop a conceptual grammar of a cultural phenomenon they call "minor literature." The term refers to the use of a "major" or high-status language by a community whose members are outsiders in the realm of this language. In the voices of minorities, marginal enclaves, and others that inhabit the exteriority of a dominant or national culture, the major language is inflected by a sense of self-alienation that questions its representational certainty.[2]

Franz Kafka's work, a continuous allegory of the linguistic and cultural estrangement of a Czech Jewish writer in Prague writing in German, illustrates the use of a major language in this self-reflexive mode. Kafka's writing constitutes a textual island colonized by German, where German rules as a stranger estranged from itself. The minor literature dislodges the major language from its geographical and cultural environment, thus relativizing its status and problematizing the inviolability of its identity:

> We might as well say that minor no longer designates specific literatures but the revolutionary conditions for every literature within the heart of what is called great (or established) literature. . . . There has been much discussion of the questions "What is a marginal literature?" and "What is a popular literature, a proletarian literature?" The criteria are obviously difficult to establish if one doesn't start with a more objective concept—that of minor literature. Only the possibility of setting up a minor practice of major language from within allows one to define popular literature, marginal literature, and so on.[3]

The notion of generating the possibility of self-critique from within, from a first principle, has a long history in the context of Romantic idealism. Johann Gottlieb Fichte, who detected the greatest weakness of Kant's critical philosophy in its inability to represent the self to itself, endeavored to correct this perceived failure by positing a "not-self" (*Nicht-Ich*). The "self" (*Ich*) sees itself reflected by the not-self and recognizes its own status as representation. For Novalis, however, this self-recognition fell short of understanding the otherness of the not-self. Novalis understands the self-positing of the self and its op-positing of the object as an activity of signification, of naming, of language. If selfhood is the ground of language, then it should also represent the principle of highest diversity that is not the not-self but *Du* (thou). *Du* transforms *Ich* into "a social, liberal, universal principle."[4] Furthermore, the principle of all self-understanding is the encounter with our otherness: "Wir verstehn natürlich alles Fremde nur durch *Selbstfremdmachung*" [naturally we understand every-thing foreign only by *making* ourselves *foreign*] (3:429, no. 820). In Noval-is's two novel fragments, *Heinrich von Ofterdingen* and *Lehrlinge zu Sais* (Isis's apprentices), the respective protagonists achieve self-recognition through a confrontation with an unknown, foreign language and their attempts at understanding this radically different mode of representation.

In Freud's work, greatly indebted to German romanticism, the encounter between the familiar and the strange turns into a heuristic tool for the analysis of repressed memory. Freud's psychoanalytic theory trans-lated the abstract grammar of Fichte's subjective idealism into a concrete semantics of remembering and recognition through close readings of liter-ary texts. Psychoanalysis participates very consciously in the hermeneutic tradition of Romantic idealism and its emphasis on linguistic interpreta-tion and understanding. In "Das Unheimliche" (The uncanny), an in-depth analysis of E. T. A. Hoffmann's "Der Sandmann" (The sandman), Freud demonstrates that the notion of the uncanny (the other, the double) was inherent in the many uses of the word *heimlich*. After a lengthy etymo-logical and comparative analysis of the words *heimlich* and *unheimlich*, Freud comes to the conclusion that in German usage, *unheimlich*, denoting strange, foreign, unfamiliar, anxiety provoking, is a derivative of its ambi-guious antonym *heimlich*, meaning familiar, at home, and secret. In other words, the semantic domain of *heimlich* houses two apparently opposed fields, one denoting familiarity and comfort, the other the hidden and the unknown. In a play on words, Freud notes that this "little word" (*Wörtchen*) *heimlich*, "in one instance of its many nuances, coincides un-cannily with its very opposite" [unter den mehrfachen Nuancen seiner Bedeutung auch eine zeigt, in der es mit seinem Gegensatz unheimlich zusammenfällt].[5] Basing his argument on this philological genealogy, a reading of Hoffmann, and references to other literary texts, Freud makes two observations. First, if psychoanalytical theory is correct in showing that fear arises from the repression of any aspect of the affective life of the individual, then among instances of anxiety there must be those in which fear is repeatedly repressed. These instances of anxiety assume the form of the uncanny, regardless of whether they were originally threatening or took on that affect. Second, if this is the real nature of the *Unheimliche*, then it is easy to understand how in language usage the first term flows into its other, for this *Unheimliche* is in fact nothing new or unfamiliar. Once an intimate part of psychic life (*Seelenleben*), it has now become distanced and alienated through a mechanism of repression (254). Ultimately,

Freud's analysis validates the recognition of the other, the foreign, and the unfamiliar in our inner lives as a form of self-understanding. In philosophical terms, the derivation of the *Unheimliche* from *heimlich* would denote subject division. The primordial self, not yet differentiated from the outside world, projects into an alien double all that is threatening and unpleasant to itself. This not-self, which is posited by the self in Fichte and separated from the self through repression in Freud, becomes a condition of self-reflexivity. Freud "teaches us how to detect foreignness in ourselves."[6] We analyze ourselves by analyzing the "foreign." "The ethics of psychoanalysis implies a politics," writes Julia Kristeva; "it would involve a cosmopolitanism of a new sort that, cutting across governments, economies, and markets, might work for a mankind whose solidarity is founded on the consciousness of its unconscious (192)."

Like Freud, who constructs the *Unheimliche* as a conduit from the inside to the outside, to the unknown, as a path to discovering "our disturbing otherness,"[7] Deleuze and Guattari locate in minor literature the repressed and censored dimensions of the major language. What are the conditions for the production of minor literature? According to Deleuze and Guattari, minor literature is characterized by deterritorialization, political engagement, and collective articulation. The concept of a deterritorialized major language as a vehicle of self-expression for a community coincides with the use of German by the Jews of Prague before the First World War. Since they no longer have access to their "primitive Czech territoriality," they appropriate a major language—German—that serves them in the capacity of a " 'paper language' "[8] and is "appropriate for strange and minor uses" (17). The Jews of Prague were a part of the German-speaking "oppressive minority" whose idiom was "cut off from the masses." Yet at the same time they were excluded from the German community, "like 'Gypsies who have stolen a German child from its crib' " (16–17). Although the paper language—like the English of the Indian subcontinent—may have originated in a distant geography, it becomes in its migrated (or transposited) form a language of formal education, national newspapers, trade and scholarly publications, and bureaucracy. This first feature of minor literature is certainly characteristic of modern postcolonial literatures written almost exclusively in English and French in India, Pakistan, and the former British and French colonies in Africa. It also characterizes, for example, the status of literature written in Russian by Uzbek, Kirghiz, or Azerbaijani writers. Understood in a strictly geographical sense, however, deterritorialization cannot be a relevant feature of English, French, and German works written by nonnative authors in the United States, England,

Canada, Australia, France, and Germany. Their medium is not a "deterritorialized" major language but one that still occupies its natural territory and has annexed the textual domain of the foreign writer who contributes to the literary history of the host country in the currency of its national language. Thus, when Deleuze and Guattari compare Black English to Prague German (17), they find an escape route from their own law of category and genre. Black English, Spanglish, or Nuyorican are deviations from standard American English, but they do not work with an imported language in another geography. They are rooted in their locales of origin and often export new accents and inflections of the standard idiom to the domain of the dominant or national language.

What is of critical interest in Deleuze and Guattari's concept of minor literature is that it uses Kafka as a pretext to outline a conceptual framework and to legitimize a historical context for modern literary works that challenge boundaries of genre, monolingualism, and national character. It is not surprising, therefore, that the conceptual flexibility of Deleuze and Guattari's model has served as a blueprint for many critics in their reading of nonterritorial, transnational, diasporic literatures. However, although Deleuze and Guattari articulate their theoretical project through an apparently specific geography, history, and writer, they abstract the theory away from a genuine encounter with particular political contexts and historical situations. The second feature of minor literature, its strong political orientation, is not readily discernible in Kafka's work. Kafka's political agenda unfolds in a highly ritualized performance of writing, where parable and allegory can portray the political only nonmimetically. Nevertheless, drawing on Kafka's diaries, Deleuze and Guattari conclude that the individual and psychological concerns of minor literature are articulated in terms of a "political program" (17). Here "political" refers neither to an act of social intervention nor to a confrontational critique of political oppression. Rather, it implies a condition where the danger of disappearing national and collective consciousness outside the nation urges the writer to forge alternative alliances, to participate in different configurations of identity. The "cramped space" of minor literature

> forces each individual intrigue to connect immediately to politics. The individual concern thus becomes all the more necessary, indispensible, magnified, because a whole other story is vibrating within it. In this way, the family triangle connects to other triangles—commercial, economic, bureaucratic, juridical—that determine its values. (17)

Although Kafka's parables and stories implicate this triangulation of oppressive familial, commercial, and bureaucratic systems in the collective anxiety of the modern age, the highly allegorized nature of his writing conceals any imaginable political agenda. This is perhaps why Georg Lukács read Kafka's work as a portrayal of the fragmented subjectivity of the modern individual, a condition that rendered an effective formation of politicized consciousness impossible. Although "[t]he diabolical character of modern capitalism and man's paralysis in the face of this force is the real subject matter of Kafka's poetry," writes Lukács, "the ultimately allegorical character" of his work transforms the world into an atemporal abstraction of a transcendent loss, "an allegory of transcendent Nothingness."[9]

Although the political effectiveness of Kafka's work is highly debatable, Deleuze and Guattari not only view his writing as a site of radical politics but also overstate the political case for minor literature by dismissing any claims a major literature may have on social engagement: "In major literatures . . . the individual concern (familial, marital, and so on) joins with other no less individual concerns, the social milieu serving as a mere environment or a background."[10] Any overview of contemporary diasporic or postcolonial literatures readily reveals that political critique is a requisite condition of their formation. However, it does not follow that a "major" literature is, by definition, depoliticized. Every rhetorically gifted writer presents language in its contestatory and revolutionary stations and transitions. Closely linked to the political disposition of minor literature is its practice of collective articulation. In fact, Deleuze and Guattari's definition of political suggests nothing other than a gesture of collective will. Since the writing of minor literature originates in communities marked by a loss or erasure of national or collective identity, memories and other fragments of historical and cultural repositories need to be pooled. Here "literature finds itself positively charged with the role and function of collective, and even revolutionary, enunciation" (17).

Writers of exile often endeavor to reclaim and preserve cultural legacies destroyed and erased in their own countries by oppressive regimes. Intellectual goods are smuggled across borders and transplanted in foreign soil. However, their reinscription often takes the form of a negotiation between the contesting and conflicting ideologies of national and ethnic minority groups in exile. In this sense, any minor literature is inescapably the expression of a collectivity in all its agreements and conflicts. In contemporary diasporic discourses the negotiation between deterritorialization, the social imaginary, and literary imagination leads to the formation of communities bound together by improvised loyalties beyond the reach of tribe, sect, or nation. "[W]here once improvisation was snatched out of the glacial undertow of habitus," notes Appadurai, "habitus now has to be painstakingly reinforced in the face of life-worlds that are frequently in flux."[11] In Appadurai's view, the links between social life and imagination have become increasingly deterritorialized due to the ubiquitousness of mass media and the effects of globalization.

Although Deleuze and Guattari conclude correctly that a critical use of one's language generates a polyvalency of idioms, they do not pursue the implications of this language out-of-bounds as a lived social experience. In the face of the growing body of underrepresented, lesser-known, and emergent literary discourses, their model falls short of offering a satisfactory range of reading strategies. Understandably, any model that is explanatory in terms of a delimited field of cultural production—be it the writing of the Prague Jews in German during the beginning of this century, American slave narratives, the Chicano border ballad, Nuyorican poetry, or Turkish-German film—would prove inadequate, if we expect it to account for "multiple-other" forms of expresssion. Nevertheless, we need to break through criteria that can be too easily stretched. In a general sense, most exemplary works of literature can be understood as deterritorialized, politicized, and expressive of a collective ethos. A new critical inquiry has to move beyond the deterritorialized foreignness of the text. We need to read and understand other literary traditions in their diachronic and synchronic contexts, that is, in terms of both their historical development and conceptual foundations. How can we preserve the critical insight that otherness can be experienced in and through a self-reflexive use of one's own language without erasing the specificity of cultures and the heterogeneity of nonnational literatures? Can we go beyond the limiting adjective in "minor literature," reassess its semantic field, and situate it in the broader context of the politics of identity, representation, and memory? Thinking through these questions could help us gain a better understanding of the transitions and transformations at the shifting borders of history, politics, and culture.

The problematic gesture of transplanting Western theories in outlandish locations and attempts to locate or recover so-called indigenous theories retain their currency and urgency. I do not propose any final answers here. Nevertheless, I am interested in the unobtrusive theoretical gains made in those areas of inquiry situated in the cross-disciplinary currents of cultural studies. These include translation, semiotics, cultural memory, island and borderland cultures, traveling cultures, and ethnographic allegory. Investigations in these fields yield critical insights that help the reader detect the rich variety of cultural accents and decode the mythologized and memorialized alphabets of other cultures. Deleuze and Guattari discover in the revolutionary tenor of minor literature the "polylingualism of one's own language" and the "linguistic Third World zones by which a language can escape."[12] The escape of language, that bursting out of territorial borders into vertiginous space, takes the form of "pop— pop music, pop philosophy, pop writing—Worterflucht [sic]" (26).

"Language's lines of escape" may end in silence, interruption, dead ends, and even worse places. "But until that point, what a crazy creation, what a writing machine!"[13] Can the lines of escape go beyond zones of silence and interruption and reclaim discursive rights? Can the writing machine write identities that have been fragmented through historical trauma, cannot be remembered, and, therefore, need to be narrated? The escape routes may lead to sites of silence, interruption, and forgetting, but they can also point the way to hidden or forgotten linguistic and cultural capital. In our chaotically fast-paced history, minor literatures, which are increasingly transnational and bi- or translingual, assume the form of memory banks where fragments of different histories and languages, traces of cultural accents, and images of lost geographies are deposited. The German spoken in Prague constituted a language island. What we call language islands—for example, the Ladino of the Sephardic Jews in Istanbul, the archaic German of the Pennsylvania Amish—are memory archives of a language that has wandered away from its homeland and is spoken in small ethnic or religious minority communities. Likewise, dialects preserve the historical versions of the standard language and form the cultural memory of its lexicon. Transnational writing transports these compact archives of memory across borders, redistributing their contents as idioms, metaphors, and discourses around which diasporic communities can forge new, nonterritorial alliances.

Memory and Its Discontents

> The true sense for the stories [and histories] of human be-
> ings develops late and rather under the quiet influence of rec-
> ollection than under the more aggressive impressions of the
> present. The immediate events seem to be only vaguely re-
> lated but they sympathize all the more beautifully with the
> more remote ones, and only when one is in a position to sur-

vey a long series [of events] and to avoid not only taking
everything literally but also confusing the actual order with
wanton dreams, does one apprehend the secret union of
the past and the future and learn to piece together history
out of hope and memories.

Novalis, *Heinrich von Ofterdingen*

[T]he picture he had of the city was reduced to what she
said of it, and finally it was her speech alone that could call
up and protect that picture. He came to the conclusion that,
once abandoned by words, the city would fall into ruins.

Abdelkebir Khatibi, *Love in Two Languages*

Memory is a phenomenon of conceptual border zones. It is an intersection
and an interdiction. It dwells at the crossroads of the past and the present.
It bans the recall of certain events and prohibits entry into cordoned-off
areas of the past. What is remembered and forgotten in the larger social
world and the public sphere in which the individual dwells is controlled
by public, political, and educational institutions. The study of history implies a moral dictate. History serves as an exemplum that urges us to learn
from the achievements and mistakes of the past. History as a form of public
and institutional memory not so much speaks for the past but rather
presses the present into the service of an officially sanctioned version of
the past. This is perhaps nowhere better articulated than in Nietzsche's
essay "Vom Nutzen und Nachteil der Historie für das Leben" (The use and
disadvantage of history for life). History, as a discipline of knowledge,
writes the past in the modalities of the monumental, the antiquarian, and
the critical. These three models of history serve the needs of the active
and striving, preserving and honoring, and suffering and freedom-desiring
human beings, respectively.[14] Monumental history declares the memorable
achievements of the past as the standard-bearer for all times. The present
has nothing to contribute to the glory of the past; its mission is to eternalize
that glory and strive to emulate it. Antiquarian history sees all time and
events in a continuum; every identity and each life is understood only in
terms of its larger history. The antiquarian sees in the history of his city,
in its monuments and its festivities his own past; the events in the life of
the city resemble a colorful diary of his youth. His talent lies in an instinct-
ively correct reading of an overwritten history, his quick understanding of
its palimpsests (225–26). The critical historian, on the other hand, sees
history as a history of mistakes, failures, and wrong moves and attempts

to construct an a posteriori past from which he hails, as opposed to the history that he inherited. This is always a risky undertaking, "because it is so difficult to set a limit on the denial of the past, and because second natures are mostly weaker than the first" [weil es so schwer ist, eine Grenze im Verneinen des Vergangenen zu finden, und weil die zweiten Naturen meistens schwächlicher als die ersten sind] (230).

Here Nietzsche does not valorize any particular art of reading history, nor does he condemn any. He agrees that every individual and nation needs an understanding of history. This understanding could be monumental, antiquarian, critical, or a combination of these depending on the needs, fears, and goals of societies. However, because of "an excess of history" [Übermaße von Historie] (215), which knows of no forgetting, and an unexamined acceptance of scientific (*wissenschaftlich*) (282) history, which allows for no omission, the living, whether they be individuals, nations, or cultures, move progressively away from life toward self-denial. To live the present moment means to enjoy a healthy dose of forgetting (213). Critics have looked in vain for a resolution in Nietzsche's essay in the form of an alternative model of reading history. Paul de Man, for example, sees in Nietzsche's radical move to transcend history to reach a new point of origin "the full power of the idea of modernity."[15] This attempt to overcome history turns upon itself, for the dilemma of modernity, de Man claims, lies in its "generative power that not only engenders history, but is part of a generative scheme that extends far back into the past" (150). Thus, "Nietzsche finds it impossible to escape from history," and this paradox slips into an aporia, leading Nietzsche to the realization that his own critical attempt "can be nothing but another historical document, and finally he has to delegate the power of renewal and modernity to a mythical entity called 'youth' to which he can only recommend the effort of self-knowledge that has brought him to his own abdication" (151).

It is rather surprising that de Man, an astute reader of texts, who so skillfully unpacks metaphors, gives up so fast on Nietzsche after reading his statement, "history itself *must* resolve the problem of history" [die Historie *muß* das Problem der Historie selbst auflösen].[16] In fact, Nietzsche prescribes a very specific antidote to the malaise of the historical: "The unhistorical and the superhistorical (*das Unhistorische und das Überhistorische*) are the natural antidotes to the overproliferation of history in life, to the historical sickness" (282). Nietzsche explains that by "unhistorical" he means the art and the power to forget, that is, to delimit the horizon of remembering. "Superhistorical," on the other hand, are those forces, such as art and religion, that direct our concerns away from passages and lend existence an eternal and stable character (281). At this point in Nietzsche's essay it becomes clear that he is, in fact, suggesting the screening as well as the regenerating power of memory as an antidote to the doctrinaire rigidity of scientific history. The problem in the monumental, antiquarian, and critical modes of history lies in the reduction of historical phenomena to an intellectual exercise. If history is understood as a sovereign science, then its knowledge renders the knower powerless, for history cannot be used in formulaic terms. Scientific knowledge (*Wissenschaft*) considers art and religion hostile forces, since it validates only scientific observation. But this "observation of things" sees everywhere "what has come to be" [ein Gewordenes], that is, the historical and nowhere "a becoming" [ein Seiendes] that is eternal. Therefore, it lives in inner contradiction with the generative powers of art and religion (281–82). Although Nietzsche never names the antidote to history "memory," all his prescriptions of counterhistory imply the reconstructive and liberating force of memory. Memory, as Freud so thoroughly demonstrated, is a process of (re)construction and is composed of forgetting as well as remembering. Nietzsche sees in the excess of history, of remembering, the pathology of life and the destruction of human beings. But if they exercise the power "to use the past (*das Vergangene*) for life and to construct history once again out of what has happened (*das Geschehene*)," they can be rehabilitated (215). This power of transfiguration is what makes us human.

If history is to be an enabling rather than a life-negating force, it can never be a finished product in a neat scientific sense but rather must be an ongoing process. This process is informed by an awareness of the paradoxes of human life and history, that is, the permanence of the contingent and the aleatory that art and religion embrace. As such, art and religion but not science can deploy the power of corrective and liberating memory. Nietzsche gives the example of Greeks who, like his contemporaries, were suffering from an overflow of the past and the exotic. Their culture was overwhelmed by Semitic, Babylonian, Lydian, and Egyptian features; their religion had become the Orient's battleground of gods. The Greeks were able to moderate this excess of history by learning to differentiate their real needs from false needs. They learned, Nietzsche says, to organize chaos (284). This involved a selective forgetting and remembering in order to open up the space for a reorganization and fructification of cultural legacies. The excess of history arises from false needs, from the need to overlay (adorn) life with scientific knowledge. The Greeks imagined culture not as an adornment of life—since all adornment hides what is adorned and becomes a misrepresentation and concealment—but as a harmonious interplay among life, thought, appearance, and desire. Nietzsche's conception of culture as a generative, life-giving power derives from a process of creative selection and organization, a process that is closely linked to the workings of memory and imagination. In the final analysis, Nietzsche implicitly classifies history as science and memory as art. Jorge Luis Borges revisits Nietzsche's version of history and memory in the allegory of "Funes the Memorious." Funes suffers from an excess of remembering. He remembers "not only every leaf of every tree of every wood, but also every one of the times he had perceived or imagined it."[17] His memory, a precise scientific instrument of observation and classification, enables him to learn several languages without any effort. However, at the end of the story Borges's narrator remarks that Funes was probably incapable of thought, for thinking requires selective forgetting, generalizing, and organizing the chaos of infinite detail.

Nietzsche's complex negotiations between history and corrective remembering are opened to a politically charged reinterpretation in Walter Benjamin's "Über den Begriff der Geschichte" (Theses on the philosophy of history). Benjamin asserts that in order for history to be transformed into emancipatory memory, its fragments need to be reconfigured in such a way as to release their revolutionary potential. The allegorical lessons of the past remain *in potentia* until the chaos of history, in a Nietzschean vein yet transcending Nietzsche's idealized Hellenic solution, can be organized to highlight those moments of danger when individuals and whole societies became victims of ruling powers. The past is neither the site of monuments nor a museum of irreplacable achievements. It needs to be understood both in its temporal context and in terms of its corrective employment for the present. As the sixth thesis states:

> To articulate the past historically does not mean to recognize it
> "the way it actually was." It means to seize a memory as it
> flashes at a moment of danger. Historical materialism is con-
> cerned with retaining that image of the past which unexpectedly
> appears to the historical subject at a moment of danger. The dan-
> ger threatens both the survival of the tradition and its receivers.
> For both the threat is the same: becoming a tool of the ruling
> classes. In every epoch the attempt must be made anew to wrest
> tradition away from a conformism that is about to conquer it.[18]

Memories need to be "wrested away" from the complacent continuum of history to break the chains of the present in whatever form they appear. The reduction of the past to an unproblematic continuum, to a representation of historical progress, has led to a dismantling of its power, deprived the future of its inheritance, and pressed a blindfolded generation into the service of fascism. A corrective remembering of the past involves detonating the revolutionary baggage of the past. History, Benjamin states in the fourteenth thesis, is an object of construction at a site that is transformed by the *Jetztzeit* (immediate present; literally, "time of the now"). To Robespierre, for example, ancient Rome was a past charged with the present that he blasted out of the undifferentiated, uninflected continuum of history (258). Revolutionary actions retrieve the explosive memory of past revolutions from the forgotten, monotonous stretches of history. Thus, memory activates the power of history to transform the present. It translates the ciphers of the past into alphabets of the present and makes history readable by relating it to the moment. Benjamin names this charged recall a "citation." Citing the past unleashes its power for the present.

Benjamin ends "Begriff der Geschichte" by stating that the historian cannot simply link events in a linear order "like the beads of a rosary" [wie einen Rosenkranz]. Instead he grasps the constellation that his era has formed with a definite earlier one. Thus, he establishes a conception of the present as *Jetztzeit* that is shot through with chips of messianic time. "The time of the now" is the encounter of the past with the present. It is the moment when the emancipatory power of memory is released. In "remembrance" (*Eingedenken*), time is neither empty nor homogeneous. For the Jews, as Benjamin observes, *Eingedenken*, which the Torah and the prayers teach, is a time through whose gate the Messiah could enter at any second (261). It seems that for Benjamin, as for Freud, the stuff of memory is indestructable, subject to resurrection or reconstruction in times of crisis—crisis as psychic and cultural pathology in Freud and political persecution and destruction of human lives in Benjamin. The historical and political implications of memory in Nietzsche and Benjamin can perhaps be more concretely imagined when reflected through Freud's analytic lens and translated into the terms of the subject—the human subject of history.

In *Present Past: Modernity and the Memory Crisis*, Richard Terdiman credits psychoanalysis as "our culture's last Art of Memory."[19] It is through Freud's work that our preoccupation with memory has moved to the center stage of modern culture (242). Freud's memory-intensive analytic theory, however, contests and complicates the question of recollection as a corrective procedure at every turn and underlines the paradox at the heart of psychoanalysis. This paradox inheres in psychoanalysis's embrace of irreconcilable extremes. On the one hand, every treatise on Freudian memory concludes with the certainty that memories are rooted in fixed impressions and contents. However, these immutable traces and fragments experience transfigurations, disfigurations, and ruptures that take the form of dreams, delusions, and repressions. In other words, memories have a definite referent. Neuroses, psychoses, and other aberrations in the psychic life of the individual that are no longer recognizable as manifestations of the referent are, nevertheless, forms of remembering. The goal of the psychoanalytic procedure is to reconstruct memory from the jumbled assemblage of its fragments. Ultimately, the art of memory, as Freud demonstrates in "Konstruktionen in der Analyse" (Constructions in analysis) is the art of reconstruction.

Analysis urges the patient to clear away the repressions of his or her early development and replace these with responses commensurate with a more mature psychic condition. The delusions and repressions are the "substitute" (Ersatz) for what was forgotten. All the clues that the patient delivers into the analyst's hands, such as dream contents, repetitive actions, and transference, constitute fragments that will help the analyst put the patient on the path to "winning back the lost memories."[20] "We all know that the person being analyzed," writes Freud, "has to be led to the point of remembering something that was experienced and repressed by him." Freud asserts that the dynamics of the patient's remembering are so engrossing that they push the other component of the psychoanalytic labor, the task of the psychoanalyst, into the background (45). The analyst is not the agent of remembering; so what is the analyst's job? It is "to guess or, to put it more correctly, construct what was forgotten from the traces it left behind." This "task of construction, or if one prefers reconstruction" of the patient's lost or occluded memories closely resembles the task of the archaeologist who is excavating ruined or buried sites of the past. In this analogy, the ruins and remains unearthed by the excavation correspond to the fragments of memories, associations, and behavioral gestures of the subject under psychoanalysis. However, the reconstruction of the physical and the psychical differ greatly in terms of what is preserved (45–46). Freud emphasizes that "all of the essentials" (46) of psychic life remain intact. Even if they appear to be totally forgotten, they are but hidden and buried and thus inaccessible to the subject. This instance of perfect conservation is very rare in archaeology. Nevertheless, the archaeologist's task is less complicated than the analyst's, for the structures of psychic experience are often shrouded in impenetrable mystery. Furthermore, the archaeologist works in a temporally linear fashion, whereby the reconstruction of each piece has to be completed before the next step is taken. Archaeological reconstruction proceeds by a diachronic analytic. The memory work, on the other hand, is both diachronic and synchronic. At any given point during the treatment, the analyst can insert the "excavated" material into the present experience of the subject, and the two temporalities can be handled in an alternating fashion and realigned during analysis.

Although the full conservation of memory remains a theoretical reality, in practice, total recall on part of the subject (or, for that matter, complete reconstruction by the analyst) is rare:

> The path that starts from the analyst's construction ought to end in the patient's recollection; but it does not always go so far. Quite often it is not possible to lead the patient to the recollection of the repressed. Instead of that, through a correct implementation of the analysis we produce in the patient a firm conviction of the truth of the construction, which yields the same therapeutic result as a recaptured memory. (52–53)

Although reconstruction succeeds in granting memory traces entry into consciousness, this "return of the repressed" [Wiederkehr des Verdrängten] (54) is also resisted by displacing it into events marginally related to the repressed fact. These forms of resistance are incorporated in delusions, for forces opposed to remembering distort the process of recall.

This insight about the therapeutic result of constructed memory and distortion of memory arising from resistance to it and resulting in delusion and madness is important in understanding mechanisms of personal and collective memory in narratives that are the subject of this study. The rejection of "reality" is triggered by a mechanism of resistance to the return of the repressed and by a drive for wish fulfillment. "This is, after all, the familiar mechanism of dreams," observes Freud, "which was believed to correspond to madness in the ancient times." Nevertheless, "there is not only *method* in madness, as the poet already knew, but also a fragment of *historical truth*" (54). The object of analysis is to relieve those suffering from their "own reminiscences" (56). This takes the form of liberating the fragment of historical truth from its distortions of reality and its interference with the present and leading it back to the point in the past where it belongs (55).

When Freud applies his theory of memory in the individual psyche to a collectivity, to a culture as a whole, his conclusions remain analogous to the insights of the psychoanalytic method. The primeval memories of human beings were transformed, transfigured, and in some sense disfigured in the course of civilization building. The delusions of humanity are equally "inaccessible to logical critique and opposed to truth." Nevertheless, they are able to exert an extraordinary power over human beings. Freud's study of the nature of personal and collective memory concludes that both individual and societal forms of delusion "owe their power to the element of *historical truth* that they have brought up from the repression of a forgotten primeval past" (56). In culture, natural drives have to be harnessed for the survival of the species. What is repressed in a society reappears as sublimation in the form of art, rite, and ritual. But this sublimation is seen as an illness, a distortion at a larger societal level. Freud's case for the immutability of collective memory remains a diagnostic observation, as the original title of *Civilization and Its Discontents* suggests—the correct translation of *Das Unbehagen in der Kultur* would be "the dis-ease in culture." Psychoanalysis implies but does not, as Kristeva suggests,[21] prescribe a politics of restoring the repressed or compensating the silenced. At least, as Paul Ricoeur suggests, not yet. For when Freud's writing is seen beyond the limited context of therapeutic prescriptions and protocols, his texts on culture provide a rigorous hermeneutics of culture. As Ricoeur observes, Freud "considers the universality of linguistic symbolism much more as a proof of memory traces of the great traumas of humanity, in terms of the genetic model, than as an incitement to explore other dimensions of language, the imaginary, and myth."[22] In the final analysis, Ricoeur believes that Freud's vision of mankind is a tragic one, for images of psychoanalytic language—the return of the repressed, the challenge of *Trauerarbeit,* or "the decathexis of censored energy"—all point to the tragedy of beginnings, the tragic fate of man's childhood, and the tragedy of repetition (156). This tragic knowledge that Freud reintroduced into modern consciousness "must be assimilated in order to reach the threshold of a new ethic which we must no longer attempt to extract from Freud's work by immediate inference. It will be slowly prepared by the fundamentally nonethical teachings of psychoanalysis" (159).

What I have tried to show in this investigation of critical texts on memory is that the stakes in the game of memory are always very high. Since memory is an art of construction and reconstruction and thus manipulable, it can be prescribed as both poison and antidote. The hermeneutic analysis of memory illustrates that memory, like language, is a double-edged sword. It can reveal as well as conceal. In *History and Memory,* Jacques Le Goff takes issue with recent trends that conflate history and memory and even validate memory as a truer form of history. He agrees that national and other ideologies influence the way history is written. He argues, however, that recent developments in critical historiography take into account the production of history in relation to the political and social forces that condition its mode of articulation. He considers memory as the raw and indispensible material of history. Since the operations of memory often take place at the level of the unconscious, however, "it is in reality more dangerously subject to manipulation by time and by societies given to reflection than the discipline of history itself."[23] Furthermore, as a discipline, history nourishes memory, accounts for what is remembered and forgotten by individuals and societies, and transforms memory into an object of knowledge (xi–xii). However, it is precisely in such claims of history on objectivity and comprehensiveness that Nietzsche and Benjamin see the danger to cultural self-reflection. Though memory can be manipulated more or less than, or as much as, the writing of history, literary texts call on cultural memories embedded in symbolic practices for alternative modes of clarification, relativize them through personal and communal experience, and rarely turn them into tools of ideology.

The current interest in memory is based, to a large degree, on the mistrust of scientific objectivity in history and psychology. Furthermore, the threat to human memory by the onslaught of information technology and the disappearance of local cultures due to modern mass migrations and globalization have contributed to the interest in issues of memory. Memory studies have gained both momentum and controversy in our times. The revisionist project to force the Holocaust out of collective memory and the controversies surrounding false-memory syndrome and delayed memory, which have wandered from the domain of psychology to the courts of law and the media, have also played a major role in generating public interest in memory. What path is the fate of cultural memory to take in an age of information superhighways, when knowledge expends itself at a dizzying speed, memory is electronically stored, and all recall is instant? Geoffrey Hartman argues that although technology has perfected the art of simulation, it has not decreased forgetfulness or the pace at which events disappear into the abyss of time. In fact, if anything, the information overflow enforces a speedy overthrow of what is current.

Hartman sees official history as the greatest danger to public memory: "Even the dead, as Walter Benjamin declared, are not safe from the victors, who consider public memory part of the spoils and do not hesitate to rewrite history."[24] The monologic authority of official history undermines the "only *active* communal memory we have," which lives in poetry, legends, symbols, songs, and dances. In a Nietzschean vein, Hartman argues that only art free of official intervention has a chance to transmit our cultural inheritance and provide "a counterforce to manufactured and monolithic memory." Hartman's is one of the most eloquent voices for the preservation of cultural memory through "[a]rt as a performative medium—art not reduced to official meaning or information" (30). His pioneering work in public memory is an outcome of his efforts to prevent the forgetting of the Holocaust. Perhaps the single greatest force behind the rise of memory studies during the last two decades has been the anxiety about the eventual erasure of the memory of the Holocaust. With the passing away of the last witnesses and survivors and attempts by revisionist historians to deny that the horrors happened, testimonies, interviews, and videos were put together, commented on, and publicly presented by prominent archivists, scholars, critics, and artists.[25] It is the eloquence and sophistication of the work in this area that has given momentum to modern memory studies.

In *Twilight Memories,* Andreas Huyssen sees the anxiety of memory closely linked to the culture of forgetting. The struggle for memory is the struggle for history and a resistance to the cultural amnesia that universally embraced technologies may inadvertently cause. The battle for memory "represents the attempt to slow down information processing . . . to recover a mode of contemplation outside the universe of simulation and fast-speed information and cable networks, to claim some anchoring space in a world of puzzling and often threatening . . . information overload."[26] Notions of memory invention and appropriation are now more and more linked to questions of national identity and ideology. And anxieties about the preservation of national, cultural, and ethnic legacies have been exacerbated by patterns of social and economic migration. "Struggles for minority rights are increasingly organized around questions of cultural memory, its exclusions and taboo zones," writes Huyssen. "Migrations and demographic shifts are putting a great deal of pressure on social and cultural memory in all Western societies, and such public debates are intensely political" (5). The raging instantaneity that increasingly informs our culture, disconnected atoms of temporality exploding and disappearing on the monitor screen, a dizzying discontinuity where we cannot mark time—all have understandably contributed to the anxiety about the future of communal and cultural memory.

The Art of Storytelling in an Age of Its Electronic Dissemination: Rafik Schami's *Erzähler der Nacht*

Contemporary writers of exile and diaspora display a deep awareness of the danger that globalization and the worldwide domination of technologies of communication pose to local and little-known cultures. In a series of interviews with writer-critic Erich Jooß, the Syrian-German author Rafik Schami voices his concern about the diminishing power of the storytelling tradition in Arab lands. The issues he raises in these interviews as well as the conversations between the storytellers in *Erzähler der Nacht* (Storytellers of the night)[27] bear on the future of cultural memory in an age of relentless technology. Schami believes that the widespread availability and affordability of transistor radios and television have not only made the art of storytelling obsolete but also effortlessly spread state control and propoganda to the furthest regions of Syria. Although Schami does not consider himself a "purist" and claims he is not waging a war against television, he states that television had a damaging influence on Arab lands, since this region historically and culturally had a very limited experience with images but a very wide-ranging one with words.[28] Schami's ideas on the status and destiny of storytelling, his apprehensions about the ubiquitousness of electronic media and its possibly irreversible damage on the inherited wisdom of tradition, echo the earlier insights of Benjamin's essay "Der Erzähler" (The storyteller).

"The art of storytelling is tending toward its end," observes Benjamin, "because the epic side of truth, wisdom, is dying out."[29] The epic faculty par excellence is memory. Echoing Nietzsche and Freud, Benjamin observes that epic memory is not only capable of remembering a great flow of events but also of forgetting them, remembering them selectively and coming to terms with their disappearance and death (398–99). Benjamin considers Herodotus the first storyteller of the Greeks. Citing Herodotus's story of the Egyptian king Psammenitus in *Histories*, Benjamin remarks that by limiting the information content in his accounts, the historian preserves the resonant memory of events. That is why Herodotus's tale of Psammenitus is capable of generating wonder and reflection after thousands of years: "It resembles the seeds of grain that have been preserved for millennia in the airtight chambers of the pyramids and have retained their germinative power to this day." A story "preserves its strength in concentrated form and is able to release it even after a long time" [bewahrt ihre Kraft gesammelt und ist noch nach langer Zeit der Entfaltung fähig] (392). Salim, the master storyteller of Damascus in Schami's *Erzähler der Nacht*, reveals that each story retained in his memory is bare and unadorned. Only in telling do the stories acquire "the appropriate dress, scent and gait" (*EN*, 242). The bad storytellers, however, insist on remembering a story in all its details. Salim, who is now mute and cannot tell the stories he remembers, feels that all remembering is in vain, for a story needs at least two people to survive (*EN*, 242–43).

For Benjamin, the invisible tie that binds the storyteller to the listener is memory. The listener is not a passive player, but an agent that has to reproduce the story. Memory creates the chain of tradition. The storyteller does not burden the listener with psychological explanations, for these bar the magical by legitimizing the logical. Storytelling "is not concerned with passing on the pure essence of the thing (*das pure "an sich" der Sache*) like information or a report."[30] Like Nietzsche, Benjamin rejects the concept that mere accumulated knowledge or scientifically verifiable truths can explain the complexity of human life and history. Information "lays claim to immediate verifiability." Its primary objective is to be understandable "in and of itself" [an und für sich]. It is often not any more exact than the knowledges of previous times. Yet, "whereas the latter willingly borrowed from the miraculous, it is absolutely necessary for information to sound plausible. Therefore, it proves to be incompatible with the spirit of storytelling." Benjamin concludes that the growing power of information dissemination has played an important role in diminishing the significance of storytelling (390–91). Information has use only for the moment; it is trapped in its synchronicity. The story, on the other hand, is the keeper of memory. It merges the event with the life of the storyteller. And with each retelling, the layers of circumstantial memories grow.

Like Benjamin's essay, Schami's *Erzähler der Nacht* is a memorial to storytelling in an age of its apparent demise. Each storyteller relates a story, anecdote, cautionary tale, or a segment of history with his or her own signature. Schami once revealed that he tried to incorporate into this book every known art of narrative in the world, every kind of tale, even the story the fire tells the wood. (*D*, 114). Indeed, Schami's novel, which is composed of numerous embedded tales, is a compact museum of narrative genres: allegory, chronicle, memoir, fairy tale, short story, novella, anecdote, lie, gossip, proverb, polemic, political speech, social commentary, tale of exile, and last but not the least, silence. In fact, the frame of the tale is based on Damascus's most famous storyteller Salim's sudden loss of voice. At yet another level, *Erzähler der Nacht* is a kind of narrative performance that flourishes in countries where ruthless and dangerous forms of state censorship silence and persecute writers. Writers often silently resist censorship by rewriting commonly known folktales or fairy tales with subtle twists. The late prominent Turkish humorist Aziz Nesin, whom Islamic fundamentalists attempted to assassinate for his publication of the Turkish translation of Rushdie's *Satanic Verses*, was famous for his fairy tales for grownups that, in their elusive symbolism, censured oppressive and corrupt regimes and politicians. Writing under censorship, as Heinrich Heine well knew, also has great advantages, in that storytellers develop a powerful and intimate relationship with the reader through a secret symbolic code.

In *Erzähler der Nacht*, Schami recalls a troubled era in recent Syrian history and allows censored voices to come to word through the symbolic economy of the frame narrative. Schami, a professional storyteller and writer, uses the German language as a vehicle to generate a politically committed and stylistically innovative literature that engages questions of orality, literacy, and cultural translatability. Part story, part history, *Erzähler der Nacht* interweaves fantasy with lived experience, folktale with social criticism, nostalgia with political commentary, and the Arabic idiom with the German language. The first-person narrator of the novel is a young boy who is the only child allowed in the circle of the storytellers, and the narrative frame is based on the premise of finding a cure for retired coachman and master storyteller Salim's sudden loss of speech. Twenty-one words before the onset of speechlessness, Salim's muse, the story fairy, appears to him and tells him that after sixty years of service to him she is retiring and taking his gift of speech with her. However, since she had always been very fond of him, the fairy king had relented and agreed to let her return to him if Salim were to receive seven unique gifts within three months. Thus begins the race to find the gifts that can redeem Salim. His close circle of friends, all around seventy, come from various walks of life, Ali, a locksmith; Musa, a barber; the former minister of finance Faris, nicknamed "the Red Pasha" for his radical reforms, Tuma, "the emigrant," who lived for many years in America; Junis, the coffeehouse owner; and Isam, who spent twenty-four years behind bars for a murder he did not commit. They come up with every imaginable remedy, to no avail, and finally decide to take turns telling Salim their unique stories. These six friends are "the storytellers of the night" in the book's title. In "The Thousand and One Nights," an essay of extraordinary learning and insight, Jorge Luis Borges recounts that the famous German Orientalist and translator Baron von Hammer-Purgstahl mentions certain storytellers of the Orient known as *confabulatores nocturni*, men of the night whose profession was to tell stories at night. Apparently, the first person who employed these storytellers of the night to ease his insomnia was Alexander of Macedon.[31]

Schami's novel is not just another modern contribution to the tradition of the Arabian cyclical tale whose most illustrious example is *The Thousand and One Nights*, a book by thousands of anonymous authors, none of whom knew s/he was helping to construct a masterpiece. However, Schami is quite aware that he is contributing a new chapter to this one continuous book by giving it a specific geography and a history. In his above-mentioned essay, Borges observes that history and chronology, though they exist in the East, are primarily Western inventions. "There are no Persian histories of literature or Indian histories of philosophy, nor are there Chinese histories of Chinese literature," he writes, "because they are not interested in the succession of facts. They believe that literature and poetry are eternal processes."[32] The title *Thousand and One Nights*, as Borges remarks, suggests an infinite book. Thus, not only its anonymous authors but also its many translators added their versions to it. In a Borgesian manner, Schami's tale of storytellers and tales translates history into memory, theory into story, and political censure into fairy tale.

The premise of the novel itself, Salim's sudden speechlessness, allegorizes the silencing of crucial truths under unstable and oppressive regimes, universal censorship, and senseless victimization of citizens to cover up state lies. For example, there is the heartbreaking story of a goat owner who sold fresh milk on the streets of Damascus. One day government officials, who feared that unpasteurized milk would add to the cholera cases they kept denying through state-controlled radio, confiscated the seven goats of the poor milkman. Driven to hunger and trying to eke out a living with odd seasonal jobs, he never gave up the hope that his seven darlings would one day return to him. Many of the tales are cautionary tales that urge the listener to wrest away emancipatory memory from the history of lived oppression. The stories are constantly interrupted by the listeners who insert social and political commentary and other minitales into the narrative. When Junis and Musa hear how a king in one of the tales banishes the first of his many wives, who could not give him a son, to a distant island and announces that the queen died in childbirth, they are livid: " 'May God cripple his tongue for that lie,' curses Junis; 'what kind of a cowardly dog is he!' fumes Musa. 'I have five daughters and I wouldn't exchange the nail of the small toe of my daughter for a son' " (*EN*, 224). Here there is an attempt to defuse Western notions of the low status of women in Arab society. Furthermore, in the end it is a woman's tale that exorcizes the spell. The story that cures Salim through its uniqueness and originality is told by Ali's wife Fatmeh and is the "true" life story of her mother Leila. Leila, who had settled in Damascus temporarily to raise her only child, was in fact a bewitched storyteller who had the power to heal through narrative. After her daughter's marriage to Ali, Leila leaves Damascus forever to tell her stories in foreign lands and cities. Interestingly enough, this *Erzählerin* (storyteller) as *Erlöserin* (redeemer) is herself a perpetual traveler, not rooted in any land or language but fluent in the universal language of stories.

Schami also introduces, in the person of another unforgettable woman artist, a unique cultural icon of the Arab world. Umm Kulthum, an Egyptian singer who died in 1975 in Cairo, was undoubtedly the most famous performer and cultural ambassador of the Arab world in the twentieth century. Her performing career spanned fifty years, and for forty years her Thursday concerts were broadcast live by the Egyptian radio all over the Arab world, bringing life to a stop everywhere. No self-respecting politician, the narrator observes, would have imagined giving a speech on a Thursday night, because not a single Arab would have listened to him (*EN*, 46). Umm Kulthum was a highly accomplished artist and an incredibly powerful public personality in a very complex society.[33] She was a village girl who negotiated a career through archaic and bureaucratic institutions, created a unique idiom of Arabic music, and achieved a stature that no figure of the Arab world ever came close to. She researched Arabic musical styles and poetry extensively, incorporated these into her repertoire, and consciously fashioned herself as the representative of Egyptian expressive culture. She was the unique diva of the Islamic world. Arab leaders everywhere held her in high esteem. When Egypt was defeated by Israel in the Six-Day War of 1967, Umm Kulthum went on an extended concert tour all over the Muslim world and raised over two and a half million dollars for the depleted Egyptian treasury, most of it in hard currency and gold.[34] Schami invites this unforgettable manager of the memory of Arabic music and poetry to the stage once more to introduce her to a Western audience.

In the *New York Times* review of the English translation of the novel as *Damascus Nights*, Malcolm Bradbury describes Schami's work as a modernized version of *The Thousand and One Nights*, "well digested for Western readers, for whom the tales are clearly written."[35] One can certainly read these tales for sheer entertainment. However, Schami is intent on making clear that he always hides many clues in his writing that allegorize the "history and political developments of the Orient" (*D*, 114). He subverts clichéd images of the Orient as an empty continuum trapped in a stagnant medieval worldview and turns the tables on his Western reading public by exoticizing the Occident through the eyes of his storytellers. Tuma's "real" story of his life in America, though told with humor, is a sharp criticism of Americans' unself-conscious ignorance of the worlds beyond their radar screens. Tuma reveals to his listeners an eye-opening account of the misinformations, half-truths, and stereotypes that plague the representations of Arab people. Americans cannot understand how Tuma, a Christian, can be an Arab. On the other hand, when Tuma tells that Americans have dozens of brands of dog food, people visit cemeteries for pleasure, birthdays are a cause for serious celebration, and nobody bargains in department stores, his incredulous audience is mesmerized by the strangeness of this foreign culture. For the most part, however, Schami's exoticization of the West has a light touch, and cultural misunderstandings are depicted with genuine humor. Tuma tells about an experience riddled with riddles of communication across cultures. In a department store, he asks the saleslady about the price of a jacket. She looks surprised and tells him that it is on the sticker and he can read it. Tuma responds by saying that he can read, but that "life is a conversation, question and answer, give-and-take" (*EN*, 155), and starts bargaining the price down. The salesgirl gets more and more confused. Thinking he is deaf and dumb, she shows him the sticker price, writes it down, and finally gives up hope of getting her message across.

Whether the stories of Schami's *confabulatores nocturni* are life stories, versions of handed-down fairy tales, lies or gossip, they are ultimately allegories of reading a silenced history. Salim's muteness coincides with an era of relentless state repression and censorship during the unification of Syria and Egypt under Egyptian president Gamal Abdal Nasser (1958–61). This merger, known as the United Arab Republic, was intended as a protection against a Communist takeover and to counterbalance the growing Soviet influence in the region. And overnight, the Iraqi president Abd al-Karim Kassem, who had been Syria's close ally and hailed by Radio Damascus as the hero of the Iraqi Revolution, was transformed from friend to foe. Here the narrator reports that Kassem is now depicted as a bloodthirsty demon, and the Syrian radio broadcasts daily reports of famine, uprisings, and cholera in Iraq but not a word about the fighting in eastern Syria (*EN*, 54–55). The Syrian government was consistently silent and in denial about outbreaks of cholera in the country, thus putting the people in grave danger in order to protect itself and reassure the tourists (*EN*, 91). In direct and indirect ways, all stories are cautionary tales that depict the trials of Syrian people after the independence of the country in 1946, the year of Schami's birth, and expose the corruption of successive regimes and ruthless dictators. After the Syrian army officers seized control of the country in 1961 and withdrew from the United Arab Republic, Syria witnessed two more coup d'états in 1962 and 1963. Referring to an earlier set of three revolutions in 1949 alone, Faris tells of a colonel who staged the first of these by storming first the presidential palace and then the radio station, only to be awakened himself 134 days later and executed in his pajamas by another faction. When this colonel first got Faris out of his bed in his pajamas to tell him that he had engineered a bloodless, ingenious coup, Faris replied: "You have opened a door in Syria that you can never close again. You got me out of bed. You'll see that you too will be dragged out of bed before long" (*EN*, 219). The colonel laughs at this and reminds Faris that he is not a civilian and sleeps in his uniform and with his pistols. In many coups during the fifties and sixties in the Middle East, the radio, as the magnifying, authorizing, and disseminating agent of the human voice, became the indispensible can(n)on of military revolution and its rhetoric. Time and again, people woke up one morning to hear yet another army officer announcing that the armed forces had overtaken the government to restore peace and order. In many cases that was all it took to legitimize the new government.

For Schami, committed literature (in the sense of the French *littérature engagé* or the German *engagierte Literatur*) implies making a difference, changing things. A tale, a story, or a novel that aspires to such a commitment has to appeal to the brain and the heart. Bad writing is bad politics. Boring the listener or the reader is unforgivable. *Erzähler der Nacht* pays tribute to the long line of Arabian coffeehouse storytellers, the *hakavati*. The themes, motifs, and rhythms of oral storytelling traditions rooted in gossip, magic, folklore, dreamlore present multiple readings of an event, since tales are understood in relation to other tellings of the tale. This intersubjectivity of retelling and relating offers ways of confronting crisis, loss, and violence in a community.

Erzähler der Nacht is also a memorial to Damascus, the city of Schami's birth, childhood, and early youth. (Coincidentally, in Arabic *Schami* means "from Damascus.") The city's long history was witness to the peaceful coexistence of a vast variety of cultures, religions, and ethnic enclaves. At the time of the novel, Damascus is a city of political oppression and poverty but not of despair. It is a city that embodies the memories of diverse religions and cultural traditions. The old city still resonates with the distant sounds of a remembered past and is woven in its enduring colors like a rugged Oriental rug (*EN*, 105). Unlike Beirut and Jerusalem, other multicultural centers of the Middle East, Damascus resisted becoming a modern-day battleground where neighbor turned against neighbor in bloody conflict. In one of his interviews with Eric Jooß, Schami recalls with nostalgia the Damascus of his boyhood and of a much more remote history, a place where Orthodox Christians, Roman Catholics, Maronites, Muslims, Druses, Baha'is, and Jews lived in peace under the protection of a "historical unwritten treaty" (*D*, 34). A Christian who grew up in the Christian district of Damascus, Schami recalls with wonder and admiration how during the Crusades the predominantly Muslim city protected its Christian minorities while fighting off the Christian enemy. The fast-paced rise of Islamic fundamentalism since the mideighties led to "a betrayal of this historical consensus" (*D*, 34) and to religious conflicts. Around this time, the Damascus of peaceful interfaith constellations disappears and becomes a part of the writer's memory. The religious conflicts, as Schami correctly observes, are no longer about religion as a system and practice of belief; they are about economics, domination, and political corruption. Schami boldly reiterates a well-known but often censored fact, that "Saudi Arabia, the rich land that always saw itself threatened by the poorer, more or less republican regimes, covertly and overtly supported the Islamists with its mighty petrodollars" (*D*, 33). Schami's anxieties about the political developments in the Middle East and the erosion of cultural tolerance in a place with a long history of peaceful multiculturalism and his hopes for the interventionist power of narrative are foregrounded in allegorical transfiguration in all his works.

In Damascus, "Every street has its face, its smell, and its voice" (*EN*, 85). Although smell is generally considered one of the most powerful instigators of recall and the many smells of Damascus streets waft through the narrative, the storytellers of *Erzähler der Nacht* regard voice and speech as the most effective agents of public memory, propoganda, and subversive intent. "The presidents talk longer and longer, and the people become more and more silent," (*EN*, 32–33) complains Faris. But Musa is taken by the speeches of the president broadcast throughout the land: "What is the most beautiful script against the divine tone of the voice? Just the faint shadow of words on paper" (*EN*, 33). Both the real and the fantastic characters that populate this novel reflect frequently and at length on speech in its various manifestations: "Don't waste your words. . . . Words are responsibility" (*EN*, 27); "Gossip has a will of its own, it changes form, becomes more and more colorful, and its origin recedes more and more" (*EN*, 40); "Lies and spices are sisters" (*EN*, 99). The veneration of words comes to word most emphatically in Tuma's account of exile: "I didn't know how valuable the word was until I became voiceless in exile. Words are invisible jewels that are seen only by those who have lost them" (*EN*, 151–52).

In literary cultures with a long history of oral tradition, in modern societies that suffer from low literacy rates, the spoken word rules in the realm of communication. This brings with it the problem of propoganda, which is always controlled by the state and broadcast into the remotest village coffeehouse or living room. *Erzähler der Nacht* articulates the palpable anxiety about the death of communication arts by the radio, especially transistor radios which had become ubiquitous, since they required no electricity and could be listened to anywhere. Junis complains that the radio has replaced the spoken wisdom of men, that it fills the coffeehouse with its drone, silences the customers who in the old days were not afraid to speak their minds (*EN*, 111). In the final analysis, Salim's speechlessness, as the narrator observes in the final chapter that closes the frame, may have been a feigned one, a lesson he wanted to perpetuate. The moral of the story was that silences and silencing can only be broken by the reassertion of the human voice and its reinsertion into narrative and story.

Schami now writes and tells his stories in exile. Coincidentally, a recent article in the *New York Times* reported that the tradition of Syrian storytelling (which had been eclipsed for fifteen years from 1975 to 1990 by other more popular forms of entertainment) has made a comeback and holds nightly audiences under its powerful spell in this "era of uncertainty about Syria's future."[36] The oral storytelling tradition, though seriously diminished in a global sense, lives on locally and has enjoyed a comeback in diasporic writing. However, in an age of global transformations and transitions, oral storytelling, in order to survive as a source of wisdom, consolation, and sense of continuation, needs to be written down. Writing, as Hans-Georg Gadamer has shown, is the only means of updating tradition and making the past contemporaneous with the present (heeding Benjamin). Only in writing is there "a unique co-existence of past and present" [eine einzigartige Koexistenz von Vergangenheit und Gegenwart].[37] "Written tradition is not a fragment of a bygone world," writes Gadamer, "but has already raised itself above it into the sphere of meaning that it expresses." What is written is not a mere document of the past, merely a bearer of tradition, but "the continuity of memory" [die Kontinuität des Gedächtnisses] (368). Writing marks a will to be remembered. Following G.W.F. Hegel, Gadamer sees the beginning of history coinciding "with the emergence of a will to hand down, 'to make memory last' " [mit der Entstehung eines Willens zur Überlieferung, zur "Dauer des Andenkens"]. Gadamer acknowledges that there can be a will to continuity without writing; however, only a written tradition can transcend mere continuity. Therefore, writing enables literature to acquire "its own contemporaneity with every present" [eine eigene Gleichzeitigkeit mit jeder Gegenwart] (369). Faris, the most learned man in Salim's circle, contradicts the barber who claims writing is but the mere shadow of words on paper: " 'Writing is not the shadow of the word but the trace of its steps. Today we can hear the voices of ancient Egyptians and Greeks as clearly as if they were speaking to us, only through the script. Yes, my dear, only writing can let the voice travel through time and grant it the immortality of gods' " (*EN*, 33). Hélène Cixous imagines "x-ray-photo-eco-graphing" the time of a conversation between two people, conserving "the radiation of this encounter in a transparent sphere," listening to "what is produced in addition to the exchange identifiable in the dialogue," and recording invisible events and signs that contradict the message of the dialogue as the unique accomplishments of writing. In other words, writing captures signs, gestures, and a whole web of semiotic economies that elude speech. The art of writing and not the art of theater can make invisible events, "silences," "mute words" appear at the edges of writing, "at sentence-corners." What is not said but "expressed with means other than speech" can "be taken up in the web of writing."[38]

Islands of Memory/Memories of Islands

Perhaps the most kaleidoscopic form of cultural memory is concentrated in island nations that mark stations of transit in diasporic movements. In a recent study on Caribbean cultures, Antonio Benítez-Rojo observes that "the culture of the Caribbean, at least in its most distinctive aspect, is not terrestrial but aquatic, a sinuous culture where time unfolds irregularly and resists being captured by the cycles of clock and calendar."[39] Just as language islands are linguistic and cultural memory archives, so are actual islands, especially those that have been occupied and colonized by different powers. The memories of violence that are the legacy of bloody colonial conquests are transcoded into the human and natural habitat of the islands. Benítez-Rojo argues that "the cultural discourse of the Peoples of the Sea attempts, through real or symbolic sacrifice, to neutralize violence and to refer society to the transhistorical codes of Nature." Since these codes are neither rigid nor finite, "the desire to sublimate social violence" can only be realized in a poetic space (17). This leads me to an inquiry into the implications of cross-cultural literatures of island nations and reconfigurations of cultural memory in a hermetic space. The collision, confrontation, and conservation of different cultural influences acquires a tangible intensity in delimited zones of time and geography such as islands and borders. In *The Island of the Colorblind*, Oliver Sacks describes islands as "experiments of nature, places blessed or cursed by geographic singularity to harbor unique forms of life." These unique species follow "a separate evolutionary path in their isolated habitats."[40] As with species and genera, so with human cultures. This is particularly true of the Caribbean islands, where ghosts and deities of the past have never departed but followed distinct and divergent r/evolutionary paths to become variously memorialized. Literally and figuratively at crosscurrents, island nations of the Caribbean, such as Haiti, Cuba, Puerto Rico, and the Dominican Republic are caught in a bond(age) of proximity to lands that themselves were long-term colonies. The Caribbean islands have been sites of clash and conflict centering around issues of national, religious, and ethnic identity, independence and mandated status, capitalism and socialism. Structures of power and influence that are engaged in overt and covert struggles are many—memories of Spanish, African, and French pasts, African shamanism and sorcery, voodoo and Spanish Catholicism, American and Russian imperialisms, patriarchal dictatorships and Independentista movements. Loyalty to the island and the desire to escape to the mainland or back to the original homeland also exist in a state of unresolved tension. These islands are palimpsests of histories, and often each archeological layer can be uncovered in almost intact form. The burden of political and religious memory consistently maintains high levels of intensity, since the geography of a small island affords the perfect site for preservation, and time likes to sit still in the tropical heat.

The following Haitian and Puerto Rican tales depict the intensity, color, taste, and smell of personal and collective memories born of the islands and passed on in the voices of the daughters of the islands. Although intimately allied in their vision of comparable pasts, these stories inscribe history in different symbolic registers, thus challenging any assumption about the relative homogeneity of Caribbean cultures. This diversity of rhetorical strategies is engendered by a visible resistance to the notion of "cultural hybridity," a resistance that aspires to preserve the specificity of migrated cultures, veneration of ancestors, and loyalty to original languages. The different narrative voices accentuate historical, political, social, religious, and linguistic ruptures and factions throughout the region. Edwidge Danticat's *Breath, Eyes, Memory* is a coming-of-age novel narrated in a voice of poetic sovereignty, innocent of theoretical intervention. And in her first English novel, *The House on the Lagoon*, Rosario Ferré offers an almost perfect metanarrative in which two writers fight for the restoration of the Puerto Rican past with oppositional techniques of history and story writing, as they contest each other's version of their family histories. Since many Caribbean storytellers write in ex-i(s)le, they necessarily occupy a fragmented and contested geography as subjects, a space of conflicting loyalties to language, nation, and cultural values. Although she makes no apologies for rewriting her personal experience of Haiti, Danticat admits to self-questioning, when confronted by Haitians who criticize her for not really knowing what is going on in Haiti, eschewing the hard truths, and not writing in her own language.[41]

Breath, Eyes, Memory

> I come from a place where breath, eyes, and memory are one, a place from which you carry your past like the hair on your head. Where women return to their children as butterflies or as tears in the eyes of the statues that their daughters pray to.

> **Edwidge Danticat, Breath, Eyes, Memory**

These lines toward the end of Edwidge Danticat's tale bear testimony to the indestructable matter that is the stuff of memories. Everything lives but in transfigured form, women as butterflies, stars, or larks, the living as ghosts, history as prison, French as Creole, lived experience as recurring nightmare, and the world as Guinea (netherworld). Sophie Caco, a young girl in the impoverished village of Croix-des-Rosets in Haiti, is raised by her illiterate aunt Atie and does not know her mother, who left her in infancy to live in New York. As young Sophie crosses the border into adolescence, she is summoned by her mother to join her in New York, to cross another thorny border into a world of ambiguous promises. Atie tells Sophie that when she wakes up in New York, her life in Haiti with her aunt will appear to be a distant dream. Yet this dream-memory clings to every fiber of Sophie's American reality. Her life in America turns into an ongoing quest of reconstructing from the shards of her mother's nightmares her troubled history in order to reclaim and redeem her. The quest ultimately fails, for memory does not self-destruct but can destroy its prisoners.

Danticat's story is characterized by several important insights common to many tales of migrancy and dislocation. Memory is irascible and unerasable when inscribed into matter. As inscription in flesh, it resists all forms of exorcism. In order to stay one step ahead of confinement in an asylum, Sophie's mother requests an exorcism before she dies of a self-induced abortion. The experience of deprivation and violence suffered in the Haitian homeland lives on as material memory in exile in the scars of women's bodies, in their accents, in the taste of their cooking. It is ironic that Sophie and her mother, removed from the suffering of Haiti in the relative comfort of Providence and New York City, are subjected to the physical assaults of memory on their bodies, whereas Sophie's grandmother and aunt in Haiti survive the hardships of their homeland without bodily harm. Sophie learns that she was conceived when her mother was raped by a masked assailant in Haiti. His invisible face becomes visible in Sophie's features. The mother, unable to face the face of her rapist in the child and the site of the crime, flees her country for good. But the visions of both the crime and its scene haunt her incessantly. When the mother sends for Sophie, the reunion heals some of the scars of her rape and cancer temporarily. The cancer that slowly ravages the mother's body, entrapping it in a web of pain and despair, becomes an added metaphor for the insidiousness of embodied memory. Eventually, both mother and daughter become hostages of the same nightmarish past that takes its toll on their bodies.

Obsessed by the fear that Sophie may incur the same fate as herself, the mother "tests" her periodically to make sure that her virginity is intact. The pain and the shame of this practice drive Sophie into a self-inflicted violation of her hymen with a pestle. As a result, she is thrown out by her mother and is free to marry Joseph, a Creole musician from Louisiana, and has a daughter. Although she finally finds a relatively safe haven in her small family, the traces of her mother's violation and her own self-violation reappear in Sophie in the form of anorexia, bulimia, and sexual phobia. The past is displaced into the present through the body. There is an inescapable irony in the fact that an immigrant from an impoverished land where food is a great luxury would suffer from anorexia, a decidedly Western disease of affluence and wastefulness. " 'How does that happen?' " asks Sophie's mother in astonishment,

> I have never heard of a Haitian woman getting anything like
> that. Food, it was so rare when we were growing up. We could
> not waste it. . . . When I first came, I used to eat the way we ate
> at home. I ate for tomorrow and the next day and the day after
> that, in case I had nothing to eat for the next couple of days.[42]

The extra pounds on women in poor lands signify wealth and health and are a cultural determinant of desire. But Sophie falls into the habit of eating unhealthy and fattening foods that would evoke "[n]o memories of a past that at times was cherished and at others despised" (151). Although deep lines of suffering permeate this story, they do not prevent the narrator from poking fun at life in America, a land of excess obsessed with losing weight, an overworked and overfed nation full of underloved souls spending their extra time and money in support groups and therapist's offices. The dialectic of remembering and forgetting is played out in its many nuances in this tale. Both Sophie and her mother want to erase the traces of origin in their voices. Sophie is irritated when people inquire about the faint accent in her speech. Her mother's answering machine speaks its instruction in English and French:

> "*S'il vous plait, laissez-mois un message.* Please leave me a message." Impeccable French and English, both painfully mastered, so that her voice would never betray the fact that she grew up without a father, that her mother was merely a peasant, that she was *from the hills.* (223).

Like Lady Macbeth, who tries to rub off the scent of blood from her hands with the finest oils of Arabia, the mother tries to erase the black memory of her skin with various lightening creams. This obsession with erasure only ends in more remembering. A conversation with a taxi driver upon Sophie's return to her home in Haiti is revealing with regard to the modes of resistance to remembering and forgetting in exile. The driver praises Sophie:

> "I find your Creole flawless," he said.
>
> "This is not my first trip to La Nouvelle Dame Marie. I was born here."
>
> "I still commend you, my dear. People who have been away from Haiti fewer years than you, they return and pretend they speak no Creole."
>
> "Perhaps they can't."
>
> "Is it so easy to forget?"
>
> "Some people need to forget."
>
> "Obviously, you do not need to forget," he said.
>
> "I need to remember." (95)

In this vein, Rosario Ferré provides a critical insight into the socioeconomic determinants of selective forgetting among Puerto Ricans in the United States. She argues that Puerto Ricans who come from a privileged class and are part of the recent brain drain from the island "can afford to keep memory clean and well-tended," but "[t]hose who come fleeing from poverty and hunger . . . are often forced to be merciless with memory, as they struggle to integrate with and become indistinguishable from the mainstream."[43] For Ferré, this violation of memory among the poor Puerto Rican youth in the States amounts to cultural suicide, for by refusing to learn Spanish, a language that remains a memorial to their disadvantaged origins, they cordon off the main road to their history and literature.

For Sophie's mother, the power of destructive memory drowns the potential of enabling cultural memory (which resides in the healing power of stories, prayer, rites, magic) and leads to a tragic death. Pregnant with a male child from her lover of many years, she is violently seized by the return of the not so repressed. Following a botched attempt at self-abortion she bleeds to death. The mother's valiant struggle to put the violence she suffered behind her, to try to reconcile herself with her American life, and her efforts to make a go of things silently allegorize the fate of Haiti. Although the political tone of this "memoir" is very subdued, the metaphorical dimension evokes the larger historical and political parallels to the life of Sophie's family.

In 1804 only the second nation after the United States to win independence in the Western Hemisphere, Haiti is today the poorest nation in the Western Hemisphere. It is the only nation whose birth came about as the result of a successful slave rebellion. The turbulent history of the nation's birth is steeped in lore and legend and memorialized in the Citadel and the Palace of Sans Souci, both built by Christophe, who led Haitian troops against the French, British, and Spanish forces in a twelve-year revolt that ended in Haiti's proclamation of independence in 1804. Reputedly the largest fortress in the Western Hemisphere, the Citadel, Christophe's "legacy of stone and arrogance,"[44] is considered a symbol of the Haitian spirit of independence. After the liberation of Haiti, Christophe crowned himself King Henri I in 1811. "Memories are made of stone," writes Michel-Rolph Trouillot, "and Henry I built more than his share of forts and palaces."[45] The enormous amount of labor expended on the fortress and several other mountaintop forts by an isolated and war-torn country testifies to the determination of the former slaves to hang on to their newly found independence. Christophe suffered a stroke in July 1820 from which he never recovered, killed himself a few months later, and was buried in the Citadel, which had claimed twenty-thousand lives through the cruelty of forced labor.

In the course of its history as an independent nation, American intervention, internal political strife, and widespread corruption have eaten away at the economic and spiritual fabric of Haiti's island community. François Duvalier ("Papa Doc") and his son Jean-Claude ("Baby Doc") raped and plundered the island from 1957 to 1976, when Baby Doc was finally forced to flee. After 1986 many attempts at civilian democracy were aborted by military coups.[46] Political unrest and economic hardship have driven floods of Haitians to the shores of the United States, yet those who stay home remain committed to the preservation of their fragile democracy. Partly because of their early independence, the Haitians have a strong sense of their own place in history and a commitment to the survival of a free, just, and democratic nation. Feelings toward the United States in the Haitian community of exiles are often in conflict. "Never the Americans in Haiti again" shouts a man during a heated discussion among immigrants in a Haitian restaurant in New York, where Sophie is having dinner with her mother and her mother's boyfriend Marc. "Remember what they did in the twenties. They treated our people like animals . . . they made us work like slaves."[47]

In the long run, Sophie's mother does not survive the violence, but Haiti, raped and plundered by imperialist ambitions and corrupt politicians, does. Danticat dedicates her book to "the brave women of Haiti" who "have stumbled but . . . will not fall." However, her work articulates the political only in the realm of the personal and only as a chapter of cultural history recalled allegorically in the lyrical tales of the circle of Haitian women—grandmothers, mothers, aunts, sisters, daughters. How does Haiti survive? The charm of Danticat's tale lies in its simple and elegant ability to demonstrate how narrative transforms trials and pain into empowering wisdom. When the young Sophie has to leave her beloved aunt Atie in Haiti, she asks her how to avoid "chagrin" from happening to them. Atie answers that we don't choose chagrin, rather it chooses us. Yet she assures her niece that the capacity to bear pain is the privilege of the strong. "She told me about a group of people in Guinea who carry the sky on their heads," Sophie recalls; they were given the sky by their Maker because they were strong. "These people do not know who they are," continues Atie, "but if you see a lot of trouble in your life, it is because you were chosen to carry part of the sky on your head" (25). In a fundamental way, folklore and fairy tales are practices of "collectively remembering the significance of what a language is to a particular culture, of privileging certain explanations above others."[48]

Danticat's language resonates with traces of several other accents. Her parents spoke English, but the everyday language of the family was Creole, not French. She and her brother conversed in a mix of English and Creole. She is very appreciative of the efforts of French Creole writers who are striving to find a voice. Danticat's own voice is an accomplished and polished instrument capable of registering an eclectic range of linguistic memories. "I learned a great deal from reading Jacques Roumain," she says, "because he captured so much of Creole in French. That's what I try to do in English, so that our voices can still come across, so that people can recognize a different voice even if I'm translating myself when I write."[49] Trouillot attributes the silences in Haitian historiography to the inability of most Haitians to participate in the production of their own history. "[T]he writing and reading of Haitian historiography implies literacy and formal access to a Western—primarily French—language and culture," states Trouillot. But since "[m]ost Haitians are illiterate and monolingual speakers of Haitian, a French-based Creole," they are effectively silenced in the writing of a history that has been dictated by Western conventions and practices.[50] Danticat's sociopolitical engagement with her Haitian origins assumes the form of giving her people a voice, offering their lyrical wisdom to a wider audience. In *Krik? Krak!* a collection of stories Danticat published in 1995, she "shows the violence and poverty existing alongside a defining love and hope that keep life going in Haiti regardless of the holocaust surrounding it."[51] Ultimately, in Danticat's work, all therapy is narrative therapy where the occulted memories of many cultures shimmer through in a tapestry of shared sounds and images. She unpacks for the reader shards of rite and ritual embedded in the many speech forms of the island—sounds of French and of Haitian Creole, African nature gods, voodoo magic—and translates the material of this discovery into an idiom of recovery.

The House on the Lagoon

Toward the end of Rosario Ferré's metafictional novel *The House on the Lagoon*, Isabel, the main narrator, reflects on the generic status of her own writing: although she has filled pages and pages, she is not certain whether she has been "working on . . . a biographical novel, a diary, or just a handful of notes which would never take a definite form."[52] Ferré crafts ingenious allegories of history, memory, nationhood, and gender roles in stories about her native Puerto Rico. In one of her dreams, she finds an apt image for her status as an island writer afloat between the island and the mainland in the currents and currency of two languages. Upon returning to San Juan from Washington, D.C., after a five-year stay, Ferré has a dream in which she is still in Washington, carried away by the cool waters of the C. and O. Canal. She catches a glimpse of the shore of Washington to her right and the shore of San Juan to her left. Her interpretation of the dream concludes in the reflection that as a writer her true habitat is neither shore, but rather the water of words, "neither Washington nor San Juan, neither past nor present, but the crevice in between." The dream tells her that "one has to learn to live by letting go, by renouncing the reaching of this or that shore, but to let oneself become the meeting place of both."[53]

The House on the Lagoon is the story of the long and ill-fated marriage of Isabel Monfort and Quintín Mendizabal. At another level, it is the history of Puerto Rico, embodied in the fortunes of the two families that are the major actors in this novel, the Mendizabals, rich, upper-class merchants, and the Aviléses, their servants who are descendants of slaves. In middle age, Isabel starts writing a multigenerational novel about the Monfort and Mendizabal families, the story of the arrival of their Spanish, Basque, and Corsican ancestors in Puerto Rico, and the personal, communal, and political contexts of their experience of Puerto Rico's historical destiny. Isabel presents in lush colors the variegated culture of the island, its mixture of African, Spanish, and Native American styles and mythologies. She parodies the insistence of the island's racist elite who defy history and geography to maintain pure bloodlines in this compact meeting ground of races, and she registers their astonishment at being treated as colored folk by the Americans during their trips to the mainland. Isabel, a Vassar graduate who majored in Romance literatures, uses historical facts selectively in putting together a colorful memory album of her family. Quintín, a historian by training and businessman by vocation—and clearly by avocation—finds his wife's manuscript and is bothered both by her imaginative use of historical facts and her representations of the family. He is outraged by the autobiographical nature of the novel, its potential for airing the family's dirty linen, and Isabel's misappropriation of the historical facts he had given her. Isabel is truly declaring her independence from the constraints of her family and culture, and Quintín is determined to put an end to her flagrant behavior. Initially, he responds by writing alternative chapters to those in the manuscript, hoping Isabel will come to her senses. At first, Isabel ignores Quintín's "corrections" of her history, but things get complicated, as history itself spins out of control.

Throughout the novel itself, ambivalent viewpoints on the self-contained status of (I)land experience appear as island (in)sights. After his fall from grace as the first Puerto Rican chief of police, Quintín's grandfather Arístides wanders alone in Old San Juan, gazing at the sea and finding comfort that "[a]t the water's edge there was nothing to hold you back; nothing to remind you that you had lost everything."[54] He celebrates the promise of the waters to rearrange borders, change lives, nurse wounds, and let one sail to the world beckoning at the horizon, without money or a ticket, simply in "imagination, the sailboat of the soul" (134). The simultaneously desired and contested relationship of the island to the mainland is aptly expressed in the metaphor of a marriage of convenience: "The way I see it," Isabel remarks about the uneasy commonwealth status of Puerto Rico, "our island is like a betrothed, always on the verge of marriage." If Puerto Rico becomes a state, it has to accept English, her future husband's language, as her official language (184). Throughout the novel, Isabel champions the freedom of bi- and multilingualism, the preservation of linguistic memory on the island. In recounting the story of Bernabé, an African chieftain brought to the island as a slave from Angola, Isabel makes a passionate case for peoples' inviolable right to their languages. Slaves were forbidden to speak their native Bantu, a cruel ban that Bernabé could not accept, for "[o]ne's tongue was so deeply engrained, more so even than one's religion or tribal pride; it was like a root that went deep into one's body and no one knew exactly where it ended" (60).

One of the most contested issues in the never-ending debate about the island's status is language; in the absence of a synthesizing allegory of nationhood, language becomes the unifying force of community identity. Nurturing language—by magic incantations, writing and reciting poetry, and gossiping—is the dominant activity in the circles of women. In fact, rumor is the other narrator of the story. As John Berger once observed, rumor rules in places where life flows with the currents of unpredictability and incertitude. It is "worse than myth for it is uncontrollable." It "is a mass reaction to trying to follow, anticipate and hold together events which are always on the brink of chaos."[55] Islands are sites of the kind of gossip that sprouts and grows like the native foliage. Rumor and gossip are transmitted instantly without the need for electronic devices. "Gossip is like Spanish moss," writes Quintín on the back of Isabel's manuscript, "it knots itself around every telephone pole and hangs from the eaves of houses in no time at all."[56] The water locks the words in, separates the discourse of the island from the outer world, but currents can transport words and memories to faraway worlds. The water around the island functions in Ferré as a metaphor of hyphenated selves and cultures; it separates and connects at the same time. "Every time we wet our feet or wade into the sea, we touch other people, we share in their sadness and their joys," Isabel's son Willie tells her at the end of the novel. "Because we live on an island, there is no mass of mountains, no solid dike of matter to keep us from flowing out to others. Communication is possible, Mother" (389).

The House on the Lagoon is a polished and well-crafted metanarrative that contests the master status of historiography over story. The troubled history of Puerto Rico's peculiar status as a commonwealth, the never-resolved debates about statehood and independence are told through the perspectives of multiple narrators who voice their opinions in Isabel's text, which is contested and interrupted by Quintín's commentaries. Isabel is "commissioned" by her grandmother Abby, who wishes her granddaughter to be the memory of the family, to script the multigenerational narrative. "Now you can write the story of our family," she tells Isabel, as she prepares to die, "with the dead and the living to help you, and I can rest in peace" (203). Isabel is not only a fledgling novelist but also a self-conscious literary critic. It seems that she has been keeping abreast of poststructuralist theories after graduating from Vassar. The following observation testifies to her dabblings in reader-response theory. "Each chapter is like a letter to the reader," she says of Choderlos de Laclos's novel *Les liaisons dangereuses*; "its meaning isn't completed until it is read by someone" (311). Quintín regards fiction as a web of lies and history as the true account of human endeavors that can change the course of events. A proponent of scientific historicism, Quintín finds history an ethically superior mode of narrative. What ensues is a theoretical debate about historiography and its discontents, about history and fiction, fact and construction in which Isabel has the postmodern theorist's upper hand:

> History doesn't deal with the truth any more than literature does. From the moment a historian selects one theme over the other in order to write about it, he is manipulating the facts. The historian, like the novelist, observes the world through his own tinted glass, and describes it as if it were the truth. But it is only one side of the truth, because imagination—what you call lies—is also a part of the truth. Like the dark side of the moon, it's no less real because it can't be seen. Our veiled passions, our ambivalent emotions, our unaccountable hates and preferences can best be understood through novels, and heard across the centuries. But I know you'll never agree with me, so we may as well drop the subject. (312)

Isabel takes her place in the age-old contentious debate between fiction and historiography and follows in the footsteps of the likes of Aristotle, Novalis, and Michel de Certeau. "In its struggle against genealogical storytelling, the myths and legends of the collective memory, and the meanderings of the oral tradition, historiography establishes a certain distance between itself and common assertion and belief," writes de Certeau; "it locates itself in this difference, which gives it the accreditation of erudition because it is separated from ordinary discourse."[57] For Novalis, "A historian must necessarily be a poet, for only the poets are likely to perfect the art of skillfully configuring events." As long as the events and characters of a narrative reflect the spirit of an age, it is of no consequence whether or not they are invented.[58] Novalis stresses that history is produced at various sites, and its articulation is subject to different regimes of memory with conflicting visions. To the seasoned person, history makes the unknown world familiar by means of telling images. These images need literary re-membering and narrative coherence to become knowledge (257–58). Poetry enables the reader to understand the complexities of experience through image, analogy, and allegory, whereas history explains through analysis. In de Certeau's terms, historiography "is always attached to an ambition to speak the 'real.' This ambition contains the trace of a primitive global representation of the world."[59] Fiction, on the other hand, "in any of its modalities—mythic, literary, scientific, or metaphorical—is a discourse that 'informs' the 'real' without pretending either to represent it or to credit itself with the capacity for such a representation." Because literary texts do not aspire to a "univocal" discourse and eschew empirical solutions, they can draw upon a larger database of possible combinations and configurations of events (202). This (poetic) configuration allows for a critical transformation of historical phenomena.

As Quintín continues to eagerly and surreptitiously read each new chapter of Isabel's novel, his anger at her customized alterations of their family histories grows, and he attempts to bargain with her not to publish it, for not only history but reputations are at stake. When Isabel resists, he threatens to destroy the manuscript. Although families, friends, ideals, trust, and political hopes perish, Isabel's manuscript comes out of the inferno of history intact, and fiction (or rather metafiction) proves mightier than fact. Isabel and Quintín's only biological child, Manuel, who was supposed to take over his father's highly successful business, falls in love with Coral, a mulatto's daughter, and joins a terrorist nationalist organization, leading the attack on his father's house. The elders die; Quintín drives his own brother Ignacio to suicide; Perla, the beautiful daughter of Isabel's friend Esmeralda and Coral's sister, is accidentally killed during a shootout between the National Guard and the slum people; Quintín unleashes his dogs on his own sons and disinherits them and finally dies a horrrible death.

In his final attempts to wrench Isabel's manuscript from her, Quintín belittles his wife's work by telling her that it is "not a work of art.

It's a feminist treatise, an Independentista manifesto; worst of all, it distorts history."[60] Isabel's measured answer that this novel is not about political freedom but personal freedom, about her independence from Quintín, metaphorizes Puerto Rico's desire to claim cultural independence from the United States. Although for the past century Puerto Ricans have been divided over their political status, they have shared a strong sense of pride in their language and cultural heritage. In the plebiscites of 1967 and 1993 the majority voted for the status quo, thus dashing the hopes of the Independentistas. In a nonbinding referendum on December 13, 1998, "the none of the above" option on the ballot—which included the choices (a) U.S. commonwealth, (b) free association with U.S. commonwealth and independence, (c) statehood, (d) independence, (e) none of the above—got the majority of the votes. Today Puerto Rico remains a self-governing commonwealth and enjoys a certain amount of authority over its internal affairs. However, the United States controls all the areas that come under the jurisdiction of the federal government in the United States, including the constitutionality of laws, foreign relations, treaties, declarations of war, customs, immigration, citizenship, military service, social security, and postal service. Yet the island has no voting representatives in either house of Congress, and Puerto Ricans cannot vote in presidential elections.

The space of freedom in the text appears at the meeting of the personal and the emotional with the collective and the political. Whereas Isabel never weakens in her will to preserve the familial and communal life in the empowering texture of imaginative narrative, Quintín, a failed historian, wants to preserve his art collection, the displaced memory, in a museum. The desire to build a museum as his legacy is a telling commentary on a man whose medium is not language. The museum rigidifies memory and, like historiography, it orders and stabilizes lived experience, whereas memory preserves the very fluidity of history. The unrelenting contest between Isabel and Quintín for the appropriation of family (hi)stories represents what David Middleton and Derek Edwards call "the rhetorical organization of remembering and forgetting." This can primarily be understood as an "argument about contested pasts and plausible accounts of who is to blame, or to be excused, acknowledged, praised, honoured, thanked, trusted and so on."[61] Rhetorical practices of ordering the past underline an ideologically motivated desire to remap the present.

Although this novel is a highly accomplished attempt at metafiction, a commentary on history and memory in island cultures, and a subtle and powerful critique of American intervention in Puerto Rico's political, historical, and cultural destinies, it suffers from a certain rigidity of binary oppositions. In spite of the framing devices that allow for a multiplicity of narrative voices, most male characters and in particular Quintín are drawn as caricatures. This abstraction in the portrayal of male characters interferes with the complex work of memory or perhaps with the proper function of poetic historiography by unintentionally reproducing an ideological version of history strictly divided along gender lines that are not so subtle gender typologies. Quintín is not altogether unjustified in his gripe that Isabel has depicted the men in both their families as either brutes or weaklings. There is a twist, however, that somewhat rectifies this all too self-conscious caricaturization of men. The only living witness to Isabel's story is her adopted and much beloved son Willie, Quintín's illegitimate child with a black servant. After all the tragedies, Isabel does decide to leave Puerto Rico and settles with Willie in Florida. Manuel disappears into the oblivion of history, whereas Willie, an artist, lives on in Isabel's life and text, presumably ready to add his own color to her story.

Ultimately, the language of modern dislocations cannot be accommodated within borders of time and place but yields to the idiom of memory, where times collide, are scattered in fragments that then merge in reconfigurations. Isabel's uncertainty about the genre of her own text has come full circle. Memory derives its interventionary force from its freedom from fixed perspectives and "sustains itself by *believing* in the existence of possibilities and by vigilantly awaiting them, constantly on the watch for their appearance."[62] Celia, the family memoirist and matriarch in another novel about a Caribbean island, in Cristina García's *Dreaming in Cuban*, never gives up the memory of Castro's successful revolution. Her belief in the possibilites of the future is conditioned by the liberatory configuration of island geography: "If I was born to live on an island, then I am grateful for one thing: that the tides rearrange the borders. At least I have the illusion of change, of possibility."[63] Isabel's multigenerational memoir survives the inferno of history. It does not allow for the certainty of historical representations but offers alternative forms of explanation. As a fragment—a manuscript in progress in the form of a contestatory dialogue—"a handful of notes"[64] without a definite form—Isabel's text assumes the structure of dream and memory. It negotiates between genres and generations as it develops on the multiple registers of a diary, a family biography, and a theoretical fragment. Writing appears at the site of a lost sovereign history and resists the silencing of the past by its capacity for relationships and reconstellations. Likewise, memory—as a property of plural temporalities, the past, the present, and the future—has "an aptitude for always being in the other's place without possessing it." Thus, it does not exhaust itself yet can effect subtle transformations of tradition. "Memory is a sense of the other," writes de Certeau. "Hence it develops along with relationships—in 'traditional' societies as in love—whereas it atrophies when proper places become autonomous."[65] The stories of the islands illustrate how contested and embattled histories are preserved in protected zones of trop(e)ical memory. The literary text embodies this memory in its various narrative shadings. It reaches out beyond its formal boundaries, beyond the shore/borders of the island to the mainland(s), to a larger world. It evokes the complexity and contested nature of the political and cultural context that gave rise to it and that it allegorizes.

3

Autobiographical Voices with an Accent

> All biographies like all autobiographies like all narratives tell
> one story in place of another story
>
> Hélène Cixous, *Rootprints*

To live "elsewhere" means to continually find yourself involved in a conversation in which different identities are rec-
ognized, exchanged and mixed, but do not vanish. Here differences function not necessarily as barriers but rather as
signals of complexity. To be a stranger in a strange land, to
be lost (in Italian *spaesato*—"without a country"), is perhaps
a condition typical of contemporary life. To the forcibly in-
duced migrations of slaves, peasants, the poor, and the ex co
lonial world that make up so many of the hidden histories of
modernity, we can also add the increasing nomadism of modern thought. Now that the old house of criticism, historiography and intellectual certitude is in ruins, we all find ourselves
on the road. Faced with a loss of roots, and the subsequent
weakening in the grammar of "authenticity," we move into a
vaster landscape. Our sense of belonging, our language and
the myths we carry in us remain, but no longer as "origins"
or signs of "authenticity" capable of guaranteeing the sense
of our lives. They now linger on as traces, voices, memories
and murmurs that are mixed in with other histories, episodes, encounters.

Iain Chambers, *Migrancy, Culture, Identity*

In *Migrancy, Culture, Identity,* Iain Chambers presents a well-orchestrated medley of personal memory, philosophical reflection, anthropological and literary theory, cultural criticism, social commentary, well-positioned quotations, and photographs to communicate how notions of identity and geography shift and shape as they travel through myriad languages and cultures, across borders and histories. At one level, this book can be read as the long version of Chambers's curriculum vitae, his own *Bildungsroman.* Evocative of early German romanticism's *Bildungsroman* that recounts the protagonist's *Bildung* through different stations of his journey in prose, poetry, song, anecdote, letter, philosophical reflection, and free associations of dream and memory, Chambers's text infuses the theoretical with the poetic. The theoretically imagined memoir has emerged as a genre of choice for many academic writers of exile.[1] Its force resides in the interest it holds for many fields and disciplines including literary and cultural criticism, history, anthropology, ethnography, and gender studies. Contemporary memoirs written in exile and migrancy are rarely expressions of a unified voice. The term *autobiographical voices* defines the nature of life stories composed in diasporas more accurately than *autobiography* or *memoir,* since it suggests an explicit or implicit dialogue between the writer and the community, ancestors, or family.[2] Anthropologist Michael M. J. Fischer maintains that this term prevents the problem of defining autobiography as an unambiguous genre by addressing the question of "subject positioning" in personal narratives and autobiographical fictions.[3]

In an earlier article on American ethnic autobiographies, Fischer refines and redefines the concept of ethnicity through a psychoanalytic framework of dream interpretation and memory construction. He rejects an essentialist history and structure of ethnicity but rather understands it as a component of cultural identity that is reinvented and reinterpreted by individuals in every generation. Ethnicity is a dynamic force, even when not consciously instilled in the individual. In its doctrinaire forms of expression, however, it can turn chauvinistic, defensive, and sterile. Because ethnicity is "a deeply rooted emotional component of identity, it is often transmitted less through cognitive language or learning (to which sociology has almost entirely restricted itself) than through processes analogous to the dreaming and transference of psychoanalytic encounters."[4] Fischer analyzes Maxine Hong Kingston's *The Woman Warrior* as an "archetypal text" (208) of ethnic identity construction, where narrative order mimics the fragmentary logic of dreams: "simultaneously the integration of dissonant past fragments and the daydreaming 'trying-on' of alternative possible identities" (212). Fischer argues that contemporary ethnic autobiographies are informed by an accentuated metanarrative mood that calls attention to their linguistic and fictive status and to the authorial privilege of the narrator. The self-reflective tenor of the text, which encourages the reader to "participate in the production of meaning," differs greatly from earlier conventions of autobiography "as a moral didactic form" (232). Texts that call for a dialogue foster an ethical disposition, for they awaken in the reader "a desire for *communitas* with others, while preserving rather than effacing differences" (232–33).

Modern anthropology's growing interest in the literary dimensions of its writing has shifted the concern from the veracity and accuracy of personal narratives to an understanding of these texts as a microcosm of larger political and sociocultural issues. They are no longer regarded as records of individual lives but as the story of a life embedded in a particular history. "Just as the travel account and the ethnography served as forms for explorations of the 'primitive' world . . . and the realist novel served as the form for explorations of bourgeois manners and the self in early industrial societies," notes Fischer, "so ethnic autobiography and autobiographical fiction can perhaps serve as key forms for explorations of pluralist, post-industrial, late twentieth-century society" (195). The interpretive strategies of a given culture inevitably color personal narratives and determine the conditions and constraints of their articulation. However, Fischer argues that ethnic autobiographies cannot be adequately understood in terms of sociological categories, such as "group solidarity, traditional values, family mobility, political mobilization" (195). Likewise, the diversity of diasporic lives cannot follow standard rules of classification. Françoise Lionnet has noted that many autobiographies by women of non-Western cultures use the concept of *métissage* to foreground relationships between historical and personal circumstances, to investigate and illustrate linguistic hybridizations, and "to generate polysemic meanings from deceptively simple or seemingly linear narrative techniques."[5] Lionnet invokes Martinican poet, novelist, and theorist Edouard Glissant's notion of *métissage* to illustrate an important critical dimension of the autobiographical texts she analyzes. *Métissage* is a braiding of "cultural forms through the simultaneous revalorization of oral traditions and reevaluation of Western concepts." The investment in the recovery of their unrecorded histories helps writers to imagine the past "in the absence of hard copy," to rectify "ideological distortions" (4), and to free their ancestors from catacombs of silence.

A textual space "will support more life," that is, generate more significant meanings, "if occupied by diverse forms of life (languages)," observes Lionnet (18). Fischer maintains that autobiography constitutes a "three-fold" object of desire for the anthropologist. First, as an intersection of the speaking subject and the social context, it negotiates between the modernist notion of the autonomous individual and the postmodern de-centered self. Second, autobiography allows access into a world of authentic cultural experience that is often the blind spot of traditional social theory. And the third enduring attraction of autobiography for the anthropologist lies in its ability to foreground "the reflexivity of human storytelling."[6] Since one of the characteristic features of the postmodern age is the coalition of deterritorialized and transnational groups—Indians and Filipinos working in the Persian Gulf, Turks and Arabs in Germany, Mexicans in the United States—contemporary ethnographic practices are informed by a profound cross-cultural critique that would have been impossible even fifty years ago:

> Compare the impact of the style of cross-cultural critique prac-
> ticed by a Bronislaw Malinowski or Margaret Mead, in which
> an exotic pattern of child-rearing could be held up as a foil to
> our own patterns of child-rearing to show that they were not
> "natural," but alterable cultural conventions. Contrast the
> degree of intellectual control necessary under contemporary
> conditions of multiple readerships, where what one writes is
> read by those one writes about as well as by one's colleagues
> or cultural fellows. (82)

It comes as no surprise, then, that a great number of contemporary "autoethnographies" are written by native anthropologists, philosophers, literary critics, and novelists well versed in the arts of theory and memory. The late Libuše Moníková, a highly acclaimed Czech-born writer and critic and a Germanist by training, has commented eloquently on questions of national identity and linguistic diversity by writing her life story, in part, as a dialogue with a national literary history. Maxine Hong Kingston and Eva Hoffman are academically and poetically well positioned to give voice to serious and responsible cultural criticism in their personal narratives. Kingston is professor of creative writing at the University of California, Berkeley. Hoffman, a Harvard Ph.D., journalist, literary theorist, and historian, writes in an academically trained language of great sophistication and insight. Oscar Hijuelos, the prolific and accomplished novelist of the Cuban-American literary scene, infuses notions of cultural and linguistic memory with poetic resonance. The autobiographical voices of Hijuelos, Kingston, Moníková, and Hoffman sound neither "ethnic" nor like traditional autobiography but resonate in both the poetic and the theoretical praxis of writing. The autobiographical narratives of this chapter show us that modern cultural identities are forged from many interrupted (hi)stories whose traces are reconfigured in new environments. They are not in search of identifiable origins and traceable lineages and, in this sense, embody Kristeva's notion of the philosophical stature of the "foreigner." Like a philosopher, the foreigner does not place much emphasis on origins, for although "[h]is origin certainly haunts him, for better and for worse . . . it is indeed *elsewhere* that he has set his hopes, that his struggles take place, that his life holds together today. *Elsewhere* versus the origin, and even *nowhere* versus the roots."[7]

The long-standing debate about the generic status of autobiography and its standing in literary history has produced volumes on the written art of self-portraiture. In *The Forms of Autobiography*, William C. Spengemann names "historical self-explanation, philosophical self-scrutiny, poetic self-expression, and poetic self-invention"[8] as the defining formal strategies of self-representation in the genealogy of autobiography. These strategies are incorporated into diasporic writing in varying degrees and recast in terms of performative acts, such as playing the chorus to the community, projecting multiaccented voices, and improvising identities. The common denominator of many autobiographies of exile is the interweaving of personal, familial, communal, political, mythological, and poetic voices. The autobiographical voices of Hijuelos, Kingston, Moníková, and Hoffman are registered here with particular attentiveness to (*a*) the testimonial, confessional, and biographical dimensions of exilic writing; (*b*) the celebration of bilingualism and polyglot identities; (*c*) the reimagination of geography and genealogy; and (*d*) the nature of their "collective" authorship that reflects the diverse sentiments, aspirations, and politics of the groups they represent. The notion of collective authorship also takes into its purview the decidedly intertextual character of these stories that crisscross between their own narratives and references to other works of imaginative and documentary literature. The naming of these features, however, should not be seen as quantitative or qualitative markers on any absolute scale. They are, at best, compact allegories subject to revision and supplementation.

The memoirs of migration and dislocation discussed here are characterized by multiple, ambiguous, and contestatory voices and by a desire for redefinitions that commission acts of poetic self-reflexivity. They are composed of varying degrees of revelation, fictionalization, veiling, and unveiling. Maxine Hong Kingston's *Woman Warrior: Memoirs of a Girlhood among Ghosts* is one of the best-known, celebrated, contested, and theorized accounts of growing up female in Chinese America.[9] *The Woman*

Warrior locates communal memory not so much in the commonality of remembrances as in the real and reimagined lives of kin and in family traditions and stories. Here, the status of autobiography is one of willed self-invention, constructed in dreamlike sequences. Similarly, Moníková's story does not follow any chronological order but rather forms, by her own account, a sequence of images, dreams, daydreams, mythological and historical visions, all framed, interrupted, and interpreted by literary texts. All four memoirs are situated at the intersection of intimate self-portraiture, linguistic travels and travails, and a poetically nuanced triangulation of dislocation, memory, and human agency. For Hijuelos, Kingston, and Hoffman migration was not a matter of choice. Kingston and Hijuelos were both born in the United States; Hoffman was twelve when her parents took her and her sister to Canada. Moníková, on the other hand, had come to Germany of her own accord as a first-generation émigré. These life stories offer a diversity of strategies for writing about loss and critical insights into the vicissitudes of personal and communal remembrance. Here the object of nostalgia (a remembered, recovered, or invented homeland)[10] is displaced into writing and is no longer locatable in a particular geography. Kingston's China is a memorial site for ancestors known to her only through her mother's cryptic revelations. Moníková's Prague resembles Heinrich Heine's tongue-in-cheek metaphor of literary history as a morgue where critics look for their favorite dead.[11] It is situated within a pathography of contested geographies and genealogies that complicate her efforts to find emotional and intellectual moorings. And Hijuelos's Cuba is a (pre)text for a biography of his mother (and, to a lesser extent, of his father).

Autobiography as Parent/Family Biography

The Woman Warrior

Maxine Hong Kingston's *Woman Warrior*, dedicated to "Mother and Father," is an autobiographical story as a series of dialogues with a parent, an aunt, and spirits of ancestors. In an essay on *The Woman Warrior*, Joan Lidoff notes that many contemporary women's autobiographies are written as biographies. The early 1980s saw a proliferation of what she calls "the forgiving genre,"[12] where daughters foreground the story of the parent(s) and write themselves as an appendix to their text. Interweaving the story of the self with that of parents and family, engaging the m/other in a dialogue, and speaking for a collectivity underline the fundamentally relational character of identity. Lidoff sees in the collective articulation of modern women's autobiographies a gesture that is more compassionate and self-effacing than the dramatization of the self as the starring actor (117). Furthermore, speaking through the other(s) grants the author of the autobiography freedom from the fixity of circumscribed positions and self-definitions. I do not believe that an autobiography speaking through the m/other is necessarily a more just, compassionate, or democratic form of self-representation than a "self-ish" autobiography. In *The Woman Warrior*, Maxine finds a route of escape from the dictates of suffocating convention through an appropriation, understanding, and radical reinterpretation of the collective voices that haunted her through childhood, adolescence, and young adulthood. She purposefully recasts her mother's accounts of their family history in alternative, fablelike, dreamlike settings in order to imagine a forgotten past as an infinitely re-presentable present. In this re-presentation, she is freed from her double bind (and hyphenation) as a Chinese-American girl-child, from the ghosts of a culture that considers raising geese more profitable than raising daughters[13] and is much too fond of aphorisms such as, "When fishing for treasures in the flood, be careful not to pull in girls" (52). "There is a Chinese word for the female *I* which is 'slave,' " observes Maxine. "Break the women with their own tongues!" (47). So she sets out with a vengeance to claim, in a powerful language, a life of honor, valor, and accomplishment, which cultural dictates had prevented her from pursuing.

The *Woman Warrior* adds a very significant dimension to autobiographical imagination and theory. It is not only the story of a life as part of a family, community, and history, but also the programmed invention of the self through autobiography. The memory of her "girlhood" engenders Kingston's (auto)biography; however, the autobiographical project itself determines the (after)life of the subject. In "Die Aufgabe des Übersetzers" (The task of the translator) Benjamin maintains that a translation emerges not from the life (*Leben*) of the original but from its afterlife—literally its survival or endurance (*Überleben*). In other words, translation grants a second life to the original. If autobiography is seen as a form of self-translation, then Maxine gets a new lease on life in her "memoirs." The dialectic of life story and reinvented destiny informs every passage of Kingston's narrative and offers a highly original conceptualization of the autobiographical act. The reinvention of Maxine is facilitated by the talk-stories her mother, Brave Orchid, tells her. In one such story, Brave Orchid narrates the tale of Fa Mu Lan, the woman warrior. In the person of this legendary figure, Maxine imagines the context that links her both to her native culture and to her American life. Like Fa Mu Lan, Maxine has words on her back that need to be avenged. However, Maxine's revenge involves "not the beheading, not the gutting, but the words" (53). Here, the sword returns to life is as a pen.

Kingston once stated that we all had the burden to figure out the reconfigurations of so-called facts in poetic imagination, to understand how "raw human event" is put through "the process of art."[14] Her poetic pilgrimage starts with the objective of restoring to language and memory a disgraced aunt who killed herself and her illegitimate child after giving birth. The family erased the (hi)story of this aunt from memory by denying her a story and a name. "We say that your father has all brothers because it is as if she had never been born,"[15] her mother tells Maxine at the very beginning of the memoir. This recalled incident bears a great tragic irony, for Kingston tells us both in this memoir and more poignantly in *China Men*, a biographical history of the men in her family, that her grandfather had so desperately wanted a girl, as his wife kept producing a string of boys, that he even attempted to exchange her father for a baby girl.[16] The aunt's story is a cautionary tale that Maxine is not allowed to repeat to anyone. The tale is of twofold significance. It renews the ban on memory and imposes another one on Maxine's living speech. Writing becomes the measure to counter speech prohibitions that haunted young Maxine's Chinese-American girlhood. Maxine now rewrites the story of the No Name Woman not in terms of what has been said about her in her mother's narrative but as a tale that provides alternative scripts of her life, where she is portrayed as a rebel with a cause. In the eye of the writer's mind, the aunt is transformed from a hapless victim of rape to a seductress. Through these imagined scripts, Maxine reestablishes her familial links with her aunt in an attempt to reach her own cultural past: "Unless I see her life branching into mine, she gives me no ancestral help" (8). This invented biography-autobiography re-members a life and events, even though the actual life and events may have been very different. "We can change the past by figuring out new meanings of events that took place,"[17] states Kingston, and this is precisely what happens in *The Woman Warrior*, where the oppressed and forgotten women, Maxine, her aunt, and even her mother, are given a new history (an afterlife) through the legend of Fa Mu Lan.

Kingston's memoir has been the object of much passionate dispute among Chinese-American writers who have accused her of fabricating an exoticized version of Chinese culture, an exoticism designed to appeal to Western expectations and preconceptions. As a "guided Chinatown tour,"[18] the book was dismissed by its critics as an exercise in masking the complexities of Chinese cultural traditions. Criticisms focus on willed mistranslations, such as the translation of the Cantonese *kuei* as "ghost," which neutralizes the derogative connotation the word carries for white people, and on liberties taken with Chinese legends, especially that of Fa Mu Lan. Here Kingston is charged with tampering not only with the letter but also the spirit of the legend.[19] Sau-ling Cynthia Wong maintains that Kingston's reinterpretation of Fa Mu Lan's story differs radically even from its popularized version in the "Ballad of Mulan." "[T]he spirit marriage to the waiting childhood sweetheart, a wish-fulfilling inversion of the No Name Woman's fate, is utterly unlikely in ancient China, considering the lowly status of women," writes Wong. "The traditional Fa Mu Lan is never described as having been pregnant and giving birth to a child while in male disguise. . . . The Fa Mu Lan of 'Mulan Shi' [or "Ballad of Mulan"] is a defender of the establishment, her spirit patriarchal as well as patriotic, a far cry from a peasant rebel." Wong cites a Chinese-born scholar, Joseph S. M. Lau, who "dismisses the book as a kind of mishmash, a retelling of old tales that would not impress those having access to the originals."[20] A more sympathetic critic calls the second chapter, "White Tigers," where the Fa Mu Lan tale is retold, "a literal exercise in Chinese myth revision." Kingston's is the last one in a long line of renarrations of the "The Ballad of Mu Lan" in storybooks, novels, plays, and movies. On the received narrative memory, Kingston imposes strands of " 'the [kung fu] movies at the Confucius Church in the 1950s, the Berkeley subculture of the 1960s, and the gender politics of the 1970s."[21]

These criticisms lend support to the view that *The Woman Warrior* depicts cultural memory as a variable, as women's work, and as the mother of invention, in a manner of speaking. It exemplifies the full repertoire of shifts and tensions that the memory of a community is subjected to during the trials and tribulations of passages. The criticisms of Chinese-American scholars provide an interesting reflection because they illustrate a prescribed line of communal memory to which Kingston's tale supplies a form of countermemory. In an earlier article, "Kingston's Handling of Traditional Chinese Sources," Wong concedes that Kingston's artistic enterprise concerns the legitimization of a unique Chinese-American cultural heritage, not the representation of a Chinese-Chinese culture.[22] *The Woman Warrior* is a book about the Chinese-American rites of passage as experienced by the women's line in the family. Here remembrance is creative and interpretive, interlaced with dream, madness, reflection, and the audible whispers of the ghosts of the past. The narrator's commentary offers new ways of understanding linguistic terror, rupture of communication between generations, the stronghold of communal memory, language loss, and madness rooted in speechlessness. What Kingston undertakes may in fact not be any different from the way Chinese culture has been passed on—in parables that form an inscrutable semiotic. The Chinese-American children cannot decode the system that may be perfectly clear to the Chinese, or maybe not. "I think that if you don't figure it out, it's all right. Then you can grow up bothered by 'neither ghosts nor deities,'" muses Maxine. The Chinese have been writing and rewriting culture for an eternity without bothering to supply an owner's manual. She surmises that they probably kept improvising, as they went along. "If we had to depend on being told," she figures, "we'd have no religion, no babies, no menstruation (sex, of course, unspeakable), no death."[23] Maxine's musings bear out Fischer's view of ethnicity as a cultural construct subject to generational definition and ongoing revision.[24]

The immigrant parents cling to a language on which their children have only a tenuous and disintegrating hold. Their cultural habits are ingrained and allow for no recasting. The burden of refashioning cultural practices to avoid embarrassment and misjudgment falls on the children. Maxine has to modify her mother's insistence on receiving reparation candy from a druggist who accidentally had medicine intended for another Chinese family delivered to them. Brave Orchid sees this mistake as a curse cast on her family and insists that Maxine tell the druggist to rectify his crime by sweetness. The child tries to make herself "cute and small" (170) and tells the druggist that her mother asked that he give her candy because that is the way the Chinese did "things." As a young child, she "felt the weight and immensity of things impossible to explain to the druggist" (171). Her cover-up or alteration of Brave Orchid's misplaced demand succeeds, and the druggist gives her a handful of lollipops, not understanding the mother's intention and probably thinking this is a typical child's "thing." In fact, every time Maxine and her siblings go to the drugstore afterward, the druggist showers them with candy. Brave Orchid gloats over her victory of teaching the druggist a lesson, but Maxine is embarrassed and thinks that the druggist feels sorry for them, believing them to be poor and homeless, living in the back of the laundry.

"My mouth went permanently crooked with effort," she writes, "down on the left side and straight on the right" (171). She finds it ironic that Chinese-American girls become almost permanently mute, when emigrant villagers constantly shout. Everyone talks at once, making "guttural peasant noise" (171–72), irking the Americans who hear them. Chinese women's voices were loud and strong and so embarrassed Chinese-American girls that they were reduced to whispering. "Most of us eventually found some voice, however faltering," Maxine remembers, by inventing "an American feminine speaking personality" (172), except for a girl who never spoke even in Chinese school. This mute Chinese girl becomes the scapegoat for Maxine's repressed fury. One day she corners her in school and physically assaults and tortures her to get a word, any word, out of her—and fails. After this incident, Maxine is afflicted by a mysterious illness that keeps her confined to bed for months. Physically and emotionally, the prize for demanding speech, demanding to be heard, is too high and exacts its toll on Maxine's body: "Even now China wraps double binds around my feet" (48).

Women are silenced doubly, first as having no say in any matter, then as linguistic cripples in another tongue. Maxine's tongue was literally cut by her mother at birth. Brave Orchid sliced the frenum of the baby's tongue, so that she could be bilingual (two-tongued), in a manner of speaking. "The tongue has no bones, it turns wherever you turn it," a Turkish saying goes. However, the boneless (and forked) tongue becomes a bone of contention between the mother and the daughter. "Why did you do that to me Mother?" asks Maxine.

> "I told you."
>
> "Tell me again."
>
> "I cut it so that you would not be tongue-tied. Your tongue would be able to move in any language. You'll be able to speak languages that are completely different from one another. You'll be able to pronounce anything. Your frenum looked too tight to do those things, so I cut it."
>
> "But isn't 'a ready tongue an evil?' "
>
> "Things are different in this ghost country." (164)

The Turks also say that someone whose tongue can twist can master languages with ease, communicate well, is glib and smooth (has a "ready tongue"). The implications of this metaphor run through many tales of migration and dislocation.

Although in Maxine's accounts, her mother emerges as an irrational, intolerant, and inflexible figure in her American life, she is redeemed in Maxine's narrative by the memory of her Chinese past. Maxine studies an early photograph of her mother at the age of thirty-seven on the diploma awarded from To Keung School of Midwifery. The retelling of Brave

Orchid's life reveals a competent, liberated, intelligent, and well-educated woman. Before coming to America to toil away in the laundry, she was a competent midwife and doctor held in high esteem by family, friends, villagers, and patients. This narrative provides a form of reparation memory, for here the mother is portrayed as a rational and commanding figure, quite different from her migrated/translated Chinese-American persona. It becomes clear that she and her family were doubly disenfranchised first by the Communists' appropriation of their property and then by her devastating fall from the position of a respected doctor to that of a laundress. The hyphen in *Chinese-American* divides and weakens Brave Orchid's logic of adaptability and resourcefulness. And it reinforces the "neither here nor there" status by drawing her to a place that no longer exists. "We have no more China to go home to" (106), she mourns.

When history and geography are irrevocably lost, the past has to be reinvented to make the present bearable; it has to take on the form of a narrative, a fabulation. The misplaced nostalgia has to be dismantled and restructured as a tale of survival. "We belong to the planet now, Mama. Does it make sense to you that if we're no longer attached to one piece of land, we belong to the planet?" (107), Maxine asks her mother in exasperation. The immigrant child has to clean up the overflowing attics of obsolete ritual to make place for the present:

> To make my waking life American-normal, I turn on the lights before anything untoward makes an appearance. I push the deformed into my dreams, which are in Chinese, the language of impossible stories. Before we can leave our parents, they stuff our heads like the suitcases which they jam-pack with homemade underwear. (87)

Kingston has to translate "the language of impossible stories" into a usable idiom. She realizes that diversity in speech is a prerequisite for survival. The story of Brave Orchid's sister Moon Orchid is a poignant illustration of how losing the nuances of language/narrative ends in madness. After Brave Orchid sends for her sister, whose husband had started a new life and family in the United States, Moon Orchid starts experiencing the devastating effects of being uprooted from her home and relocated in a strange world at an advanced age. She slowly loses her grip on reality, endlessly repeats stories of being followed by Mexican ghosts, and finally has to be confined to an asylum. When Brave Orchid realizes that "all variety had gone from her sister," the narrator gives her what is probably the best line in the book: " 'The difference between mad people and sane people,' Brave Orchid explained to the children, 'is that *sane people have variety when they talk-story. Mad people have only one story that they talk over and over*' " (159) (emphasis added). And the daughter hears the mother's lesson clearly. Survival in an alien culture depends on the ability to translate stories to reclaim, as Benjamin observed, their lessons anew for each age (and place).

In one of the metafictional moments of the book in the final chapter, the narrator presents a reflection on her strategy of rewriting: a radical fragmentation, selection of fragments, and their complex reconfiguration as new narratives, a strategy so complicated that it can "blind" its practitioner. Long ago in China, knot makers tied string and rope into many forms. There was one knot that was so difficult to make that it blinded the knot maker. An emperor finally outlawed this knot. "If I had lived in China," writes Maxine, "I would have been an outlaw knot-maker" (163), drawing attention to her intention to resist transparency and preserve the polyvalency of symbolic retelling. In the end, she offers the further insight that cultures and cultural memories can survive if they are masterfully translated. In the final section of the last chapter, "A Song for a Barbarian Reed Pipe," the Chinese-American girl "who skirted the edges of madness only to ascend, after great pain, triumphantly into voice"[25] offers an account of her own entry into the order of cultural translation through the story of the Han poetess Ts'ai Yen, born in A.D. 175. Daughter of the famous scholar Ts'ai Yung, Ts'ai Yen was captured at twenty by a Hsiung-nu chieftain who made her his concubine. The Han considered the Hsiung-nu, who were from the south and spoke no Chinese, barbarians. During her twelve years in captivity, Ts'ai Yen bore the chieftain two children and tried to teach them Chinese without success. But the Hsiung-nu were masters of a haunting flute music that made Ts'ai Yen "ache," and she could not escape its overwhelming force. Ts'ai Yen taught herself to imitate this music in her own words. One day, the barbarians heard a voice coming from her tent that matched the sound of their flutes. Ts'ai Yen sang in Chinese, but the barbarians could understand the sadness and anger of her words and "could catch barbarian phrases about forever wandering."[26] Ts'ai Yen was finally ransomed off after twelve years in exile and brought back her songs, three of which have been passed down to our day. One of her compositions, "Eighteen Stanzas for a Barbarian Reed Pipe," became a part of the music culture of her own people. "It translated well," the narrator says of the song, and with this last line of the book, she declares herself, in a metanarrative vein, a cultural translator. In a poetically resonant voice, Kingston succeeds in giving us a classic of diasporic writing that raises issues of cultural memory and its discontents, cultural translation, and linguistic exclusion and eloquently portrays the painful passage from an inflexible— because rooted—cultural idiom to life in a bilingual medium.

Our House in the Last World

Oscar Hijuelos's first novel, *Our House in the Last World,* is a fictional biography of his parents, who immigrated to New York as a young couple from their hometown Holguín. Like Kingston, Hijuelos dedicates the book to his mother and the memory of his father (Alejo Santinio, the father in the book, dies in 1969). A big, burly man with a voracious appetite for food, alcohol, and women, Alejo is a very physical presence in the book. Although his life in America turns into a series of disappointments and failures and wealth constantly eludes him, he is generous to a fault toward fellow Cubans, friends, and family. Alejo dies a death of poverty and excess. Too much food and alcohol and lack of adequate medical care lead to a sudden and relatively early death. His only moment of glory under the American sun comes during Soviet premier Nikita Khrushchev's visit to the United States in 1961. Khrushchev attends a luncheon in his honor at the hotel where Alejo is working as a cook. A photograph of Alejo and another cook with the premier is published in *Daily News,* transforming Alejo briefly into a minor celebrity. The memory of this event fades fast, and a yellowed newspaper clipping on the basement kitchen wall remains as the only reminder of Alejo's brush with celebrity.

Relatives of the Santinio family who arrive in America much later find their way to prosperous lives. They do "not allow the old world, the past, to hinder them."[27] Immigrants who are not bound by diasporic loyalty to homeland and compatriots learn to live the American dream. Alejo and his wife Mercedes's attachment to Cubanness and a romanticized past prevents them from attaining the dividends of migration and labor. Nevertheless, Alejo, who never returns to Cuba, constructs a liveable Cuban-American hyphenated identity—although the right side of the hyphen carries very little weight in his case—through his work and the camaraderie with other exiles and immigrants of New York and remains committed to the welfare of his homeland and compatriots to the very end.

This story of immigration, which, like many narratives of passage, gives a graphic depiction of the woes of the displaced, their dashed hopes, marginalization, and perpetual sense of homelessness, turns ultimately into a tribute to Mercedes, to her guardianship of family memories and of Cubanness. Hector, the younger of the couple's two sons, who was born like Hijuelos in 1951 in New York, narrates most of the story. However, Hector's voice often and willingly yields to that of his mother, Mercedes. Mercedes is the bearer of family memories. A sheltered daughter of a once affluent, prominent Cuban family, she was an aspiring poet with a boundless lust for life. In American exile, where her high-voltage Spanish endures as the last physical tie to her past—Hector calls it her "thousand-words-a-minute Spanish" (122)—she becomes literally speechless in the public sphere. As family members left behind in Cuba pass away, Castro's revolution closes the door on hopes of return, and exile thus becomes permanent, Mercedes slips into an apparent madness. She sees and speaks with ghosts of departed family members everywhere. In many stories of immigration, the loss of voice leads women to encounters with voices and visions of ghosts.[28] Ghosts become the ethereal metaphor for losses sustained through passages. They are the invisible markers of a past visible only to those who suffer from an overload of memory.

Mercedes suffers from an excessive remembering and mourning of a departed life. Psychoanalysis sees in the pathology of misremembering, in the delusions and repressions that serve as a substitute for repressed memory, the failure of the work of memory. In "Erinnern, Wiederholen und Durcharbeiten" (Remembering, repetition, and working through), Freud describes the goal of psychoanalytic technique as "filling out the gaps of memory" [Ausfüllung der Lücken der Erinnerung] to overcome resistances put up by repression mechanisms.[29] Repressed memory leads to irrational fears, compulsions, and in cases of more advanced psychosis to hearing voices. During analysis, working through the patient's resistance becomes often a daunting task for the analyzed and a test of patience for the analyst, since the patient, instead of remembering, mostly repeats and gets agitated by what resists remembering, by inhibitions or pathological characteristics. And were the analyst to determine and name these mechanisms of repression, the patient is not necessarily freed from them. The patient has to work through this resistance to remembering.

However, Mercedes's ghosts are immune to analytic probing, for they represent a willed pathology of survival in exile. Hector, who is often driven to playing the realist analyst, tries in vain to exorcize her ghosts and bring her to the present. After Alejo's death, Mercedes takes up with his ghost. She impersonates Alejo, talking in his voice like a ventriloquist, and staging fights with him. She also creates a set complete with props, a pack of Alejo's cigarettes, his shoes under the bed, his hat on the bureau, in order to transform the ethereal into the material and the ephemeral into the eternal. "Ma, why do you try to make it look like Pop was here?" asks an exasperated Hector.

> "Not me, it *was* your papa!"
>
> "Ma, that's impossible."
>
> "No, no no, no."[30]

Ghosts from her ancestral land, Spain, and her Cuban homeland accompany Mercedes to her "last house in the world" and offer her a world where she can live in the comforting parameters of her own idiom and on her own terms. Mercedes's pathology—the obstinate refusal to give up her ghosts, paralyzing visions, irrational behavior—generates her poetic rememberings. Mercedes is the voiceover for the past, for what has become invisible. And although she acts the ventriloquist, speaking for the dead, imagining their desires and terrors, even poeticizing them, she would have remembered in vain had Hector not given her a voice, become a ventriloquist for her. Writing originates at the site of a piercing memory or a silent mourning or the overwhelming sorrow of *Vergänglichkeit*—that untranslatable idiom of fear and awe in the face of the ephemerality of all things. We try to recover through the materiality of writing that which faces the ravages of time. "When I write a book," Cixous reveals, "the only thing that guides me in the beginning is an alarm. Not a tear (*larme*), but an alarm. The thing that alarmed me at once with its violence and with its strangeness."[31] The violent strangeness of Mercedes's world marks the beginning of Hector's story of his mother. The *Unheimliche* of her experience captures both meanings of the German word: her uncanny communication with the dead and her irredeemable homelessness.

Ventriloquist, mad poetess, biographer of departed souls, Mercedes finds her only home in metaphors of her own making. When Hector becomes seriously ill after a trip to Cuba, Mercedes is convinced that Cuba is the origin of the disease, and the land she glorified in dream, memory, and imagination turns into a house of the dead. She sees "tiny coffins, cemetery stones, flowers, stoic-faced families walking through cemetery gates and down winding paths, heads bowed . . . children crying and her mother crying . . . her father's funeral winding through the cobblestone streets of Holguín."[32] She likens the ill body to "a huge house with winding walls and endless rooms where food was eaten and blood pumped and where little monsters like micróbios swarmed in thick streams through the halls, a house where the walls were on the verge of collapse" (88). Disease becomes symptomatic of the bitterly conflicting forces of remembering and forgetting, the pathos of exile, and the unhappiness at home. The cherished images of Cuba are marred by Hector's illness: "Cuba gave the bad disease. Cuba gave the drunk father. Cuba gave the crazy mother. Years later all these would entwine and make Hector think that Cuba had something against him. That it made him sick and pale . . . and excluded him from that life that happy Cubans were supposed to have" (94).

Hector's illness pulls him violently away from his early childhood Cuban identity nurtured by Mercedes's maternal devotion, the love of his woman relatives, sweet drinks and fruits of Cuba, and the sounds of Spanish. The nurse at the home for terminally ill children in Connecticut, where Hector stays for nearly a year, punishes him for speaking Spanish and forces English upon him. She makes him "suspicious of Spanish. Spanish words drifted inside him, he dreamed in Spanish, but English began whooshing inside. English forced its way through him, splitting his skin" (95). The split skin (and the forked tongue) become extended metonymies of the damaged body and fragmented identity. Thus begins Hector's imprisonment in his hyphenated self. Alejo has "his people, the Cubans, his brothers," Mercedes has her dreams and ghosts, and Hector's older brother, Horacio, escapes the family circle early on by joining the army and getting married. But "Hector always felt as if he were in costume, his true nature unknown to others and perhaps even to himself. He was part 'Pop,' part Mercedes; part Cuban, part American—all wrapped tightly inside a skin in which he sometimes could not move" (175).

Mercedes passes on to her sons her gift of dreams, prophecy, and imagination. When Hector tries to re-member his Cubanness and his Spanish in anticipation of his beloved aunt Luisa and her family's visit, he invokes images of Cuba, "as if memory and imagination would make him more of a man, a Cuban man" (161). Cuba comes back to him through Mercedes's stories and memories:

> The day before Luisa arrived he suddenly remembered his
> trip to Cuba with Mercedes and Horacio in 1954. He remem-
> bered looking out the window of the plane and seeing fire spew-
> ing from the engines on the wing. To Cuba. To Cuba. Mercedes
> was telling him a story when the plane abruptly plunged down
> through some clouds and came out into the night air again.
> (161)

Hector cannot stop remembering. He sees his maternal grandmother, "Doña Maria, now dead, framed by a wreath of orchids in the yard, kissing him—so many kisses, squirming kisses—and giving advice. She never got over leaving Spain for Cuba and would always remain a proud Spaniard. 'Remember,' she had told Hector. 'You're a Spaniard first and then Cuban' " (162). Horacio, the tough-minded, independent son, is visited by his father in a strange and comforting dream, which he interprets as a sign of being at peace with his father's soul. And Hector, after moving from his parents' house, still sees his father. Although he was infuriated with Mercedes for talking to Alejo's ghost, Hector admits that "in that house, which is memory, I can't escape him" (226). In spite of the never-ending trauma of the loss of her Cuba, Mercedes survives, a memorial to memory. In the final passages of *Our House in the Last World*, she travels back not only to the Cuba of her memories but also several centuries back to the Spain of her imagination and sees herself in a former reincarnation as a handmaiden in Queen Isabella's court.

If the handing down of family culture is a part of women's work, then Mercedes's legacy to her son Hector is the inspiration to write her memories. Hector writes down his thoughts in a composition notebook like the ones his mother writes poetry in. He feels "mesmerized" (226) by memories of his Cuban past, which take on a literary reality in his notebooks: "And when I write in my notebook I feel very close to her and to the memory of my father. I go back to that certain house, I go back to my beginning" (228). In negotiating the trials of passage in dream, memory, and imagination, in scripting dialogues with the ghosts of the past, Mercedes succeeds, perhaps unknowingly, in instilling in her son a receptiveness toward the creative powers of forgetting and remembering. As such, the writing self is no longer the lone agency of autobiography but a participant in a larger family and community history.

Autobiography as Heuristic Fiction

What is designated as fiction in such novels as *The Woman Warrior, Breath, Eyes, and Memory*, or *The Mixquiahuala Letters* has "the status of remembered fact."[33] Of course, autobiographical features in works of fiction have always been a part of literary convention and do not undermine our expectations of the genre of fiction. On the other hand, autoethnographies and contemporary memoirs of migration and exile have radically transformed reader expectations of autobiography. Paul de Man has rigorously investigated the intricate negotiations between autobiography and fiction to thematize the sense of undecidability that challenges the assumed unity of the autobiographical subject. The genre of autobiography has traditionally been the form of the account of a life actually lived and factually experienced. It "seems to depend on actual and potentially verifiable events in a less ambivalent way than fiction does. It seems to belong to a simpler mode of referentiality, of representation and of diegesis." Although autobiographical elements contain dreams, fantasies, and illusions, such fabulations, nevertheless, "remain rooted in a single subject whose identity is defined by the uncontested readability of his proper name." On the other hand, the weight of this proper name does not necessarily insure an unambiguous referentiality. We may assume that the facts of one's life produce autobiography, but is it not equally possible "that the autobiographical project may itself produce and determine the life and whatever the writer *does* is in fact governed by the technical demands of self-portraiture and thus determined, in all its aspects, by the resources of his medium?"[34]

Pavane für eine verstorbene Infantin

Libuše Moníková's *Pavane für eine verstorbene Infantin*, an experiment in autobiographical writing as a form of literary self-refashioning, indeed "produces" the life of its author. The imagined autobiographical self charted a successful path to literary success for Moníková, who, before her premature death in 1998, had moved from the obscurity of a young Czech émigré lecturer's life to the center of critical acclaim. At the end of the novel, the protagonist, Francine Pallas, Moníková's alter ego, is released from the ruthless pain that held her in its grip since her departure from Czechoslovakia. Francine's freedom from her crippling exilic melancholy comes about through performative acts realized in imagination and writing that are governed by the demands of her own willed self-invention. Like its heavily coded title, the book abounds with hidden allusions, artistic and literary references, and culturally specific notations.[35] "My life is a sequence of literary and filmic scenes and arbitrary quotations that I cannot put in an order,"[36] laments Francine. This statement forms the structural principle of the book. The events of Francine's life in Göttingen, where she is employed as a part-time lecturer on German literature, are not narrated in any logical order. Rather, the narrative moves between

Prague and Göttingen, lecture halls and catacombs, dream and daydream and through a pastiche of film and television images, literary biographies, depictions of illness and madness, and somber reflections on reasons for exile and a perceptive outsider's biting satire of the host country. Like the author Moníková, the narrator Francine is a scholar of German literature and a specialist on Kafka. And like the author, she leaves Czechoslavakia after the Soviet invasion in 1969, triggered by Soviet fears in the face of the fast-moving democratization process known as the Prague Spring under the Communist Party leader, Alexander Dubček.

Moníková works historical fact and detail as well as exilic predicament into the narrative in direct and oblique ways. Literary and visual references structure the story within an allegorical plan. The book begins with an image of *Findelkinder* on the television screen. These were children who were separated from their families during the Second World War. After the war, the surviving children began looking for parents, siblings, and relatives they had lost. Most did not know their place of birth or their age, and many were given several names. Some were reunited with family members after many years through the efforts of the Red Cross. Many never found out to whom or where they belonged. These children reflect a larger picture of populations that have lost genealogy and geography in the shuffle of history. This introductory clip sets the stage for the performance of a narrative of exile. The writer's autobiography takes the form of a re/dress rehearsal for a drama of loss and restoration. It is a performance of the *Trauerarbeit* (work of mourning) necessary for the recovery of the subject suffering from the death or disappearance of a loved one. Freud defines *Trauer* as a normal reaction to the loss of a beloved person or an abstraction such as Fatherland, freedom, or an ideal that takes the place of the loved being. Although *Trauer* can lead to radical departures from one's lifestyle, it is not considered a pathological condition and is expected to pass in due time. In individuals with a weaker psychic disposition, however, *Trauer* gives way to melancholy. Freud sees in the condition of the melancholic "a deeply painful mood, a waning of interest in the world brought about by the loss of the ability to love, constraints on any form of achievement which find expression in self-blame, self-cursing and lead to a maniacal expectation of punishment."[37] *Trauerarbeit* requires a long process of working through memories of the lost object of the libido. Sometimes an ersatz object alleviates the pain of loss. In negative cases, the loss leads to a rejection of reality and a fixation on the absent object through a hallucinatory psychosis of desire. If the *Trauerarbeit* is carried out successfully, however, the self (*Ich*) becomes free and unrestrained once again (430). The beginning of Francine's *Trauerarbeit* coincides with her departure from a Czechoslovakia crippled by sadness and lethargy: "I left the sorrow of a whole nation behind. . . . She [Czechoslovakia] was then no longer in mourning, only lethargic; I would have never taken leave from mourning."[38] It ends after her performance as a cripple on a wheelchair. Francine's disability allegorizes the ills of the homeland she leaves behind and those of the hostland, where she falls into a profound melancholy. The physical enactment of this real or imagined paralysis becomes one of the two decisive factors in the successful completion of her *Trauerarbeit*.

Francine's voice is inflected variously by a sensation of emptiness, a rejection of wordly joys, an inability for love and compassion—she finds no happiness with either of the two men in her life—and a ruthlessly satirical view of Germans. Her mourning, which often borders on melancholy, has as its implicit object the lost Czech land. Even a very basic understanding of what was once a familiar geography eludes her. When she projects a map of Prague during a lecture on Kafka, she gets disoriented and cannot understand why the river (Vltava; German Moldau) flows northward. Her life as a lecturer at the university is unfulfilling; she is frustrated by students who only attend her seminars to complete requirements. She is contemptuous of women who come to her lectures without books and notes, let their children run wild, object to critical literary discussions, because they want to talk about real life and nurture only their own narcissism. Referring to one of them, she remarks with sarcasm: "The woman is older than me, many times a mother, soaked in practical emancipation" (*durchdrungen von praktischer Emanzipation*) (23). Her academic career deteriorates in seminars reduced to "Häkeln und Hegeln" [crocheting and Hegelizing] (22). She resents students who relieve their boredom with talk of revolution, when her own friends and countrymen had lost their lives for freedoms people in Germany took for granted.

The German society is portrayed as a place of bleak loneliness. Francine's observations of other others, Turks, Chileans, Portuguese focus on the isolation and alienation of these people. One of the sharpest critiques of the Germans is aimed at their ignorance of and disrespect for others: "I cannot get used to this audacity, this jovial stupidity, this abundance of ignorance" (42). When her French-Berber friend Genevieve visits Francine in Germany, she exclaims in her broken English: "There are so many *crippens* in Germany! How is it possible?" (11) As this spiritually and psychologically crippled society traps her in its net, Francine feels she is becoming more and more like a cripple, like her colleagues who spend all their vacation time and semester breaks nursing various ailments: "I have adjusted; sometimes I can barely walk because of pain." She develops a strange, inexplicable pain in her hip. Just as a patient suffering from clinical melancholy cannot determine what the object of her loss is, Francine cannot understand the cause of her limping, the pain that intermittently announces itself. Like melancholy, this disability causes *Lusthemmnis*, an inhibition of desire (11). She begins to identify more and more with the sick, the mad, and the disabled, and develops an interest in the literary representations of disability. She gets herself a wheelchair and masquerades as a cripple. Giving a name to the invisible dis-ase becomes a catalyst in the process of recovery. She can now meet the gaze of strangers and stare at them longer than they can stare at her. The wheelchair, her "ambulatory throne" (146), frees her from the patronizing gaze. She can finally look double marginalization—being foreign and disabled—in the face. Once the disability assumes a name and a physical form, it commands attention, compassion, and cooperation from the Germans who otherwise are very stingy with such traits. The invisible foreigner becomes visible, a presence to be reckoned with, a threatening anomaly that, unlike other anomalies like foreigners, has to be accommodated. The *Trauerarbeit* ends in an audacious performance by the protagonist, who breathlessly negotiates the threatening paths of a cold and indifferent German landscape in a wheelchair. At the end of this wild ride, she throws the wheelchair over a cliff on the third of June, the anniversary of the deaths of Kafka and of Arno Schmidt, and her deep-seated melancholy dissipates in the comforting ritual of her solitary commemoration of the two writers.

But the decisive factor in Francine's recovery is her self-induced transformation into a palimpsest of mythologized figures, texts, and heuristic fictions. She lends a mythical/literary register to her genealogy by reinventing herself both as the legendary Bohemian infante Libuše and Franz Kafka's literary heiress (she sometimes calls herself Franza). Instead of offering the reader tidbits of cultural flavor, Moníková provides generous portions of historical and literary information but also expects from the reader an informed appreciation and understanding of her project. The scene of writing is a parchment of scripted impressions, dreamed dialogues, and alternative versions of literary lives and fictions. In an imaginary conversation with Kafka, Francine objects to his depiction of the unredeemed life of the Barnabas family in *The Castle* and his decision to seal their fate as outsiders without name and identity. Kafka responds by saying that she needs to write her own version. Francine is amused to detect in Kafka's German her own Czech accent. As Kafka pages through Francine's copy of Borges, she tells him of his reception by numerous modern authors such as Borges and Nabokov. In a new beginning, Francine decides to leave her meaningless job as a lecturer and devotes herself to the rehabilitation of the Barnabas family by changing the final chapter of *The Castle*. Thus begins her own rehabilitation through a re-vision of a fragment of literary history.

In her reading of Hélène Cixous, Mireille Calle-Gruber stresses that for Cixous writing is a way of expressing "mourning through the traces left by others—books, writers, whose reading has excited an emotional and scriptual journeying. Writing is making (the journey) *with*. In honour of. In memory."[39] This intertextual working through the memory of literary lives and tales is, in the end, what rehabilitates Francine physically and mentally. In the beginning of the book, as Francine is reimagining Kafka's Prague and his contemporaries, she reflects: "If this 'rectification of literary lives' would take hold, like Stoppard and in a different way Borges had imagined, than I would have something more concrete to work with."[40] The *Trauerarbeit* comes to a closure with an imaginatively choreographed ritual. Francine celebrates by dancing the *dupák* and its Slovak variant *odzemok*, stomping gaily with the "incriminating" leg (141). This dance embodies echoes and rememberings of themes running through Francine's entire narrative: "pavane for the dead princess" is translated into another cultural idiom that resurrects the dead princess as the new literary heiress Libuše. Now she can remember without pain and celebrate, not mourn, her history. "It is the third of July, the winter is long gone, I have expelled death" (146), she says after throwing away the wheelchair. The disposal of the wheelchair is also a symbolic reenactment of a piece of cultural memory. In certain parts of Bohemia, Francine tells us, winter is driven away in a rite where a mask or strawman is carried and thrown into the water by children. Village boys jump into the water and take the mask to the other shore to be burned: "Winter goes up in smoke, and people also say that death is driven away" (143). In remembering the rites and rituals of her past, Francine translates the experience of exile from a state of irreparable loss into one of creative distance that enables self-understanding. This understanding requires a new interpretation of our relationship to the past and to passages, an interpretation that takes into its purview repressions, forgetting, anamnesis, as well as affects, emotions, and physical pain aroused by spatiotemporal distances.

> We need to triangulate to something—the past, the future,
> our own untamed perceptions, another place, if we're not to
> be subsumed by the temporal and temporary ideas of our
> time, if we're not to become creatures of ephemeral fashion.

Eva Hoffman, *Lost in Translation*

Just as Kingston's *Woman Warrior* rewrites the past in the code of poetic imagination, Eva Hoffman's *Lost in Translation* transcodes self, history, and geography into new language. In *Fictions in Autobiography,* Paul John Eakin notes that "the writing of autobiography emerges as the second acquisition of language, a second coming into being of self, a self-conscious self-consciousness."[41] For the writer whose medium is literally a second language, the writing of autobiography goes beyond the "second acquisition of language." It also becomes a metanarrative account about the acquisition of the second language in which the autobiography is written. Writers such as Maxine Hong Kingston, Eva Hoffman, Sandra Cisneros, Meena Alexander, and Richard Rodriguez, born into a language other than the language of the country they live in, have written eloquently about their desire for the mastery of the national language. They recount with relish and nostalgia their dream of creating a space of comfort and privilege in the acquired language.[42] Kingston, for example, transcends her perceived marginalization in two cultures by transforming the tradition of the talk-story and recharging it with new meanings. She creates a new identity for herself and her forgotten aunt by translating her mother's talk-stories into written stories and resituating them in her hyphenated culture.

The new language is the most distinct marker of the cherished public identity in the new culture. For writers of exile and diaspora it is also a compensation for the absence of a supporting native culture. The acquired language makes them often aware of their privileged status with regard to those who are voiceless in their own language. Hoffman reminisces about filling herself "with the material of language"[43] and is constantly reminded that mastery over language is the passport to visibility, presence, and power. In a telling account, she reflects on the rage bottled up in the lame four-letter words brandished by ghetto youths:

> In my New York apartment, I listen almost nightly to fights that
> erupt like brushfire on the street below—and in their escalating
> fury of repetitious phrases ("Don't do this to me, man, you fuck-

ing bastard, I'll fucking kill you"), I hear not the pleasures of macho toughness but an infuriated beating against wordlessness, against the incapacity to make oneself understood, seen. (124)

Language is not only an empowering but also a redeeming practice. "Anger can be borne—it can even be satisfying—if it can gather into words and explode in a storm," continues Hoffman. "But without this means of ventilation, it only turns back inward, building and swirling like a head of steam—building to an impotent, murderous rage. If all therapy is speaking therapy—a talking cure—then perhaps all neurosis is a speech dis-ease" (124). Hoffman collects and stores words for nourishment: "I've become obsessed with words. I gather them, put them away like a squirrel saving nuts for winter, swallow them and hunger for more" (216). She knows that language can be a strategically deployed counterforce to prejudice, exclusion, and repression: "I believe that language will become a crucial instrument, that I can overcome the stigma of my marginality, the weight of presumption against me, only if the reassuringly right sounds come out of my mouth" (123). The pride of mastering the second language better than the native speaker becomes the ultimate reward. Rushdie justifies British Indian writers' choice of English as their medium of literary expression by claiming, "To conquer English may be to complete the process of making ourselves free."[44]

Hoffman's memoir is less a story of one individual's life than a many-faceted account of conquering an alien and unyielding language and the subsequent necessary transformation of self and identity in this conquered space. Barely in her teens, Eva is transported from her history-book picture of Cracow to a suburb of Vancouver, Canada, where the family settles. Hoffman's memoir is more a portrayal of the North American culture of the late sixties and the seventies than of life in postwar Cracow either as memory or as experience. Eva's experience of Cracow during her visit there underlines the coincidence of dream and memory:

> I remember Cracow, literally, from my dreams. Usually in those dreams, I have been baffled in my desire to get where I want to go—an elusive homing place just beyond the edge of sleep. Now, in actual Cracow, it turns out that the dreams, repeated so often over the years, enable me to find my way. I move from street to street not by map or rational plan but because I've memorized them in my night wanderings. I come upon spots and buildings and streets which I recognize without knowing that they've been encoded in some region of my memory.[45]

Hoffman often deploys metaphors of psychoanalysis and codes of dreamwork as analogues of the task of translation. She thereby illustrates that reassembling shards of memory to form a coherent identity in another idiom is a necessary requisite for healing the neurosis of physical and psychic dislocations. But this is never easy. It a long-term and costly process of therapy:

> For me therapy is partly translation therapy, the talking cure a second-language cure. My going to a shrink is, among other things, a rite of initiation: initiation into the language of the subculture within which I happen to live, into a way of explaining myself to myself. But gradually, it becomes a project of translating backward. (271)

In therapy, Eva attempts to trace her way back to what Freud called elements of "historical truth" in "Constructions in Analysis" in order to free the present from "anomie, loneliness, emotional repression" (268). These instances of truth are embedded in the memories of her first language, Polish. Yet, she can no longer reclaim Polish in any coherent manner. "In Polish whole provinces of adult experience are missing" (272), she notes and has to accept that "Polish is no longer the one, true language against which others live their secondary life" (273). For Hoffman, concepts can never fully coincide in translation, because not only words and phrases but feelings, signification systems, structures of knowledge, in short, a complicated semitotic map of a given culture has to be reconstructed in another one, an equation that proves unresolvable: "You can't transport human meanings whole from one culture to another any more than you can transliterate a text" (175). Eva regards the American notion of dating, for instance, as a highly standardized semiotic practice that she can never quite decode (149). On the other hand, she is embarrassed and frustrated when her Polish jokes do not translate well into English and realizes that failed translation, like a joke that falls flat, makes a case for the poor self-judgment of the speaker. Later, as Polish begins to gradually leave her, she cannot quite manage intimacy in English. The distance from the borrowed language affords measured appreciation and even poetic mastery but no sense of "losing oneself" in the language (of the other), a necessary condition of "falling in love." On the other hand, love in the first language also yields to the force of forgetting and the tyranny of irreversible sequence in time. Upon her reunion with Marek, her "fantasy lover" of long ago, she realizes that it is not possible to "get further than the vividness of [their] remembering . . . [to] beat [their] way back through the wall of accumulated time" (229). "Culture shock can be real shock" (268), she keeps telling her therapist, who does not seem convinced of the fact. Nevertheless, at some point she claims that stepping into the past through "the Looking Glass"—being back in Poland—released her "to go on into the present" (241), although her story does not fully corroborate this claim.

In Algerian novelist and critic Abdelkebir Khatibi's *Love in Two Languages* a radical finale to a similar tale of living and loving in another language is suggested. Here, there is a definite gendered difference in degrees of embracing the other('s) language. In this novel of love cum meditation on language, the unnamed "he" welcomes his divided subjectivity and enjoys its pleasurable pain by playing with it in language. The "she" lives with the undiminished loss of exile from self, language, and space, imprisoned in the oppressive fog of memory. Finally, as melancholy threatens to drive her to the brink of madness and death, she finds the courage to return to her mother tongue. But to "beat" her "way back through the wall of accumulated time," to use Hoffman's felicitous phrase, is to land in a no-land—a place no longer classifiable as origin, a station of no memories:

> Her past resembled nothing at all and no known, recognizable face was assigned to this past. Not only did she not resemble her parents (where did she come from in that case?), but even in her own language, her body's native land, she made herself unclassifiable. Other-thought: she saw no living place, nor any dead one either, and had absence been invoked, I believe that for her this word would only have been a joke, the revenge of a presence without a name.[46]

Upon her return to her mother tongue, "she" found no ancestry and no registry that contained her name. Words she had forgotten to say in her mother tongue were legion. When she finally could say her name with joy, "that day was the festival of the language" (112). Despite her ultimate return to the mother tongue, she cannot put a closure on translation and presents "the chasm of her memory to this future which is continually translating itself. She is overjoyed by this new experience" (113). Hoffman, on the other hand, has consciously taken another turn on this exilic road, an exit where connections to the mother tongue are not clearly marked but the signs to the other tongue are unmistakable and lead to a point of no return. Unlike the "she," who now has to translate the memories that defined the state of exile into a recovered originary language, Hoffman has to abandon the mother tongue to a growing erasure in order to apply herself fully to a different task of translation—into the other tongue. She changes her name from Ewa to Eva, and in that transliteration of one letter, she inscribes a negotiated identity in another alphabet.

Ultimately, Hoffman's text is a conceptually rigorous meditation on translating oneself. In this memoir, structures of re-membering, reminiscing, forgetting, and refashioning the self from shards and traces of cultural and linguistic memory operate in intertextual spaces. Hoffman refers to other memoirs, such as Mary Antin's diary, as an example of one immigrant's experience, to the *Education of Henry Adams*, which tells the (hi)story of a "native son" of America, and to *Speak, Memory* by Vladimir Nabokov, a writer who translated well into English. Her text is situated at the intersection of these (pre)texts. Hoffman finds a home in the company of these writers who have crossed many boundaries of time and space. Her tribute to them is a tribute to another kind of ancestry that is not a parentage but a lineage of vocation. Although Hoffman's family leaves Poland because of the history and memory of Jewish persecution, this book does not engage in questions of the Holocaust or the Jewish Diaspora. Nevertheless, one brief reference to the death of her mother's sister in a gas chamber speaks volumes about the indescribable pain and suffering of Polish Jews. The account of her young aunt's horrendous death strikes Eva as more cruel, fantastic, and grim than anything in the Brothers Grimm. In her typical fashion, Hoffman juxtaposes received story and memory with textual reference. The reference to the Holocaust is precariously poised at the edge of the child's memory and hemmed in so as to be almost invisible. The literary footnote fleetingly alludes to the historical event. Here language falls silent, recalling Adorno's pronouncement that there can be no poetry after Auschwitz.

In the end, the narrator does not fully translate herself, her past, memories, and stories and learns to live with "the relativity of cultural meanings"[47] on her skin. She will now live in the free space of ideological absence, "in the chinks between cultures and subcultures, between the scenarios of political beliefs and aesthetic credos" (275). In this way, the narrator puts the past into perspective and can theorize the personal in terms of the larger question of cultural translation. Danuta Zadworna Fjellestad observes that Hoffman's memoir "is full of marked tensions between her intellectual understanding of her condition and her experience of loss." Fjellestad reads Hoffman's tale as a highly theorized account of the questions of language, exilic consciousness, and self-refashioning, "saturated with self-conscious reflections on her consciousness. Her vocabulary is surfeited with self-conscious references to literature and postmodern theory and philosophy."[48] There is an underlying sense of unease in Fjellestad's article with the excess of self-reflection in Hoffman's story, which threatens to turn the cultural specificity of the experience of exile into an abstraction. Nevertheless, in the final analysis, Fjellestad compares Hoffman's memoir, "in its various modes of expression, in its abundance of metacommentary, in its awareness of structuralist and poststructuralist theories, in its predominant concern with linguistic and cultural constructions of the self" (143), favorably with such memorable tales of exile as Ihab Hassan's *Out of Egypt* and Kingston's *Woman Warrior.*

Hoffman's multiple migrations from Cracow to Vancouver, Rice University in Houston, Harvard, New York, and to Cracow and back give her "an Archimedean leverage from which to see the world."[49] Through it, she gathers insights that have often been missed by others. The weight of the world, she thinks, used to come from the hierarchy of the past and its cultural heritages. The present was shaped through the vertical thrust of time. Now, however, the weight of the world rests on a horizontal axis with a dizzying multitude of events taking place all at once. We live simultaneously at the centers and the peripheries. "Dislocation is the norm rather than the aberration in our time" (274), she observes. The emotional matrix of Hoffman's life is at the intersection of many places and intellectual roads. However, even those who remained in their ancestral homes are not assured of stability but are jolted and dislocated by the shifting fortunes of time in the postmodern world. In the final analysis, Hoffman finds her home in English, in an acquired language. As Fjellestad notes, "For Hoffman, the space between the *memory of her selfhood* and *her intellectual understanding of herself as a script* becomes the space of exile."[50] In Hoffman's concluding reflections, we find out how time and memory are redeemed in language and release us from existential shackles:

> When I image, imagine those shimmers of nonexistent possibility suspended on a thread of purely mental light, time expands and creates a breathing space in which sensations can be savored, as I once savored the churning of butter or the minor triad. If images, as some philosophers theorize, congeal out of the matrix of language, then perhaps I've had to wait to have enough linguistic concentrate for hope to arise.[51]

The dialogic and self-reflexive tone of exilic writing marks a space of intervention in the cultural contexts in which it moves. This writing registers its distance from social and cultural norms by questioning the logic of the traditions it has inherited as well as those it is subjected to in the new world. As a presentation of a pastiche of conversations, of parable and allegory, it further defies any form of controlled narrative. These diverse languages manifest themselves as a conversation between opposing voices or as conflicting self-perceptions of diasporic or ethnic groups. The exile's text of self represents a desire both for liberation and for transgression and danger. The writer is caught in an ambiguous, self-ironic discourse of doubt, conflicting loyalties, and even guilt. These ambivalences operate through such tropes of double meaning as metaphor, allegory, and irony.

Kingston uses the allegories of the fantastic to subvert the order and logic of her family stories. The ghosts that populate her own versions are "the bizarre fragments of past, tradition, and familial self-overprotectivenesss that must be externalized and tamed."[52] These nebulous figures set off a process in language that engages meaning with indeterminacy. The subject becomes an intertextual agency, reaches beyond the cultural text of parents and ancestors, endeavors to fill in the gaps in the texture of ancestral memory, or interrupts or pries open the latter to reinscribe new memories. Upon revisiting her native Cracow, Eva Hoffmann observes that

> one has to rewrite the past in order to understand it. I have to see Cracow in the dimensions it has to my adult eye in order to perceive that my story has been only a story, that none of its events has been so big or so scary. It is the price of emigration, as of any radical discontinuity, that it makes such reviews and re-readings difficult; being cut off from one part of one's own story is apt to veil it in the haze of nostalgia, which is an ineffectual relationship to the past, and the haze of alienation, which is an ineffectual relationship to the present.[53]

This irony toward memory and nostalgia provides the space of self-reflexivity. The writing agent knows that the present consciousness of the past is stored in word and image, and remembering, therefore, cannot "offer a faithful and unmediated reconstruction of a historically verifiable past; instead, it expresses the play of the autobiographical act itself, in which the materials of the past are shaped by memory and imagination to serve the needs of present consciousness."[54] By reclaiming in poetic space a lost history and subjecting its memory to interrogation, the writer "opens a new inferencing field" in which to "re-present the crisis of cultural foundations in a critical light."[55]

To find their own critical voice, writers of diasporas often distance themselves from the practices of the dominant culture as well as from those of their own families, communities, and ethnic groups, and strike out alone. The struggle against language (of oppression and exclusion) goes on in language (of interrogation, of discovery). In their pursuit of creative and critical writing, these writers invest the knowledge gained in language back in language and keep vigil at the boundaries of social, cultural, and political consciousness. This often lonely vigil is the price of self-reflexivity. Ultimately, autobiographical accounts of exile are predicated on a moral vision, for they maintain a dynamic and critical exchange between the self and the national and ethnic community. They problematize the issue of representation at many levels and highlight its relational character through the use of multiple narrators—parents, ancestors, literary or historical alter egos—and narrative genres such as myths, legends, criticism, literary fictions, intertexts, or anecdotes. These narrative conventions contest and relativize representational authority. In *The Woman Warrior*, as one critic observes, the narrator's "fantasies, different versions of the same memory ... Chinese mythology, historical narrative, and anecdotal reporting hold equal ontological ground."[56] The metanarrative tenor of these self-representations illustrates how memory, speculation, and individual and group psychology frame all accounts of the past. "What thus seems initially to be individualistic autobiographical searchings turn out to be revelations of traditions, re-collections of disseminated identities," comments Fischer. "These are a modern version of the Pythagorean arts of memory: retrospection to gain a vision for the future. In so becoming, the searches also turn out to be powerful critiques of several contemporary rhetorics of domination."[57]

In "Resisting Autobiography: Out-Law Genres and Transnational Feminist Subjects," Caren Kaplan argues that "out-law" genres such as women's prison writing, *testimonio*, ethnography, lesbian identity writing, cultural autobiography, and psychobiography "challenge Western critical practices to expand their parameters and, consequently, shift the subject of autobiography from the individual to a more unstable collective identity."[58] Kaplan maintains that an oppositional stance toward autobiography characteristic of out-law genres fosters closer links between the individual and the community and propagates the cultural survival of a collectivity. Cultural autobiographies, which are here defined as personal histories that connect the subject to a particular group at a certain historical juncture, play an important role in creating coalitions and solidarity in communities. The out-law genres offer a deconstructive strategy against "the individualism of autobiography's Western legacy" (132) and pave the way to a consciousness of transnational coalitions. Transnational feminism, as one of these coalitions, can resist the powers of patriarchy and capitalism. Critical and interventionist discourses can undoubtedly affect the nature and direction of political formations. However, Kaplan overstates her case by insisting on the "Westernness" of a very narrowly defined notion of autobiography as the expression of a unified subject. Ironically, all her examples of out-law genre subjects and critics are Western or English-speaking writers. Thus, her speculation about the formation of transnational feminism becomes a global abstraction. Furthermore, ethnographies and *testimonios* are, by her own account, "heavily mediated" colloborative projects where the writer-recorder is ultimately the editor-commentator (123). That the so-called out-law genres give voice to collective subjects cannot be disputed. However, in Kaplan's argument there is a conspicuous absence of any reference to the role of bilingualism or cultural multilingualism in cultural autobiographies. A critical appreciation of the transnational dimension of modern autoethnographies and bilingual memoirs would demand, as Gómez-Peña makes clear, learning other languages, histories, and cultural idioms. Solidarity among groups comes at the price of bilingual dialogue. The (auto)biographical narratives of bi- and multilingual subjects offer the most direct access to cultural histories and cross-cultural coalitions.

Autobiography, the genre of choice of many writers of diaspora, is an out-of-bounds genre that captures the fluid character of memory, migration, and transition in an appropriately nuanced fashion. In an age of shifting perceptions of national and ethnic identity, destabilized borders, and nonterritorial coalitions, autobiography, precisely because it is a genre that defies definiton and comes under many guises, is uniquely positioned to give voice to structures of experience that resist naming. Autobiographical voices conjugate all the tropes of exile. The basic structure of the narratives of this study is (auto)biographical. Autobiography and autoethnography variously or simultaneously assume the form of a confessional idiom, biography of a parent, parents, family, ancestors, or community. They can also appear as the diary of a place (often a city); a polyvocal history; a meditation on language, love, and metaphysics (Khatibi's *Love in Two Languages*); or, as in the case of Özdamar's *Life Is a Caravansary* or Sara Suleri's *Meatless Days*, what I call "an unauthorized biography of the nation."

PART TWO

4

At Different Borders/On Common Grounds

> Other Turks were also waiting at the Gate to Germany
> (*Deutschland-Tür*). A man with a sheep, a hodja with a mina-
> ret. An illegal worker masqueraded as a soccer player hoping
> to get through the border control into Germany. The farmer
> and his donkey waited too. They waited and waited. The
> Gate to Germany opened and then immediately closed. A
> dead Turkish man came out carrying his coffin.
>
> Emine Sevgi Özdamar, *Mutterzunge*

> To cross the linguistic border implies that you decenter your
> voice. The border crosser develops two or more voices.
> This is often the experience of Mexican writers who come
> to the United States. We develop different speaking selves
> that speak for different aspects of our identity.
>
> Guillermo Gómez-Peña, "Bilingualism, Biculturalism,
> and Borders"

An active European site of fiery debates, where stakes in labor migration, immigration, patriation, and national and ethnic identity politics are very high, is the reunified German state. At this historical juncture, over six million foreigners, including *Gastarbeiter* (guest workers), refugees, asylum seekers, writers, artists, and professionals are permanently settled in Germany. In the embattled Europe of the post-cold-war era, Germany, with its economic power, political stability, generous welfare system, and what until recently were very flexible asylum laws, has become, perhaps quite unwittingly and unwillingly, the destination for a growing body of displaced peoples. This unprecedented presence of the foreign has seriously challenged and aggravated the relative homogeneity of German society and culture and led to intermittent acts of violence against ethnic and national minorities. The change in German citizenship law effective January 1, 2000, allows children born to non-German residents of Germany to automatically become German citizens. However, the path to citizenship is still not easy for their parents and grandparents, who have lived, worked, and paid taxes in Germany for decades and for children born to non-German parents before January 1, 2000. For almost half a century, Germany's foreign-born population had virtually no representation in the public and political life of their hostland.

In order to meet the labor needs of its postwar industrial growth, West Germany began importing workers from the countries of the Mediterranean basin in the midfifties. The first treaty to recruit short-term workers was signed in 1955 with Italy. Bilateral agreements with other countries followed in quick succession. Under the terms of the treaty signed with Turkey in 1963, the first crew of one hundred thousand Turkish workers arrived in West Germany. Less than a decade later, more than one million Turks were living in Germany. Although initially only Anatolian farmers without land comprised the corps of recruits, later teachers, artisans, civil servants, small-business owners, all increasingly frustrated with the economic hardship in Turkey that was eroding the middle class, boarded the train to Munich. In 1973, when the need for workers had stabilized, recruitment was frozen (*Anwerbestopp*). However, whenever the economy demanded a larger labor force, employers devised ways of letting more foreign workers in through the loopholes in the system.

In the course of time, most of the workers and their families decided to settle in Germany. During the last two decades, many Turkish political refugees fleeing military and right-wing regimes and police brutality arrived at German borders. Today close to three million Turks reside in Germany. Most Germans are, at best, oblivious to this culture in their midst and, at worst, openly hostile to it.[1] Although the Turkish community in Germany has been transformed from a migrant labor force into a national minority, and fast-growing Turkish businesses employ a great number of Germans, the Turkish-Germans have virtually no political voice.

When the labor force was recruited more than three decades ago in the name of economic expediency, employment was stipulated to be short term, and policymakers apparently envisioned that the Turkish workers would remain segregated from German society and would be conveniently free of human traits and needs. They were the *Gastarbeiter* of the

great economic machinery. The word was possibly intended to circum-
scribe the conditions of employment; that is, the guest is expected to follow
the ground rules of the host's household, not outstay his welcome, and—
here the appellation becomes a contradiction in terms—work for the host.
Something was wrong with this metaphor. It is an oxymoron in Turkish,
where *guest* means someone the host welcomes, attends to, and serves. In
fact, the expression makes no sense in any idiom. Emine Sevgi Özdamar
remarks in her incorrigibly ironic tone: "The word *Gastarbeiter:* I love this
word. I always see two people in front of me; one sits there as the guest
and the other works."[2] The host kept reemploying the guest, as long as the
market demands necessitated extra labor. The guest obviously could not
become a member of the household. After more than forty years of residency, neither the guests nor their children and grandchildren are inte-
grated into the German society.

For generations, the Turks of Germany have been consigned, physically and figuratively, to a life of detention at the border. The literary works
of many Turkish-Germans depict in naturalistic, parodistic, and allegorical
genres the waking life of the Turkish subject as an uninterruped nightmare
of applying and reapplying for passports, visas, residence and work per-
mits. One of the stories in Özdamar's *Mutterzunge* (Mother tongue) is a
comic performance of the border trauma of Turkish workers who are ad-
mitted to Germany when Germany requires a larger labor force but are
deported, detained, and persecuted when their services are no longer
needed. A poor peasant, Karagöz, is a frequent traveler between Turkey
and Germany with his talking donkey. The donkey, who once worked as a
carrier and a vehicle of transportation in his native village, now accompa-
nies the farmer on his travels to and from Germany. He can no longer
practice his former trade and retrains himself as a chronicler, philosopher,
and parodist of the border experience. The donkey tries to comfort the
downtrodden, impoverished, and broken workers waiting at the border
with the words of Karl Marx: "The kingdom of freedom comes into being
only when work dictated by need and purpose ceases to be; it is the nature
of this kingdom to exist beyond the sphere of actual material production."[3]
When the worker who masquerades as a soccer player to gain entry to
Germany is turned away, he and other workers pay a Yugoslav taxi driver
to take them to the Italian border. He drops them off in the middle of
nowhere, they walk to the Italian border, bribe the border police, try to go
to France, ask for tickets to France ("Fransa, Fransa"), but the man who
sells them the tickets thinks they want to go to Florence ("Florenza, Florenza"). Finally, they go to Munich, where the worker works illegally as an

apple picker and sleeps in the auto-wrecking yard. When Karagöz and his donkey see him again at the train station, he is in handcuffs and waiting with a policeman for the Orient train (76–77).

The Turks wait for days in long lines in front of the German consulate in Istanbul, wait for papers to travel through Bulgaria, Greece, Austria, and all other transit routes. Holders of Turkish passports have to acquire visas for all European and East European countries. These perpetual migrants are welcome neither in Germany nor in Turkey. In Turkey, they are disliked because they have more economic power than most upper-middle-class, well-educated Turks who work their lives away for sheer survival. In a world where nationalist and patriotic sentiments have shown little sign of retreat, those who flee their lands are often marked as traitors. "We know only too well that many Mexicans consider Chicanos renegades, sellouts or simply foreigners," writes the Chicano literary critic Juan Bruce-Novoa.[4] Caught in the interstices of geographical and cultural borders, the Turkish residents of Germany embody an essentialist "foreignness" marked by an otherness of speech, custom, and mannerism. In tones resonant of the lament of the eternally "foreign" Turk, the Chicana poet, novelist, and critic Ana Castillo writes in "A Countryless Woman" that she is commonly perceived as a foreigner everywhere she is, including the United States and Mexico.[5] Gómez-Peña, a Mexican who, for the most part, lives and writes in America but is not (yet) a Chicano, maintains that living the history of border crossings, deterritorialization, and reterritorialization dismantles the core of monolithic national or ethnic identities. He sees himself as a Latin American, a Mexican, and a Mexican in the process of Chicanization. In America, he does not have a grasp of Chicano slang; in Mexico, his speech betrays patterns of *pocho* idiom; in Spain, he is called *Sudaca*; and in Germany he is mistaken for a Turk.[6] Like Castillo, who embodies the "transcendent homelessness" (Lukács) of the mestiza, and Gómez-Peña, who has settled into the permanence of transition, the Turkish-Germans—neither Turkish nor German—wander forever along the Möbius strip of cultural borderlands. Their social, cultural, and linguistic nomadism has produced a literature of powerful resonance at the periphery of German society.

The cultural activism of Turkish and other non-German artists and writers is both a response, and a form of resistance, to the social intolerance and injustice that daily confront foreign residents of Germany. In spite of the high degree of critical sophistication the literary works of many nonnative German writers have attained, their writing is still often labeled *MigrantInnenliteratur* in academic and publishing circles. Like the term

Gastarbeiter, this designation diminishes the impact and distorts the parameters of this body of writing. The word *Migrant* houses connotations of impermanence, instability, detachment, and lack of social commitment and eschews empowering notions of adaptability, resilience, and synthesis. In order to more fully examine the critical and historical implications of this literature, I would like to draw on the transitive momentum of the concept of borderlands writing. This heuristic metaphor marks a turning point in contemporary cultural criticism, for it transforms the notion of a geographical space to include historical sites and passages. It generates a conceptual field where word and act, varying idioms, intellectual legacies, and cultural memories are engaged in confrontation, negotiation, and conversation.

Gómez-Peña defines the experience of rupture and disjunction characteristic of border crossings as "a quintessentially contemporary experience." He notes that in Tijuana any essentialist construct of Mexican identity exists only as a myth. "Crossing the border—that in itself is involuntary postmodernism," he observes. "You cross the border and in a matter of seconds you move from Catholicism to Protestantism, from the past to the future, from Spanish to English, from pre-Columbian to high tech, from hedonism to Puritanism."[7] These instant moves from one culture to another are not confined to national border sites. They exist within the boundaries of a national map or even show up on the map of a single city or street. Sandra Cisneros and Ana Castillo, two renowned Chicana writers, are both from Chicago. Their allegories of border are sometimes space bound but also temporally and imaginatively free floating.

In *The House on Mango Street* (1991), Cisneros's narrator Esperanza experiences Gómez-Peña's notion of cultural and historical border crossings in one neighborhood. Geographically far removed from the culture of her ancestors, she lives at the crossroads of several languages and idioms linked in their common destiny of (economic) destitution. She has neither lost nor found a home. Esperanza's physical distance from her Mexican origins intensifies the desire and hunger of memory for her ancestry. She is bound to an invisible ancestral memory through Mexican words and accents, and the demands of this memory become the stuff of her dreams and poetry. Her passion and talent for writing are nourished in the reterritorialized borderlands of Mango Street, where Anglos, Blacks, Hispanics, and various groups of immigrants enter an ongoing dialogue. In this new space of speech, a more resilient identity is forged for the displaced subject. The juxtaposition of speech patterns in the borderlands of geography, time, and memory lends the writing of dislocated peoples its poetic urgency. "Esperanza inhabits a border zone crisscrossed by a plurality of languages and cultures," comments Renato Rosaldo. "Multiple subjectivities intersect in her own person, where they coexist, not in a zone of free play but each with its own gravity and density."[8] In expanding the range of borderlands idioms, preserving diverse life memories, and formulating "alternative moral visions" within the framework of the short-story cycle, Cisneros's work represents a trend "against earlier versions of cultural authenticity" that honor the patriarchal dictates of a homogeneous and unchanging originary culture.[9]

"To make themselves the master of memory and forgetfulness," writes Jacques Le Goff in *History and Memory*, "is one of the great preoccupations of the classes, groups, and individuals who have dominated and continue to dominate historical societies."[10] When those minority groups that are often perceived as *personae non gratae*, such as Arabs in Europe and the United States, Mexicans in the southwest United States, Turks in Germany, or Koreans in Japan, become objects of critical, academic, and media scrutiny, they suffer further disenfranchisement, as their own stories and histories are rewritten and reinterpreted in ways that erase their past and confiscate their present. Therefore, the necessity for remembrance and its realization in writing becomes for minority cultures a strategy of resistance to forms of insistent negative representation manufactured by the media, institutions, and political interests. Remembering takes on the aura and function of a sacred ritual and bestows agency on the writer. The popular representations of Mexicans and Chicano/Chicanas in the United States and Turks in Germany show striking parallels of stereotyping, consistently portraying them as transient, unskilled, and dispensable laborers. By reclaiming agency and voice and investing their respective languages and histories with a certain archetypal authority, many Chicano/a and Turkish-German writers have countered the one-sided flow of representation and information that legitimates denying them basic economic, political, and educational rights.

The choice of writers in this comparative reading was suggested by the border situation of their respective cultures with regard to the concept of a Eurocentrically defined history. Turkey is at the eastern border of Europe, and Mexico exists at a double border, that is, geographically on the southern margin of the United States and figuratively on the western margin of Europe. Historically, both the Mexicans in the United States and the Turks in Germany constituted the backbone of imported (and often unskilled labor), though the history of Turkish labor in Germany is a much more recent phenomenon, dating only from the 1960s. Both groups have faced the most extreme forms of economic exploitation and have tradition-ally been considered undesirable aliens. Though economically indispensi-ble, they represent the *personae non gratae* among immigrant groups in their respective host countries. Whereas the Asian-American, for example, is generally regarded as ambitious, industrious, and academically gifted (the stereotypical science or math whiz), the Chicano is often represented as a wetback and a temporary or seasonal laborer. Turks in Germany are represented in almost identical terms. Since Turks are a predominantly Moslem, though a secular and Westernized people, they are considered culturally inferior to other "guest workers" from a Christian culture, such as Greeks or Italians.

Like the labor migration from Turkey to Germany that began after a revolution staged to bring down an American-backed regime, which was instrumental in dispossessing the farmers of their land, the large-scale mi-gration from Mexico to the United States is associated with the Mexican Revolution.[11] "Migration is the failure of roots," Bruce-Novoa observes; "displaced men are ecological victims. Between them and the sustaining earth a wedge has been driven. Eviction by droughts or dispossession by landlords, the impoverishment of the soil or conquest by arms—nature and man, separately or together, lay down the choice: move or die" (57). Confiscation of the lands of small farmers by big landlords, economically driven religious conflicts, and the difficulty of farming the mountainous and dry Anatolian terrain all conspired to prescribe a destiny of migration for the impoverished Turkish peasant. The dispossessed body of agricul-tural workers migrated to Germany as unskilled laborers. Farmers who lost their lands to men and nature became street sweepers, dishwashers, and assembly line workers. In Aysel Özakin's many stories of exile collected in *Soll ich hier alt werden?* (Am I to grow old here?) (1987) the loss of farming land, of small business, and the impoverishment of low-ranking civil ser-vants is matter-of-factly but eloquently portrayed. In the dream account at the onset of Özdamar's story, "Karagöz in Alamania" (Blackeye in "Ger-mania") Karagöz, an impoverished peasant, is caught stealing apples from a neighbor's tree. The neighbor goes to the peasant's father to demand compensation and asks that the son enter his service as a slave. The father is forced to give up the son and gets a sheep. A moneylender who witnesses the transaction interferes and tells the father that if he sends his son to work in Alamania (Germany), where one mark is equal to twenty-five lira and, therefore, one son to twenty-five sons, he can have twenty-five fields. In return for the money he lends the father to send his son to Alamania, the moneylender takes the only piece of land the father owns (*M*, 47–50).

The brutal challenges of "living humanely and humanly in Mexico"[12] and in Anatolia have driven huge labor armies away from their homelands to the United States and Germany, respectively.

The juxtaposed reading of the two modern literary traditions of exile in the work of Turkish-German and Chicana writers is not motivated by a mere comparatist impulse and is not meant to detract from the complex particularities of either tradition. Rather, it aspires to enhance both their uniqueness and their universal appeal by mutual reflection and by generating an awareness of the implicit dialogue that connects them. Özdamar's work portrays diverse stations of transit. Her protagonist Karagöz crosses borders as a matter of fact and necessity. She crosses borders of language and history, ancient and modern, to reinterpret and reclaim legends and lore lost or forgotten due to cultural rupture, ignorance, and misappropriation. In a similar vein, Castillo claims that Chicana writers have become excavators of their occulted cultures that were lost to "social ostracism, lack of education, migration, dispersion, and poverty" (*MD*, 166). The work of a "conscienticized" writer, in the words of Castillo, is "to be open to the endless possibilities of associations," whether using cultural metaphors familiar to the intended reader or introducing "images borrowed from other cultural legacies" (*MD*, 170).

Living Bilingually Is the Best Revenge: Resisting Monolingualism and Cultural Norm in Chicano/a and Turkish-German Literature

> We have ... reached a new phase in our poetics of self-definition. As mestizas, we must take a critical look at language, *all* our languages and patois combinations, with the understanding that language is not something we adopt and that remains apart from us. Explicitly or implicitly, language is the vehicle by which we perceive ourselves in relation to the world. If we as writers no longer necessarily feel bound to a process engendered by the Chicano movement, we are each individually accountable now for our use of language and the ideas communicated through it.
>
> Ana Castillo, *Massacre of the Dreamers*

On the whole, the transfigurations and tranplantations at cultural borders have developed in three successive and sometimes synchronic stages. The first phase in emergent diasporic literatures tends to be confessional, comprising mostly personal and collective stories of passage and immigration. These are often in the form of interpretive chronicles of a group and written in the native language. The second phase is in the language of the country of immigration and takes in its purview an aesthetically inscribed field of social observation, critique, and innovations in the use of the target language. The critically transformative third stage is a borderland of different languages, rites of passage, and negotiations between myth and reality, memory and presence, madness and reason, and factual account and revolutionary experimentations in language and style. Since these stages may emerge both diachronically and synchronically depending on immigration histories and patterns, they cannot be classified in a strictly historical order but rather are characterized by various transformations of personal and collective memory, which "is sometimes retreating, sometimes overflowing."[13]

Chicano/a literary and cultural criticism has cast its critical vision on a diverse spectrum of theoretical and imaginative writings from Latin America and from other ethnic and minority cultures in the United States. By situating their literature in a more international and intercultural context, Chicano/a literary theorists subtly state their dissatisfaction with the relatively minor critical attention paid to their cultural production in mainstream academic criticism. Angie Chabram Dernersesian has been a leading advocate of reassessing Chicano/a writing in the context of new critical frameworks and of forging transnational linkages with underrepresented and/or emergent literary traditions.[14] Castillo conceptualizes the new poetics of Xicanisma in a manner analogous to the reconfiguration of cultural legacies in contemporary ethnic and immigrant literatures. "We are looking at what has been handed down to us by previous generations of poets," she writes, "and, in effect, rejecting, reshaping, restructuring, reconstructing that legacy and making language and structure ours, suitable to our moment in history" (*MD*, 165).

The imaginative synthesis of coexisting languages and their dialogic games is a steady feature of Mexican-American and Chicano/a literature written in the United States. In creatively altering the English idiom, Gómez-Peña finds himself "in kinship with nonwhite English-speaking writers from India and the West Indies, Native Americans, and Chicanos" who likewise fire English with the passion of their native idioms and metaphors.[15] Bruce-Novoa celebrates the "interlingual" rather than the bilingual character of contemporary Chicano/a speech, which blends English with traces of Spanish idiolects, metaphors, and puns and creates highly "subtle fusions of grammar, syntax or cross-cultural allusions" that elude the monolingual reader. This practice of interlingualism is "highly sensitive to the context of speech acts, able to shift add-mixtures of languages according to situational needs or the effects desired." Furthermore, interlingualism "rejects the supposed need to maintain English and Spanish separate in exclusive codes, but rather sees them as reservoirs of primary material to be molded together as needed, naturally, in the manner of common speech." Even though some members of Chicano/a communities speak only English or only Spanish, the interlingual spectrum of expression "covers these and every potential blend."[16] "I am very interested in subverting English structures," comments Gómez-Peña, "infecting English with Spanish, and in finding new possibilities of expression within the English language that English-speaking people don't have. . . . I contain this linguistic spectrum in my experience as voyager and, inevitably it surfaces in my literature."[17]

The most striking instances of interlingualism appear in works that reflect on their own status as keepers of linguistic memory. Sandra Cisneros and Ana Castillo are distinctly vocal in their enthusiasm about the idiomatic wealth, wordplay, and metaphorical acuity of Spanish and its role in enriching their English texts. In an interview, Cisneros stated that when writing *House on Mango Street*, she did not know how to blend languages. The vignettes sport only an occasional word in Spanish. Nevertheless, Cisneros feels that the book is Spanish in spirit: "The syntax, the sensibility, the diminutives, the way of looking at inanimate objects—that's not a child's voice as is sometimes said. That's Spanish!"[18] The transportation of Spanish words and phrases into English and their seamless integration into the text allow her "to say things in English that have never been said before. . . . All of a sudden something happens to the English, something really new is happening, a new spice is added to the language." This is often accomplished by literal translation. Sometimes instead of translating, Cisneros explains the Spanish text through context—"my abuelita called me a sin verguenza and cried because I am without shame." The preference for this hybrid style—rather tame in Cisneros's prose—has helped her uncover "this whole motherlode" that she had not tapped into before (289). In Özdamar's work, the soaring imagination of Turkish lore and its imagistic force lend the abstract weight of German the impossible lightness of words in flight. Like Cisneros, Özdamar chooses to either translate her riddles or explain them in context. When Karagöz runs into the illegal worker who was dressed up as a soccer player when he first saw him, he says: "Hey, Aga, my eyes have bitten into you somewhere, but where?" "What he means by that," explains Özdamar, "is that he knew him from somewhere" (*M*, 76).

Code switching happens when a speaker switches languages midstream. Anzaldúa's *Borderlands*, which perfectly mimics spoken Chicano Spanish, offers numerous instances of code switching. Since Anzaldúa neither translates nor explains through context, code switching is her preferred mode of linguistic juxtaposition or bilingual enunciation: "Through our mothers, the culture gave us mixed messages: *No voy a dejar que ningún pelado desgraciado maltrate a mis hijos.* And in the next breath it would say, *La mujer tiene que hacer lo que le diga el hombre.*"[19] Code mixing and switching are often regarded by native speakers as a sign of the inadequate language skills of the nonnative speaker. In fact, fully bilingual and multilingual speakers frequently mix and switch codes among themselves in order to express a broader range of nuance and inflection in their speech. Whether using code switching or code mixing, Anzaldúa and Cisneros mark the transition by italicizing the Spanish text, whereas Özdamar and Castillo, who prefer code mixing, do not use italics and let the languages flow into one another. Code mixing happens when speakers change languages (codes) while not changing the topic or theme of their conversation. When some lexical items are more appropriate for the concepts that the speaker wants to express, these words are blended into the grammatical structure of the other language. For example, when the specific vocabulary of institutions and bureacratic practices of daily life in the host country are not readily translatable into the native language of the speaker, they appear untranslated in speech but are edited to conform to the syntax of the native language. The following passage from "Karagöz in Alamania" presents a perfect mimicry of code mixing in Turkish and German:

> The Turks spoke in their language, which was mixed with German words such as employment office, tax office, income tax form, vocational school. A guest worker standing there spoke: "Sonra interpreter geldi. Foremanle konustu. Bu income tax form kaybetmis dedi. Tax office cok fena dedi. Income tax yok. Bombok. Child credit falan alamazsin. Residence permit de yok. Immigration police vermiyor. Housing office de yok diyor. Employment office de permit vermedi. Ben oglani vocational school a gönderiyorum. Cok shit bu. Sen sick e mi ciktin? (*M*, 75)[20]

Not only do the German words blend into the grammatical structure of Turkish, but they are also made to conform to Turkish vowel harmony, which is a morphophonemic rule.[21] Özdamar blends not only words but also noncoincidental units of speech, proverb with verb, Koranic recitation with Persian miniature, or a whole belief system with a song.

In the tales of Özdamar and Castillo, the words in flight, that is, the shifting, mixing, and dancing codes are often linked to themes of flight from the real to the fantastic, from one realm of experience and its expression to another. The irresistibility of dancing with language is for Castillo an inherited Mexican linguistic trait: "Word-play for the Mexican Spanish speaker is contagious, a reflection of our sense of irony and humor about life" (*MD*, 168). Castillo's romance with wordplay and dance is very much in evidence in her delightfully parodistic and metafictional novel *So Far from God* (1993). Here she uses stutter, incantation, rage, despair, silence, laughter, and invective in bittersweet juxtapositions. Her code mixing has a touch of a recipe for magic. Not only English phrases and Spanish words but also idioms, prayers, everyday myths, and discourses of the occult coexist in semiotic harmony and prescribe ways of healing, recovery, survival, and peaceful passage beyond known borders to other realms of existence. In a similar vein, Özdamar illustrates that all human interaction and forms of transaction take place in the interiority of language, in its folds, crevices, ruptures, and through its ritualistic choreography. When the owner of the apple tree goes to Karagöz's father to demand that Karagöz enter his service, the two men sit down to draw up an agreement for compensation. "They spoke about this business not directly but in proverbs" (*M*, 48). In the end, Karagöz's father has to yield to the owner of the tree, not only because the latter wields the power of money but also because the father runs out of fitting proverbs and the other man does not. Like Turkish, Spanish is full of proverbs and aphorisms that offer prescriptions for relief from the inevitable burdens and curses of life. In many instances these adages are identical in their choice of metaphor and fully translatable into one another.[22] Although Castillo discovers the same treasury of idiom and humor in both Mexican and Chicano Spanish, Gómez-Peña differentiates between the behavioral and intellectual nuances of the two with a certain amount of linguistic patriotism and conceit. Although he is quick to point out that he is referring to *perceptions* of Mexican and Chicano Spanish from the respective sides of the border, Gómez-Peña reserves the gifts of dialogue, intellectual inquiry, and humor for Mexican Spanish.[23]

Wordplay and humor free all idioms from being earthbound and transport them to the realm of infinite expressibility. This flight of language often gives in to the irresistable force of parody, for parody and irony are, among other things, "major means of creating new levels of meaning—and illusion."[24] Parody is a form of rewriting or recasting with comic liberatory effect. Its object is another text, convention, code, or, in the broadest spectrum, discursive and nondiscursive practices. Alvina E. Quintana, for example, reads Castillo's *Mixquiahuala Letters* as a parody of modern ethnography, for the epistolary form of the novel unfolds as a series of observations on Mexican and American culture by the protagonist, Teresa, the writer of the letters. Quintana interprets Castillo's text as an "enterprise that provides the voices and experiences of growing up Chicana" and focuses on "what is at risk when a Chicana attempts to fashion an identity in response to two opposing cultures."[25] Castillo's writing suggests Linda Hutcheon's definition of the pragmatic range of parody: the double etymology of the prefix *para* "was not limited to producing a ridiculous effect (*para* as 'counter' or 'against'), 'but rather "the equally strong suggestion of complicity and accord (*para* as 'beside') allowed for an opening up of the range of parody."[26] Hutcheon sees parody as a bitextual and transcontextual form that stresses difference and as an effective agent of criticism (33). As a structure of repetition and re-creation, parody allows for a critical exploration of textual construction. Castillo's *So Far from God* presents perhaps the widest spectrum of parodic writing, where all cultural discourses—institutionalized religion, media, political agendas, *telenovelas,* rumor, superstition, and even constructions of ethnic identity are recast in a comic self-reflexive idiom. Referring to one of the character's boyfriend Rubén, the narrator remarks that "during the height of his Chicano cosmic consciousness, [he] renamed himself Cuauhtemoc."[27] Even the status of the narrator is not exempt from the spoof of critical distancing, as the titles of the various chapters illustrate: "What Appears to Be a Deviation from Our Story but Wherein, with Some Patience, the Reader Will Discover That There Is Always More Than the Eye Can See to Any Account" or "La Loca Santa Returns to the World via Albuquerque before Her Transcendental Departure; and a Few Random Political Remarks from the Highly Opinionated Narrator."

Özdamar had originally written "Karagöz in Alamania" as a play in 1982 and staged it in 1986 at the Frankfurter Schauspielhaus. This fantastic story of Turkey's labor migration to Germany, exemplified in the fate of Karagöz Schicksallos (Ill-Fated Blackeye), is a parody—in every sense of the genre—of other texts and discourses. In an article she published in *Die Zeit* on her direction of this play, Özdamar writes that she based the play on a letter written by a *Gastarbeiter* who had returned to Turkey for good. She did not know this man but wanted to write a play based on his life and invite him to the premiere of the play. He never made it to the play; he had died of a heart attack at the age of forty-one in his village. *Karagöz* is the name of a traditional Turkish shadow play. Karagöz, the comic main character of the shadow play, is a fast-talking smart aleck who constantly ridicules his sidekick, Hacivat. In Özdamar's story, it is the philosopher donkey who, like Karagöz, has a ready answer for everything. The donkey philosophizes, sings, smokes Camels, can belly dance, reinvents proverbs, songs, and riddles, parodies Karl Marx and the *Handbook for Guest Workers*, and delivers commentaries on Turkish and German society. On one of his trips to Germany in the company of the farmer's wife and children, the donkey meets an intellectual sitting in front of the Gate to Germany in a bathtub with his typewriter. This scene is a satirical take on the academic investigations of labor migration. The intellectual, who interviews all Turks coming out of Germany, recalls the French revolutionary and philosopher Jean Paul Marat (1743–93), who, due to a skin condition, spent a lot of time taking baths and studying in the bathtub. It was in his bathtub that Marat was stabbed to death by the young Charlotte Corday, a Girondist sympathizer. A Turkish youth, irritated by the questions of the intellectual, knocks him down with a karate kick and leaves him with the words, "The Empire strikes back" (*M*, 89). The intellectual sprinkles his questions with English phrases, talks about the culture shock of the *Gastarbeiter*, and imagines the forging of a new history and identity for the migrants. When the donkey challenges his ideas, interrupts his monologue, and ridicules his Socialist fantasies, the intellectual gets up and leaves with his bathtub. The full text of "Karagöz in Alamania" is a parodic commentary on the history of conditions that necessitated migration.

Metafiction and parody point to a critically sophisticated level of literary production. In reference to recent developments in Chicano literature, literary critic Marc Zimmerman states that the new Chicano/a writing has moved far beyond the borders of ethnic concerns. It "is inevitably more urban, more closely woven with Latino and non-Latino cultural strains, more distanced from a pre-technological , pre-capitalist world of blood bonds and sacrifices. . . . [I]t is also distanced from the world of confrontational violence with Rangers, cops, or rival gangs."[28] Similarly, the work of Turkish-German writers, especially during the early years of the Turkish migration, tended to be very confrontational toward the host society. Women writers, on the other hand, took a critical stance toward the patriarchal rules of their own societies. The recent work of Chicana and Turkish-German women writers is informed by a new consciousness of cultural memory and the ubiquitous echoes and traces of poststructuralist theory. The texts discussed here incorporate in various degrees feminist criticisms, theories of language and representation, and modern ethnography. The echoes of women's rights movements in the United States and Europe reverberate in Özakin and Castillo's stories, which openly discuss female sexuality, repression of women in patriarchal societies, and their silencing in two cultures. Women's experience of exile tends to be more alienating than that of their male compatriots, since the patriarchal dictates of their own communities ensure that they do not find escape routes to freedom in the new society.

Bruce-Novoa maintains that the Chicanos' history of experience with the police and the courts led to an aversion to social participation and to the search for alternative spaces.[29] The threat to the existence of Chicano culture was held at bay through a transformation of the lost and confiscated Mexican land into a textual space. The recovery of a lost geography and history in the construction of the imaginary nation of Aztlán, independent of both the United States and Mexico, offered a space of retreat from repression. "Mexico . . . canceled by migration and displacement"[30] was reclaimed in a trope of utopia, a sacred space beyond national borders.[31] In this instance, the practice of literary writing becomes an antidote to cultural amnesia. Literature offers culture the opportunity to reflect itself in written representation, and the symbolic action encouraged by literary imagination "can be transformed into other forms of praxis."[32] In the *Dialectics of Difference*, Ramón Saldívar translates the symbolic geography and action of Chicano literature into a radically politicized idiom. His characterization of Chicano literature challenges dominant cultural forms and translates this challenge into an affirmation of cultural difference.[33] More recently, many critics have come to see the greatest potential for the critical growth of Chicano/a literature and literary criticism in contemporary feminist fiction and theory, which resist the fixity of gender, race, and class identities. The new Chicana literature operates at the crossroads of past and present topographies and temporalities, distances itself both from "Bruce-Novoa's spatial identification" and "Saldívar's construction of machistic border and barrio defiance"[34] and examines reserves of cultural memory to dis-cover pragmatic metaphors for women's lives.

The Dialect(ic)s of *Borderlands/La Frontera* and *Mother Tongue*

The theory debates of the poststructuralist era have shown us that concepts of race, ethnicity, and gender are socially and culturally constructed and are shaped by specific historical conditions. Language is the primary tool for these constructions. Therefore, literary texts become a critical forum for understanding the conditions for the production of prejudice, discrimination, sexism, and xenophobia. The work of Anzaldúa and Özdamar is informed by a critical consciousness of how language creates dichotomies of mastery and loss and legitimizes structures of power. Through a sustained archaeology and reconstruction of the lost continents of their respective cultures, these writers produce not an imaginary or mythic space of refuge in text but a forum from which the subjects of borderlands can speak.

Gloria Anzaldúa and Emine Sevgi Özdamar portray their historical and personal destinies as gendered and ethnic subjects at the intersection of different languages, idioms, and generational and cultural terms. Women of Turkish and Mexican descent, traditionally confined to home and hearth in self-aggrandizing patriarchal family structures, struggle to reinvent, without the benefit of historical precedent, a legitimate identity in yet another foreign idiom. In what follows, I discuss how memory recovers a broken linguistic history and retells, reinvents, and repossesses it for individual and collective empowerment in Gloria Anzaldúa's *Borderlands/La Frontera: The New Mestiza* and Emine Sevgi Özdamar's *Mutterzunge*. Like many contemporary Chicana and Turkish-German women writers, Anzaldúa and Özdamar have made cultural self-assertion a priority by resisting the unilateral control over the representation of their respective cultures. Their writing represents a crossing of personal and collective and geopolitical and historical boundaries. Though not intended as a theoretical blueprint, Anzaldúa's *Borderlands* and Özdamar's stories in *Mutterzunge* illustrate how ethnic individuals and groups can situate themselves sequentially and simultaneously in contesting or overlapping positions of cultural memory. In *Borderlands*, Anzaldúa, a self-proclaimed new mestiza, offers a text in the tradition of German romanticism's *Mischgedicht* (mixed poem). A poetic performance of its own critical message and a crossover of various genres, her book presents its story in a collection of poems, reminiscences, personal and collective histories, and critical combat. Thus, the text itself emerges as a *mestizaje*, a cross-fertilization of ideas, images, mourning, and memory. It resists generic limitations that may be geographical, historical, or cultural. The act of inscription at the borders establishes a position of questioning and challenge:

> The U.S. Mexican border *es una herida habierta* where the
> Third World grates against the first and bleeds. And before a
> scab forms it hemorrhages again, the lifeblood of two worlds
> merging to form a third country—a border culture. . . . A border-

land is a vague and undetermined place created by the emotional residue of an unnatural boundary. It is in a constant state of transition.[35]

The border sites constitute zones of perpetual motion, confrontation, and translation. In writing and re-collection, the concepts of home and border become transportable, carried around in the form of political commitment and critical vision; "in leaving home, I did not lose touch with my origins. . . . I am a turtle, wherever I go, I carry 'home' on my back" (21). As a lesbian poet-writer-critic of color, Anzaldúa sees herself always transgressing/trespassing at border sites. In one of the last poems of the book, "To live in the Borderlands means you," she writes: "To survive the Borderlands / you must live *sin fronteras* / be a crossroads" (195). Anzaldúa's account is not just another postmodern self-reflexive analysis. It provides a critical space not only for political contestation and cultural clashes but also ultimately for a new narrative of dialogic understanding. "I am participating in the creation of yet another culture," she writes, "a new story to explain the world and our participation in it, a new value system with images and symbols that connect us to each other and to the planet" (81). Nevertheless, this new culture needs to preserve the memory of other languages and situate itself at polyglot borders. Anzaldúa's writing is uncompromisingly bi- and trilingual—English, Spanish, Spanglish, all inflected by the memory of the ancient accents of Nahuatl, the language of *Aztecas del norte*, the Chicanos who believe their homeland to be Aztlán. This defiant retreat from high tech to Aztec is a passionate expression of the human need to live in the comforting and accommodating diachronic structures of our histories, in the reassuring flow of continuity.

In the preface, Anzaldúa refers to her work as the representation of her "almost instinctive urge to communicate, to speak, to write about life on the borders." Indeed, the book is a testimony to the uncompromising power of a language forged at borders—of space, time, and memory—in legitimizing identity. She is relentlessly critical of those who have belittled mixed idioms born of sociohistorical necessity. "Even our own people, other Spanish speakers *nos quieren poner candados en la boca*. They would hold us back with their bag of *reglas de academia*" (54). Subjecting the Spanglish speaker to the rules of academia and forcing locks on her mouth reveal a full-blown disregard for the historical role of "border" languages. "*El lenguaje de la frontera*," the border idiom, is a living, relevant product of change. "Change, *evolución, enriquecimiento de palabras nuevos por in-*

vención o adopción have created variants of Chicano Spanish, *un nuevo lenguaje. Un lenguaje que corrosponde a un modo de vivir"* (55). This vibrant idiom, born of invention and adoption, records a diversity of social and linguistic registers.

Border culture with its valorization of many languages, idioms, and sites of translation complements Bakhtinian notions of dialogism and heteroglossia. The dialogic mode opposes monologism. Every speech form interacts with another and is subject to change and transformation. The dialogic imagination generates knowledge in the sphere of heteroglossia. Heteroglossia designates a configuration of material and historical forces inscribed in the speech memory of individuals and communities. These inscriptions reveal a diversity of social idiolects situated at certain stations of time and place. Dialogism and heteroglossia highlight and validate the dynamic flow of change, crisis, and transformation that informs human language and discourse at all cultural levels. Bakhtin argues, for example, that the various genres simultaneously employed in the novel (diary, letter, confessions, aphorisms) relativize "linguistic consciousness in the perception of language borders—borders created by history and society, and even the most fundamental borders (i.e. those between languages as such)—and permit expression of a feeling for the materiality of language that defines such a relativized consciousness."[36] The conversation between languages and voices at the heteroglot site takes on concrete form in the borderlands, where linguistic cultures clash and harmonize in social speech forms of varying currency. Borderlands accommodate many variants of unofficial, hybrid, and carnivalesque speech forms, languages for which there are no official dictionaries, which switch "from English to Castillian Spanish to the North Mexican dialect to Tex-Mex to a sprinkling of Nahuatl to a mixture of all these."[37]

Bakhtin defines the novel by its generic tendency to orchestrate

> all its themes . . . by means of the social diversity of speech types (*raznorečie*) and by the differing individual voices that flourish under such conditions. Authorial speech, the speeches of narrators, inserted genres, the speech of characters are merely those fundamental compositional unities with whose help heteroglossia (*raznorečie*) can enter the novel; each of them permits a multiplicity of social voices and a wide variety of their links and interrelationships. . . . These distinctive links and interrelationships between utterances and languages, this movement of the theme through different languages and speech types, its dispersion into

the rivulets and droplets of social heteroglossia, its dialogization—this is the basic distinguishing feature of the stylistics of the novel.[38]

Anzaldúa's richly accented, heteroglossic text is an eloquent response to the repeated charges directed at her tongue: teachers who punished her for speaking Spanish during recess, speech classes at college designed to get rid of her accent, the communal culture that denied women the right to talk back, purists and Latino/Latinas who ridiculed her "mutilated" Spanish. "I am my language,"[39] Anzaldúa declares with justified pride, for she embodies the fluency of dialogic moves, "the confluence of primordial images" and "the unique positionings consciousness takes at these confluent streams" (preface). In the final analysis, in an age of shifting centers, borders, and geographies, living multilingually is the best revenge.

Speaking for the artists creating at a time when "we witness the borderization of the world," Gómez-Peña declares that they "practice the epistemology of multiplicity and a border semiotics" and engage in "the creation of alternative cartographies, a ferocious critique of the dominant culture of both countries" and share a common enthusiasm in their "proposal for new creative languages."[40] In another borderland, thousands of miles away from the United States–Mexico border, another corps of migrant scribes, the Turkish writers of Germany, also participate in a border semiotics, as they negotiate conflicting cultural idioms. Through an identification with, or rejection, reacceptance, borrowing, and extension of, their own native myths and literary traditions as well as those of the host country, these writers rewrite cultural heritages. They write in an idiom that resists easy understanding, for it represents the conflicting voices and the fragmented collective memory of their respective ethnic/expatriate communities. The reinterpretation of native myths and national epics in their tales challenges the reader to educate herself in a new language, idiom, cultural semiotics, and history. Direct translations of obscure metaphors and frequent use of code mixing, code selection, and code switching reject appropriative analyses of their work, for they require at the very least a basic knowledge of the original code.

One of the most accomplished performers of the new German borderlands writing is Emine Sevgi Özdamar, a crossover artist, film and theater actress, dramatist, theater director, and writer. She was born in 1946 in one of Turkey's eastern provinces, Malatya, another border site where Turkish, Kurdish, and Arabic are spoken, and the legitimacy of the non-Turkish cultures is officially ignored and denied—Kurdish, an Indo-

European language, is claimed to be a mere aberrant dialect of Turkish, a Turkic language. At nineteen, Özdamar crossed several borders and cultural and time zones and arrived in Germany. After an early stint as a factory worker, she studied drama in the former East Berlin, landing roles in many theater plays and feature films. Her dramatic flair is evident in the way she directs language in performance. Özdamar's writing is about language in all its forms and manifestations, as speech and script, as language game and everyday practice, as ritual and performance, and as survival and mastery. Her first book, *Mutterzunge*, is a collection of meditations on language and fantastic satires tinged with hues of magical realism that unfold in verbal images reminiscent of a surrealistic film. In 1991, Özdamar was awarded the coveted Ingeborg Bachmann Prize in literature for her then unpublished novel *Das Leben ist eine Karawanserei hat zwei Türen aus einer kam ich rein aus der anderen ging ich raus* (Life is a caravansary has two doors through the one I went in and through the other I went out).

The first two stories of the collection *Mutterzunge*, "Mutterzunge" and "Großvaterzunge" (Grandfather tongue) illustrate how history and memory, geography and genealogy inhabit language. "In my language, tongue means language" [In meiner Sprache heißt Zunge: Sprache],[41] reads the first sentence of "Mutterzunge"; "the tongue has no bones; it turns wherever you turn it" [Zunge hat keine Knochen, wohin man sie dreht, dreht sie sich dorthin] (*M*, 7). From the onset, Özdamar underlines the latitude of language, its acrobatic skill of expression, and its possibilities of articulation and action. "Zunge drehen" (turning or twisting the tongue) is a literal translation of the Turkish idiom *dili dönmek*, often used in the negative as *dilim dönmüyor* (I cannot say or pronounce). The narrator refers to herself as one with a "twisted tongue" [gedrehten Zunge] (7), a person capable of mastering difficult sounds. After her long sojourn in Germany, she feels that when she thinks of "mother sentences" spoken by her mother in her mother tongue, they sound like a foreign language she had mastered well (7). The memories of the sounds of her language intricately linked to the sights of her homeland are fading away. Once when she asked her mother why Istanbul had become so dark, the mother replied: "Istanbul has always been lighted like this, your eyes have become accustomed to the Alamanian lights" [Istanbul hatte immer diese Lichter, deine Augen sind an Alamanien-Lichter gewöhnt] (7). In order to reclaim her mother tongue, she needs a detour through her "grandfather tongue." This grandfather tongue is Ottoman Turkish, a hybrid language of the Ottoman court and the educated classes that was mostly made up of Persian and

Arabic loan words and structures held together by Turkish connectors. Like Anzaldúa, who ventures into the memories of Nahuatl that recall the glory of a preconquest civilization, Özdamar excavates the lost accents of a language evocative of a long bygone era of power. This heady trafficking in the languages of the past and the present, "of playing with dialectical forms, playing with sounds from Nahuatl, experimenting with the phonetical structures of indigenous languges," is for Gómez-Peña "a level of absolute Otherness, the ultimate margin."[42] It is a dizzying ride on the Möbius strip of language. By reclaiming this history and expanding the memorial territories of their respective languages, Anzaldúa and Özdamar defy the low status assigned to Chicano Spanish in the United States and Turkish in modern Germany, a Turkish that is no longer the sign of nostalgia for the Orient. As Roland Barthes once remarked, "How remote it seems, that period when the language of Islam was Turkish and not Arabic! This is because the cultural image is always fixed where the political power is: in 1877 the 'Arab countries' did not exist; though vacillating . . . Turkey was still, politically and therefore culturally, the very sign of the Orient."[43]

Before 1928, Turkish used the Arabic script. In the twenties, Kemal Atatürk, the founder and first president of the Turkish republic, undertook a series of reforms designed to transform the new republic into a fully secularized and Westernized state. The Arabic writing system was replaced by a phonetic (Roman) alphabet that corresponded ideally to the sounds of Turkish, thus radically raising the rate of literacy. Özdamar's narrator cannot read the Arabic script, and her grandfather never learned to read the Roman alphabet. If she and her grandfather were to lose their speech and had to communicate in writing, "they could not tell each other stories" [könnten wir uns keine Geschichten erzählen] (M, 12). She therefore decides to take Arabic lessons from "the great master of the Arabic script," Ibni Abdullah. Thus begins her commute from her residence in East Berlin to Ibni Abdullah's small apartment in West Berlin.

This site of learning language(s) is located at multiple borders. Berlin before the fall of the Wall is a city divided, at the border of a country divided geographically, historically, and ideologically. The single room of the apartment is divided with a curtain into living and learning quarters, where Ibni Abdullah gives lessons to students of Oriental languages. The narrator and her Arabic teacher have both crossed several linguistic and cultural borders before settling in Berlin. They now engage in an effort to find common borders of language and culture. This is, among other things, a love story told in German, framed by conversations between the religious and the secular, the spiritual and the carnal, and the old and the new and punctuated by Turkish and Arabic idioms. Like Anzaldúa, Özdamar's narrator experiences the semiotic memory of language as an act of inscription on her body. "Cradled in one culture, sandwiched between two cultures, straddling all three cultures and their value systems," writes Anzaldúa, "*la mestiza* undergoes a struggle of flesh, a struggle of borders, an inner war. . . . The coming together of two self-consistent but habitually incompatible frames of reference causes *un choque*, a cultural collision."[44] In the "Großvaterzunge," the narrator's experience of both language and love through her body also marks a celebration of Arabic calligraphy. Since Islam forbade the representation of images, calligraphy became the dominant visual art form in Arabic and Ottoman culture.

The narrator's love of the picture alphabet and her desire for Ibni Abdullah intermingle and dominate her body and soul. One day he leaves her to complete her reading assignment on her own. Although he is gone, "his watchmen, his words stood in the room, some squatted sturdily on their legs" [Seine Wächter, seine Wörter standen im Zimmer, manche saßen fest über ihren Beinen]. She tries to "read" the inscribed images: "An arrow goes off from a bow. A heart stood there. The arrow gets stuck in the heart, a woman's eye bats her eyelashes. Now she has the eye of a blind woman, a bird flies and loses his feathers on the way the arrow has flown" (*M*, 42). In another scene, the narrator watches the letters she pronounces and likens some to birds, some to caravans; still others remind her of trees scattered in the wind, sleeping camels, running snakes, evilly raised eyebrows, eyes that cannot sleep, or the fat ass of a woman sitting on a hot stone in a Turkish bath (16). This is a picturesque script embellished by the speaker's imagination. The letters speak with one another "without a pause in different voices" [ohne Pause mit verschiedenen Stimmen] (24) and wake the sleeping animals in her body. She tries to close her eyes, but the voice of love tortures her body, which splits up like a pomegranate. An animal emerges from the bloody gap in her body and licks her wounds. She sees stones abandoned by the receded ocean waters under her feet. In the endless landscape, stones cry out for water. A sea flows from the animal's mouth, raising her body high, and she falls asleep on the body of water and wakes up rejuvenated. She is like "a newborn wet bird" [ein neugeborener nasser Vogel] (25).

The symbolism of the split body healed in water, an element that knows no borders and boundaries, is duplicated in Anzaldúa's text. The barbed wire of the U.S.-Mexican border is like a "1,950 mile long open wound" in her body, the memory of the rape and plunder of her culture;

it splits her, chops her up, mutilates her "*me raja me raja.*" But the sea whose "tangy smell" "seeps" into her "cannot be fenced"; "*el mar* does not stop at borders."[45] Standing at the edge between earth and ocean, her "heart surges to the beat of the sea." With the same ease with which the ocean touches the earth and heals, the narrator switches codes, a gesture that in this narrative consistently acts as a panacea for the torn tongue, "Oigo el llorido del mar, el respiro del aire" [I hear the the cry of the ocean, the breath of the air] (2). Like the body of Özdamar's narrator, her body effortlessly becomes a bridge of language between two geographies and histories, between the world of the gringo (*gabacho*) and the wetback (*mojado*), the past and the present. Like body cells that are always renewed, words are born, grow, mature, change, die, and are reborn. By employing such regionalisms and colloquialisms as *gabacho*, *mojado*, and *pa'* (for) and shifting and purposefully misplaced accents (3), Anzaldúa smuggles the variegated fabric of Chicano Spanish into Spanish and English. Thus a new language and identity free of national borders is celebrated in the borderlands:

> Deep in our heart we believe that being Mexican has nothing to do with which country one lives in. Being Mexican is a state of soul—not one of mind, not one of citizenship. Neither eagle nor serpent, but both. And like the ocean, neither animal respects borders. (62)

And neither does the bird, the image Özdamar's narrator transforms herself into. Image, metaphor, and metonomy re-member bodies of language, culture, and their inhabitants dismembered by imperialism, war, conquest, colonization, poverty, and violence. They not only restore them not only to memory but also invest them with a kind of material reality. Names, identities, and histories that expired along with passports and visas can now be brought back to life only through the potent medicines of memory: language, image, script.

But what if that script is forgotten? "In the foreign language, words have no childhood" [In der Fremdsprache haben Wörter keine Kindheit], observes Özdamar's narrator (*M*, 42). She tries desperately to correct this loss by looking for the history of her language in Arabic and by a narrative revis(ion)ing of the hybridity characteristic of Ottoman Turkish. She celebrates the visual poetry of Arabic letters. During the lessons in Ibni Abdullah's house, her Turkish and Arabic sentences, lyrics to Turkish songs, and Koran recitations by other students are simultaneously spoken, clashing and harmonizing at once. Many Turkish words have Arabic roots, and by going to the roots, the narrator can trace branches of lyric, lore, and legend intertwined in the two linguistic cultures. She recites for her teacher Turkish words of Arabic origin: "*Leb*-Mund" (mouth); "*Mazi*-Vergangenheit" (past); "*Yetim*-Waise" (orphan). Bemused, he remarks that they sound somewhat strange when spoken with a Turkish accent. "As these words got up, left your land, and ran to mine, they've somewhat transformed themselves on the way," she replies (27).

In the final analysis, this unusual love story is more than a metalinguistic commentary. It also tells a veiled political history complicated and sometimes compromised by the universal enforcement of Atatürk's hasty Westernization reforms. Atatürk has been criticized by the Left and the Right alike for the collective forgetting of Turkey's cultural past, for erasing all traces of her Islamic Ottoman heritage. Stranded in this historical lacuna, modern Turks struggle to define a cultural identity. "On anniversaries of Atatürk's death, I loudly recited poetry and cried, but he should not have had to ban the Arabic script," remarks the narrator; "it is as if this ban cut my head in two. All the names of my family members are Arabic" (*M*, 27). Nevertheless, the narrator considers herself fortunate to belong to a generation that has grown up with many Arabic words, a generation at the interstices of the past and the present of its language.

The secular sensibilities of modern Turkish education construe the study of Arabic language and the use of Arabic words as a politically reactionary act. Modern Turkish intellectuals champion the cause of *öz Türkçe* (authentic or pure Turkish). The movement to reclaim and re-create an earlier "purer" Turkish language free of the strong influences of Ottoman, Arabic, and Persian was launched by Atatürk when he established the Türk Dil Kurumu (Turkish Language Association). This association publishes a great number of books, professional journals, and dictionaries with the intention of settling the debts of modern Turkish to Arabic and Persian (and, more recently, to European languages such as English and French) and expanding its lexical possibilities through derivations of new words from root forms of modern and ancient Turkic languages. The ideology of reclaiming an "essential" Turkish language stripped of its history and organic development has come under attack, for it entails a practice of denying, forgetting, and erasing vital cultural heritages. Özdamar implicitly maintains that she can have much easier access to the study of Arabic in Germany than in Turkey, where her desire to reclaim her "grandfather tongue" could be construed as a reactionary gesture in the context of the laicist ideology that underwrites modern Turkish education. Like the Spanish academics who shudder at Anzaldúa's bastardized language,

Turkish intellectuals keep their speech and script segregated from hybridized or crossover forms, be they the legacies of the past (e.g., Ottoman) or the necessities of the present (the translinguistic lexicon of computerese, for example).

Özdamar's narrative often defies translatability, although she translates Turkish expressions literally into German. Like most languages with a long oral tradition, Turkish is an impossibly metaphorical and imagistic language that defies ready comprehension. Özdamar challenges the reader by expressions that border on the absurd when left unparaphrased. A reference to alleged revolutionaries who have been tortured reads: "They made them puke the milk they drank from their mothers through the nose" (*M*, 12). A fairy tale begins, "Once there was, once there was not" [Es war einmal, es war keinmal] (31), the Turkish version of "once upon a time," a turn of phrase that does justice to the rich ambiguity of the past. Referring to her paralysis when faced with Abdullah's seizure, she says: "I could not catch him; my hands lay on my knees like letters without a tongue" (22). During her first visit to Abdullah's apartment the narrator tells him that if her father had delivered her to his door for Arabic lessons, he would have said: "Yes, master, her flesh belongs to you and her bones to me; if she does not open her eyes, ears, and heart to what you say, hit her. The hand of the master who hits hails from paradise. Where you hit, there roses will bloom" (13). When the cultural context of this seemingly violent and misogynist statement is not translated, it can easily and understandably be misread as one man giving another the right to dismember his own daughter's body. The metaphorical economy of Turkish preserves the memory of the ancient histories of hunting, warring, conquering tribes. Therefore, it is rich in idioms that express the body in pain. In this sentence Özdamar mixes several Turkish aphorisms and proverbs. When parents deliver their children (male or female) to a teacher, they say, "Eti senin, kemiği benim" [Her/His—Turkish does not have a gendered third-person singular form—flesh is yours, the bones are mine]. This expression illustrates the great faith put in teachers in Turkish culture. A teacher is believed to play a more important part than the parent in the formation of the child. "Dayak cennetten çıkmadır" [Spanking hails from paradise] is a proverb that sanctions the necessity of punishing children who misbehave. The other aphorism in this code assembly is "Where the master touches, there roses bloom," a self-explanatory praise of expertise and learning. Why does Özdamar cut, mix, and edit metaphors, provide no explanation for outrageous (to other ears) expressions, and thus risk misinterpretation?

Both Anzaldúa and Özdamar present the reader with a text, like a map full of blank spaces. Anzaldúa will switch from English to Spanish to Spanglish and write whole poems and paragraphs in Chicano Spanish without providing a translation. Özdamar provides everything in German translation but bombards the reader with the most unheard-of turns of phrase that make no sense to a German (or any non-Turkish) speaker. Both writers expect the reader to engage in a more informed and conscientious way with another discursive practice. Though written in an accessible and visually enticing German, Özdamar's tales require translation at many levels, historical, political, social, cultural. Multicultural citizenship requires not only the admission of not knowing the other but also a willingness to learn about the other. Following Özdamar, I am reminded of a Turkish proverb that illustrates this statement better than any critical formulation I can come up with: "Bilmemek değil, öğrenmemek ayıp" [Not knowing is not a cause for shame, but not learning is]. Anzaldúa echoes Özdamar's unspoken sentiment in her preface, declaring that she will make no apologies for the unique language of her people. "[W]e Chicanos no longer feel that we need to beg entrance, that we need always to make the first overture," she states, "to translate to Anglos, Mexicans and Latinos, apology blurting out of our mouths with every step. Today we ask to be met halfway." This writing is a new challenge for the reader to join a conversation of genuine cultural bi- and multi-lingualism.

5

Writing Outside the Nation

> Leaving Pakistan was, of course, tantamount to giving up the company of women.
>
> Sara Suleri, *Meatless Days*

> Among the highlights that faraway summer of our fledgling womanhood while we studied with gringo instructors who looked for meaning in life outside a commune in Idaho, and a Mexican artisan at a contemporary market geared to attract tourists with dollars—was a weekend in Mixquiahuala, a Pre-Conquest village of obscurity, neglectful of progress, electricity not withstanding.
>
> Its landmark and only claim to fame were the Toltec ruins of Tula, monolithic statues in tribute to warriors and a benevolent god in self-exile who reappeared later on Mayan shores, and again, on the back of a four-legged beast to display his mortal fallibilities.
>
> Ana Castillo, *The Mixquiahuala Letters*

Whether removed from the subject by one or more generations, several decades, or a few years, the memory and images of nation continue to inhabit the exilic imagination. The symbolic registers of the nation usually increase proportionately to the length of time spent outside the nation, and the loyalties that bind the "imagined community" (Anderson) diverge into smaller communities bound by gender, class, caste, religion, home region, profession, language, and dialect. The concept of a sacred mythical originary nation, Aztlán, developed at the height of the Chicano movement as a source of identification and identity formation in a diasporic community that could no longer claim a Mexican homeland. However, during the 1980s and the 1990s, as different genres of cultural identification and communal memory began to emerge among Chicano communities, the politics of (national) belonging began to be variously redefined in terms of class, gender, ethnicity, and even family. The status of women in the recent history of Mexican and Turkish labor migrations has been doubly complicated. Although driven to work by sheer economic necessity to feed children and families, women workers experience a persistent degradation of their sacrifices and labors by the patriarchal hierarchy of their communities. Furthermore, as migrant and often undocumented workers, they are easy prey for employers hiring them at slave wages. The combination of loss of community and exploitation of human labor regulated by multinational economies constitutes the nonwhite woman's burden:

> Ours is a world imbued with nationalism, real for some, yet tenuous as paper for others. A world in which from the day of our births, we are either granted citizenship or relegated to the netherstate of serving as mass production drones. Non-white women—Mexicans/Chicanas, Filipinas, Malaysians, and others—who comprise eighty percent of the global factory work force, are the greatest dispensable resource that multinational interests own. (*MD*, 24)

Castillo's *Mixquiahuala Letters* and Turkish-German writer Aysel Özakin's *Die blaue Maske* (The blue mask), both autobiographical novels of passages, portray the labors of negotiating cultural and national identity in the unstable terrain of exile. In varying degrees, the two tales account for ways in which nation, narration, generation, and gender are imbricated through the topoi of transit and travel. In their nuanced portrayal of the relation of women's lives to class, race, and nation, they draw upon diverse literary heritages, disregard laws of genre, and speak across generations, geographies, and temporalities to numerous other texts. Hearing a text through another, one writer's voice in another's, allows us to stay attuned to the insights of our many languages and to appreciate the generative intertextuality that fosters dialogic imagination. The linguistic, literary, and sociopolitical range of modern transcultural texts demands critical responses that cannot be accommodated by any one national literary tradition or theoretical camp. The tension between the preservation of cultural roots and the cultivation of dreams of affluence, between nostalgia for a romanticized sense of belonging to a place, however destitute, and assimilation into a morally questionable society is a dominant trope of Turkish-German and Mexican-American and Chicano/a writing. The refiguration of Mexican and Turkish cultural identity in the American and German contexts, respectively, is informed by the double alienation of labor migration rooted in economic exploitation and border trauma.

Through a creative translation of poststructuralist, post-Marxist, and feminist discourses, Chicano/a literature and literary criticism have successfully experimented with alternative forms and fictions of self-representation that resist the homogeneity of narrowly defined ethnic concerns. Both *The Mixquiahuala Letters* and *Die blaue Maske* participate in the tradition of the *Bildungsroman*, while rewriting it in a parodic, metafictional mode to incorporate larger issues of exilic consciousness, the birth pangs and trauma of the women's movement of the 1960s and 1970s, and the radical reimagining of the state of nation.

The Mixquiahuala Letters and Die blaue Maske: Bildung beyond the Nation

In the grand tradition of the *Bildungsroman, The Mixquiahuala Letters* and *Die blaue Maske* represent the narrator/protagonist's quest for enlightenment. True to the convention of the genre, this *Bildung* (education, formation) takes place in the tropics of travel. The travelers are *Bildungsreisende* (travelers on the *Bildung* path) who during the course of their real or imaginary trips are transformed into self-reflexive agents. However, here all resemblance to the classical *Bildungsroman* ends. Whereas the late-eighteenth-century *Bildungsreisende* always returns home, for the "exiled" hero/ine, there is no return. For the typical protagonist of the *Bildungsroman* the travel begins and ends at the same point, and the protagonist incurs no real losses or scars and emerges as a learned, reflecting subject; that is, he reaches a state of conscious naïveté. By contrast, in the tales of Castillo and Özakin the topoi of travel and transit, frequently interrupted by frustration and alienation, allegorize the challenges posed by the valiant but ultimately impossible quest for the recuperation of origins. The German *Bildungsroman* was a product of the late eighteenth and early nineteenth centuries, when the concept of nationalism in a "dispersed" Germany that consisted of numerous principalities and petty states could only be realized as cultural nationalism. Thus, *Bildung*, as a form of ideal education for German youth, became intimately linked with the idea of nation.

The typical protagonist of the *Bildungsroman* is a young man who undertakes a journey, symbolic of the educational rites of passage, in order to become an *enlightened citizen*. Castillo and Özakin's protagonists are also *Bildungsreisende*. However, their quest for cultural citizenship is not affiliated with a nation but rather with intranational communities (of women, artists, exiles). The contested concepts of nation, ethnicity, and history are represented both thematically, in the topos of travel without clear-cut departure points and destinations, and structurally, in the disjunctive and circuitous narrative form that duplicates the complexity of writing new identities.

The respective narrators, both writers, take history on a trip to negotiate its burden and in the process undertake a project of cultural criticism. "History at the level of the signifier,"[1] that is, history as a register of representational practices, converts to memory as a transfigurative repertoire of the signified. This memory and its variants assume the character of what Julia Kristeva calls the "symbolic denominator," where history and geography intersect to forge cultural forces and unities that still fuel territorial conflicts between nations. However, this common symbolic denominator simultaneously transcends the nation, for its global imagination and tendency for economic standardization claim vistas that expand far beyond national boundaries. The new symbolic-social entity is inscribed into the strange temporality of a kind of "future perfect," where "the most deeply repressed and transnational past gives a distinctive character to programmed uniformity."[2] Thus, the symbolic denominator of imagined communities, rooted in their cultural and religious memories, repeatedly returns to upset globalizing strategies of socioeconomic forces and national ideologies. Sociocultural groupings, such as those that come under the rubric of "European" culture, are facilitated by common symbolic denominators of art, philosophy, and religion rather than economic status. Although Kristeva sees economics as a function of collective memory, she concedes that its characteristics are subject to intervention and alteration by external political factors. The sociocultural group formations ("of the 'European type' ") consistently face two major issues: the problem of "*identity*, which is brought about by historial sedimentation," and "the *loss of identity*, which is caused by memory links that bypass history in favor of anthropology." Kristeva sees these two issues as different temporal dimensions of time, "the time of linear, *cursive* history, and the time of another history, that is, another time, a *monumental* time (the nomenclature comes from Nietzsche) that incorporates these supranational sociocultural groupings within even larger entities" (203). This "time of another history" supports transnational and intertextual forms of representation and reproduction espoused by contemporary European feminism, as it returns "to an archaic (mythic) memory as well as to the cyclical or monumental temporality of marginal movements" (208). Socialist ideologies, based on the idea that human life is determined by its relation to production, have neglected the relationship of humans to reproduction and the symbolic order. The psychosymbolic interior structure of Western Christian culture and its secular manifestations have left women alienated "from language and the social bond, in which they discover neither the affects nor the meanings of the relationships they enjoy with nature, their bodies, their children's bodies, another woman, or a man. The accompanying frustration, which is also experienced by some men, is the quintessence of the new feminist ideology" (213).

Castillo and Özakin, positioned at various stations of a culture of migration, transport language from its nonaffective confines to a symbolic level that remains closer to the heart, the body, and the many forms of love that define human beings and let it give voice to the despair and hope of those who have suffered loss of family, home, and history. In "Un Tapiz: The Poetics of Conscientización," a chapter in her *Massacre of the Dreamers*, originally a dissertation that earned her a doctorate in American studies at the University of Bremen, Castillo foregrounds the critically transformative and corrective force of contemporary Chicana writing by discussing how it re-members mythical and poetic legacies to give melody and resonance to the unwritten voices/texts of Mexic Amerindian women:

> Choosing to be conscious transmitters of literary expressions, we have become excavators of our common culture, mining legends, folklore, and myths for our own metaphors. . . . Our cultural heritages were "discovered" in the era of our generation's rebellion. They were not directly passed on to us from the previous generation, which because of social ostracism, lack of education, migration, dispersion, and poverty, was not in a position to uncover and share such a rich and illustrious legacy. (*MD*, 166)

Castillo and Özakin's respective novels illustrate that in the self-reflexive ethos of the postnational era, the concept of nation is troped into a notion of ongoing migration. The "symbolic denominators" of nation building cross borders and restage themselves as memories of different "imagined communities," those of women, migrants, "guest workers," or political refugees. Castillo's poetics of *conscientización* is not confined to a fixed history and geography. She and her fellow Chicana writers have embraced a sense of history and temporality informed by what Kristeva calls the "dynamic of signs." Rejecting a linear and ordered account of the events of history, these writers strive to find "a language for their corporeal and intersubjective experiences which have been silenced by the cultures of the past."[3] In Castillo's words, the mission of "Conscienticized Poetics" is to take on "everything and everyone at once" (*MD*, 171), in other words, to reveal the interconnectedness of diverse cultural traditions. Castillo's vision of this universal poetics echoes the memory of a much earlier text known as the manifesto of German romanticism. In the famous *Athäneum* fragment 116, Friedrich Schlegel defines Romantic poetry as a "progressive universal poesy" (progressive Universalpoesie) whose mission is to reunite all forms of human expression, join rhetoric with logic, poetry with philosophy, and art with art criticism.[4] Although Castillo pursues the conscientious form of a universal poetics of progressivity, her interests and sympathies are justifiably aligned with the underrepresented voices and homeless cultures, those of nonwhite women, women of the Third World who in an age of nation-states "are in effect, represented by no country" (*MD*, 24).

This topos of residency in a no wo/man's land, of being "a countryless woman" (*MD*, 24) between borders, represents the paradoxical quest of Castillo's and Özakin's respective tales. The quest takes on the form of re-membering the nation from its historical traces, myths, urban visions, and, perhaps most important of all, through the experiences of women—mothers, sisters, friends, rivals. The notion of a national and/or cultural identity is reevaluated through the labors of personal memory conceptualized in a gender-specific idiom. Here women's memory assumes a genealogical posture. It imagines the past as a text of mothers and grandmothers, family anecdotes, and ancestral myths. In a very poignant biographical tale of her grandmother and mother, "My Mother's Mexico," Castillo relates that her enduring ties to her mother's land/motherland, which is neither the place of her birth nor that of her childhood and adulthood, were constituted and forged through her mother's history. Castillo inherited her maternal grandmother's love for books, writing, and recording. The mother preserved her mother's notebook through long years of migration and handed it to her daughter, the writer. As a first-generation immigrant, Castillo's mother Raquel embraces a stubbornly nostalgic and patriotic view of a nation whose destitution drove her and her guardian grandparents north:

My mami, a dark mestiza, inherited the complexes and fears
of the colonized and the strange sense of national pride that per-
meates the new society of the conquered. To this day mami
speaks only Spanish, although she has lived in Chicago for over
forty years.[5]

Herein lies one of the irreconcilable conflicts of modern migrancy. Poverty, despair, exploitation by one's own lead to voluntary or forced exile, yet the pull of place, the siren song of the homeland, transforms lived experience into a cherished past, putting the remembering agent at odds with the present. Castillo aspires to resolve the conflict of nostalgia for origins and assimilation into another land and culture in the utopian (as in nowhere and everywhere), nonterritorial space of writing. " 'Ana del Aire,' my mother calls me," Castillo tells us, "[w]oman of the air, not earthbound, rooted to one place—not to Mexico, where Mami's mother died, not to Chicago, where I was born, not to New Mexico, where I've made a home for my son, but to everywhere at once."[6] However, this writing is by no means utopian in the sense of an ideal. It is often a subversive force, for it breaks through received tradition and convention and reassembles their traces as an alternative, symbolically potent, and often more empowering version of history. In letter 16 of *The Mixquiahuala Letters*, Teresa, the author of the forty letters addressed to her friend Alicia, informs her ad-dressee of her intention to remember (read: reconstruct and interpret) their shared (hi)story in order to understand a turbulent time positioned at the crossroads of private and collective experience:

i doubt if what i'm going to recall for both our sakes in the following pages will coincide one hundred per cent with your recollections, but as you make use of my determination to attempt a
record of some sort, to stir your memory, try not to look for
flaws or inaccuracies.[7]

Unlike history, memory draws attention to its own constructed status. It does not seek to preserve the past "as it was" but, in a Benjaminian sense, revises it to release its emancipatory potential. Teresa's efforts to record and interpret her shared past with Alicia defy the boundaries of (auto)biography and underline the desire for a form of remembering that extends beyond individual experience to define the context and content of political, social, and cultural interests. Teresa's and Alicia's experiences of their conflicted relationship to Mexico, their entrapment between cultures "had to have meant something," and if they were able to understand it correctly, their insight would benefit not only themselves "but womanhood" (*ML*, 47).

The self-reflexive tenor of *The Mixquiahuala Letters*, which issues from an awareness of its own interpretive gestures, underlines its status as a metafictional text. It insists on its fictionality while simultaneously pointing to the interconnectedness of lived experience and its representation in text. The metafictional identity of the novel confers upon its author the collective roles of writer, reader, commentator, and parodist. Parody simulates the condition of intertextuality, in other words, it alternately resists, mimics, refers to, and rewrites other texts in order to recontextualize them in the present and to detonate their hidden or muted subversive power. In a sort of a prologue to the book—in lieu of a table of contents—Castillo offers alternative reading sequences for the letters, thereby transforming the monologue of the letter writer into a hermeneutic circle of writer, narrator, and readers. She declares, "It is the author's duty to alert the reader that this is not a book to be read in the usual sequence. All letters are numbered to aid in following any one of the author's proposed options." The options are presented for the conformist, the cynic, and the quixotic. Several different sets of letters are left out in each option, so that the conformist reader need only read twenty-nine of the forty letters, the cynic thirty-two, and the quixotic thirty-four. The stage for the game with the reader is set. This game itself refers to other metafictional texts, most notably to Julio Cortázar's *Hopscotch*. By dedicating her book to the memory of Cortázar—"the master of the game"—Castillo also emphasizes the intertextual character of the *Letters* in the larger context of Latin American fiction. In his theoretical speculations about the nature of postmodern ethnography, anthropologist Stephen Tyler claims that ethnography is not a field of writing where the ethnographer wields cognitive control. Rather, the ethnographer's "text depends on the reader's supplementation. The incompleteness of the text implicates the work of the reader, and his work derives as much, if not more, from the oral world of everyday expression and commonsense understanding as it does from the world of the text."[8] The figure of the implied reader as a structural device of the text is a legacy of Romantic hermeneutics.[9] Author, narrator, addressee, and reader become, alternately, both reader and writer. Since none of Castillo's suggestions regarding the sequences of the letters is chronological or consistent, the reader is led to unexpected junctures, dead ends, and labyrinthine paths, and the very act of reading mimics the labors of memory—reconfiguring a (hi)story from its fragments.

Biographical information and secondary literature point to the autobiographical status, however fictionalized, of the two novels. Castillo disavows any resemblance to a true (life) story both in the traditional disclaimer at the beginning of the novel and her suggestion of reading the letters in different orders, thus relativizing authorial truth and narrative control. When Castillo pronounces that "*The Mixquiuahala Letters* is fiction" and that "[a]ny resemblance it may have to actual persons or incidents is coincidental," she both resists autobiographical identification and raises suspicions that there is an autobiographical subject behind the mask of protest. The (auto)biographical status of *Die blaue Maske* is borne out by Özakin's other books written outside the nation which constitute perhaps a single continuous text on exile. Ülker Gökberk has eloquently argued that Özakin's work is an extended metaphor of wandering.[10] Ultimately, both narrative tales simultaneously simulate and dissimulate the autobiographical act in an attempt to negotiate the competing positions of personal remembrance and lived history. When one of the characters in *Die blaue Maske* asks the narrator if she is working on something autobiographical, her answer is: "Yes, you are the one who dreams it [the autobiography], but your dreams are full of others and of infinite possibilities."[11] In this vein, the implied collective "i" of Castillo's narrator/writer Teresa is a tribute to many "I"s and women's lives that have inspired the symbolic constitution of sociopolitical agency in *The Mixquiahuala Letters*.

It is not so much the thematic similarity but rather such common symbolic denominators as an alternative imagining of nation, dissidence through art, and a metanarrative stance that raises the critical consciousness of the reader, that set up an implicit conceptual exchange between the two novels. In both stories, the fate of the two women protagonists—Özakin's nameless narrator and Dina and Teresa and Alicia, respectively—are inextricably linked. Each pair allegorizes a fractured group identity (middle class versus working class, "white" versus "of color," religious versus secular). Özakin's narrator is from the Anatolian hinterland, whereas Dina is the daughter of upper-middle-class Europeanized parents. In Castillo, the narrator Teresa is a working-class Chicana with dark skin and Indian features. Alicia is a middle-class Latina of mixed heritage; the mark of her European ancestry is inscribed in her fairer complexion. Teresa and Özakin's narrator carry the burden of a traditional religious upbringing, whereas Dina and Alicia were never subjected to the dictates of institutionalized religion.

From the irruptive records of personal and historical experience, Özakin and Castillo form a "consciencitized" aesthetics of memory. In each story, the lives in transit are implicitly and explicitly imbricated with the psychosocial "biography" of the homeland, ties to the past emerge in a diversity of forms, and writers reflect on their role as archaeologists of a moral and social history. They recast their critical finds in a new language and idiom commensurate with their time and place in history. Nation as a particular geography becomes temporalized in memory, and the stability of its territorial ground and borders is negated in the experience of travel and multiple border crossings. Özakin's narrator is a political exile in Germany and does not have a permanent residence. In the beginning of the novel, she is in Zurich for a reading. Having neither a home nor a reason to return to any particular place, she decides to stay in Zurich to pursue a man and a memory. Teresa and Alicia travel between various locales in the United States and Mexico, and the novel closes upon Teresa's apparently final return to Mexico and Alicia's intent to go to another ancestral homeland, Andalusia.

In *The Mixquiahuala Letters*, the absence of a continuous (national) past and a motherland and travels between and within the United States and Mexico become the context of deterritorialized writing. Writing performs in the place of dislocation. This is a metageographical, an internalized space. In the closing note of *Die Phänomenologie des Geistes* (*Phenomenology of the spirit*), Hegel evokes the German word for memory, *Erinnerung*, with a hyphen: *Er-innerung*.[12] Thus, in German, memory [*Erinnerung*], when hyphenated to reveal its etymology, becomes "internalization/internalizing." Conversely, internalization in deterritorialized writing becomes memory. In Özakin's novel, the narrator, a political asylant in Germany, appears to be on the run from what ultimately proves to be an inescapable history. As a political refugee, she can no longer return to her motherland. The quest to claim a lost friend and to reconstruct their youth in terms of a shared national destiny becomes simultaneously a quest for the recovery of the lost nation. However, in the present time of the novel, which is mostly narrated in flashback, her friend Dina has been dead for some time; thus, both objects of the narrator's search are available only in the currency of memory. In this narrative economy of memory, reflections can shift imperceptibly, and a seamless merger of times, dreams, hopes emerges. This latitude enables language to record the emotional topography of the individuals in their relation to history, community, and place.

The Mixquiahuala Letters is an account of the long-standing friendship between Teresa and Alicia, their relationships with men and women, their travels in the United States and Mexico, and their work and art. Like the women in *Die blaue Maske*, who are on their own in Europe, Teresa and Alicia refuse the sponsorship of both the "home" and "host" cultures and travel alone in Mexico. This intimately personal narrative, composed of Teresa's letters to Alicia, is at the same time an unofficial social record of the women's movement of the late 1960s and 1970s in the United States and the implications of this movement for women caught between two host(ile) cultures. Although they are generations and geographies removed from Mexico, its lore, memory, and ethos hold Teresa and Alicia in their web of significances. In perhaps one of the most profound commentaries on the pull of origins, Teresa writes:

> Mexico. Melancholy, profoundly right and wrong; it embraces as it strangulates.
> Destiny is not a metaphysical confrontation with one's self, rather, society has knit its pattern so tight that a confrontation with it is inevitable. (*ML*, 59)

Whereas in Castillo's epistolary novel Mexican culture beckons to the subject across the divide of generations, in the work of Özakin and other Turkish-German women writers who are first-generation immigrants, the culture of their origins is a lived experience and a perpetual presence. Nevertheless, in each novel, women's ambivalence toward the cultural dictates of a real or imaginary homeland is represented through the juxtaposition of conflicting experiences of nostalgia, suffocation, defiance, and penitence. Travel is a topos of emancipation; however, the history of women's status in Turkey and Mexico, complicates the context of the metaphor. Travel becomes a metonymic extension, paradigmatic both for women's *Wanderlust* and women as unconsenting objects of *Lust* in the eyes of their "compatriots." Teresa reflects on the hopelessly delayed acknowledgment of women's emancipation in her conversation with a desirous suitor in Mexico. " 'I think you are a 'liberal' woman. Am I correct?' " he begins. "In that country [Mexico]," Teresa tells us, "the term 'liberated woman' meant something other than what we had strived for back in the United States. In this case it simply meant a woman who would sleep nondiscriminately with any man who came along." Teresa retorts that what he perceives as "liberal" is her independence to choose what she does "with whom, and when." It also means that she "may choose *not* to do it, with anyone, ever" (*ML*, 73). In many cultures, most notably and notoriously in those where a unidenominational and patriarchal religion holds sway, representations and perceptions of women's bodies are laden with negative cultural values and social prejudices.

The lyric, epistolary, and confessional genres favored by Anzaldúa, Özdamar, Özakin, and Castillo offer a wealth of critical perspectives on how and why women's bodies are so intimately linked with text (not merely as writing or image but as a semiotic system of sociocultural significances), language (as a repository of cultural values and preconceptions), and political awakenings. Like many writers of exile, Turkish-German women narrate their tales through a confessional idiom. This is not merely an aesthetic choice but a socially and politically resonant resolution. Although all writing is autobiographical in a broad sense, Turkish women writers, by and large, refrained from using the genre until the intellectually liberated 1960s. Writing the self (baring the soul) is an act of symbolic unveiling. This is a defiant gesture in the context of Islamic codes of modesty. In Islamic Turkish culture, the female body constituted a site of fascination as well as terror and temptation and was kept under cover. In fact, the Turkish word for prostitute (*fahişe*), a loanword from Persian, means exposed woman. Likewise, the female voice was perceived to be an instrument of seduction and evil and thus banned from the public sphere. In other words, at the level of the female subject, verbal expression is obstructed by self-erasure. Woman is absented from public spaces by being invisible and inaudible. Although Atatürk's reforms restored women's bodies and voices to their now highly visible place in Turkish history, the voice—one of the most difficult instruments to play—required the subject to spend years of hard practice to master it. Writing is participation in public discourse, and the autobiographical voices of Turkish-German writers like Özakin constitute a public statement of self-assertion.

Aysel Özakin was born in Urfa, Turkey, in 1942 and studied Romance languages and literatures in Ankara and Paris. For many years she worked as a French teacher in the Anatolian provinces and in Istanbul and was an established writer in her country, before she settled in West Germany as a political refugee in 1981.[13] Özakin wrote the *Die blaue Maske* in Germany. The novel was published first in Turkish as (*Mavi Maske*) and, subsequently, in German translation by major publishing houses in Istanbul and Hamburg, respectively. In a confessional narrative, Özakin interlinks the story of a complicated and strained friendship between two Turkish women writers in exile to the recent history of ideological clashes in Turkey and their consequences in exile. The nameless narrator is Özakin's thinly veiled autobiographical self, and the character of Dina, her onetime friend and literary rival, is based on the Turkish writer Tezer Özlü, who died of cancer in Switzerland. The two writers' search for a cultural identity coincides with the larger concern of Turkish women's struggle for voice, dignity, and freedom. The story moves between the present time and flashbacks of past events in the form of a memory work that emplots personal-historical experience as tragic destiny. The trials of a recent national past are narrated symbolically as an implicit debate between two women writers. Although the narrator is, by all accounts, the more successful writer, she cannot overcome her envy for a friend whose apparent liberation from religious and cultural constraints is made possible by her origins as the child of an educated, Westernized family. Dina is the "white" woman of the story. The self-indulgent and sexually promiscuous daughter of an Istanbul family, she studied at the German gymnasium in Istanbul, one of the many foreign-language lycées attended by the children of the well-heeled. Her stories draw on her own self-fashioned Western lifestyle. Full of ironic and skeptical dialogues, melancholy, and loneliness, they represent literary modernism in Turkish translation. The narrator remembers reading Dina's stories with delight when she lived in the provinces. Their atmosphere held an exotic attraction for her, like books translated from foreign languages. If she ever made it as a writer, the narrator wanted to write like Dina. But she couldn't. Instead she wrote about the poor district at the periphery of the city where she spent her childhood and youth. She is the "black" woman of the story and, by her own account, the writer of the people. The complicated relationship of these two women writers in exile is also an encapsulated history of the conflicts between Turkey's urban and provincial intellectuals.

Özakin's story begins when the narrator meets a man who wishes to talk to her after a reading she has in Zurich. She feels an instant attraction for this stranger, who turns out to be Dina's husband. They make an appointment to meet later, but he does not show up for the meeting. She cancels all her engagements and rents a room in Zurich to find him. The apparent plot of the story involves her amateurish detective work to track down a man whose name she does not know. Her obsessive pursuit is motivated by her desire for him and her desire to find out more about Dina's life, in particular, her last days, when she was briefly confined to an insane asylum. This obsession generates the narrative, which follows two parallel structuring themes: the actual search for Dina's husband and an ordering of flashbacks that reconstruct Dina's life in memory. This reconstruction, which is both a memorial to Dina and the narrator's coming to terms with the fractured course of her own life story, is a microcosm of the larger text about the contested issue of cultural identity, the irresolvable social class conflicts between intellectuals, and the ideological failure of the Turkish socialist movement of the 1970s.

Toward the end of the book, in a carnival scene, the narrator comments on the metafictional status of her labor of remembrance, as she tries to dance away the weight of personal and collective memory:

> My hips wanted to forget my memory. My memory that is not only burdened with my own remembrances but with those of my mother and my grandmother. With the memory of a whole history, the memory of the veiled, the memory of the woman in the harem, the memory of the teacher who sewed herself a blouse from her veil, wore ball dresses and clumsily danced tangos, waltzes, and foxtrots with her husband.[14]

Although the religious practices that imprisoned her body in a shroud of repression for centuries had been outlawed by Atatürk's reforms, the body cannot forget its humiliation and renders visible the history of corporeal and spiritual oppression. At the carnival where "mask and the repressed ego become one" [Maske und unterdrücktes Ich eins werden] (163), the narrator finally catches up with Dina's husband, who is wearing a blue mask. She realizes that Dina represents her own repressed ego, her connection to roots, and her lost history: "Between torches, trumpets, and dancers Dina appears to me to be the only mask that I can wear at the carnival" (162).

The music and the chaos of the carnival festivities deploy a free association of images and release the pent-up remembrance of things past. The sound of Istanbul's ubiquitous seagulls is the most distinct of the narrator's auditory memories. This memory begins "a whole concert," including a muezzin's call to prayer and a military officer's announcement of the coup blasting from the loudspeakers of a mosque: "The armed forces, in order to guarantee the security of the land, have taken over power" (192). These memories exacerbate the narrator's sense of alienation. An overwhelming feeling of pessimism overcomes her, "a feeling of being foreign" [ein Gefühl des Fremdseins] (194). At a show called *Caravans of Longing* featuring Turkish singers and dancers, she breaks down in tears when the sounds of her country's music envelop her "like a warm coat." Yet she is quick to add that she is not crying because of homesickness but because the melodies and the crowd that jolted her senses and memories out of their nocturnal domain made her realize that she felt herself foreign (*fremd*) in the company of her compatriots, that she was separated from the music and people of her childhood by a "wall of time" (186).

It is only when Emil, Dina's Swiss husband, tells the narrator of

Dina's final days that she is able to come to tears and truly mourn her friend's death. As Dina was dying of cancer, she suffered a psychotic breakdown and was committed to a clinic where she was put in chains. Dina's struggle for freedom as a woman in a civilized world, her struggle to write, her victory of obtaining Swiss citizenship—Emil tells how she slept with her Swiss passport, her "life insurance," under her pillow (180)—end in madness and a tragic death. The narrator can finally—if only partially—settle the accounts of the past. Freed from her obsessions, she is now "a being without memory and fear of the future" [ein Wesen ohne Erinnerung und ohne Furcht vor der Zukunft] (196). The memory work enables the narrator to finally mourn the loss of her homeland and her own past. As she goes back to her room to pack her bags, she sees a *Gastarbeiter* in an orange uniform collecting the garbage of the carnival with his loud machine. He does not hear her friendly greeting, her spontaneous and symbolic attempt at reconciliation with her land and her people. The last vestiges of regret and resentment are washed away with the debris of the carnival.

Although both the narrator and Dina chose exile to escape the oppression they experienced in their homeland, the memory of a particular geography, of Istanbul, never left them. A break with the past, the loss of "*milieux de mémoire*, real environments of memory," as Pierre Nora has shown, leads to the embodiment of memory at sites (*lieux de mémoire*) "where a sense of historical continuity persists."[15] Place is a powerful agent in the formation of cultural memory. Mexico City and Istanbul, sites of living archaeology, two megacities often anthropomorphized as seductive sirens, anchor memories of origin that reject national affiliation. These cities represent layers of civilizations, diverse mixtures of cultures and religions, scars of wars, conquests, and uprisings. They mark the final destination for their nations' impoverished and unemployed, who pour in daily from the villages and provinces, hoping to find jobs. The symbolic force of geographical locales is connected to religious memory (Jerusalem, Mecca), trauma (Auschwitz, Hiroshima), an archaic past (Byzantium in Istanbul and Aztec Tenochtitlán in Mexico City), and, most powerfully, to a real or imaginary lost home. In letter 26, Teresa writes:

> Mexico City, revisited time and again
> since childhood, over and again as a woman. i sometimes saw
> the ancient Tenochtitlán, home of my mother, grandmothers,
> and greatmother, as an embracing bosom, to welcome me back

and rock my weary body and mind to sleep in its tumultuous, over populated, throbbing, ever pulsating heart. (*ML*, 92; short line in the original)

Teresa and Alicia cannot escape the machismo and oppression of their history. The return to the "fatherland" always entails the threat of censure by the "father" (patriarchal order and religion). Teresa sees institutionalized religion as the most stubborn and pervasive perpetrator of women's enslavement. Mexican men trespass the personal space of native and gringo women, just as Turkish men in Germany insult and punish Turkish women they consider easy, women who date German men or other foreigners. Özakin's narrator is outraged and repulsed by a *Gastarbeiter* at the carnival who offers her fifty francs for sex. Such encounters always evoke nightmarish memories of being harassed and accosted by men in Turkey. She remembers herself as a young girl of barely fourteen in a packed bus where a short, fat man smelling of dust and tobacco fondles her hips. She imagines for a moment that she is still running away from his hand.[16]

As a second-generation immigrant Teresa is seeking a lost continent of alternative mythologies and discourses of liberation in a Mexico that no longer remembers that past. Writing becomes "an unrelenting search for a *different* past, to be exhumed from the rubble of patriarchal and racist obfuscations."[17] The protagonists of both novels reinvent another symbolism of national affiliation divorced from notions of territorial borders, patriarchal and religious orders, and military and state oppression. Their renewed sense of belonging is affiliated with an allegory of motherland, which embraces personal sites of memory, modes of solidarity defined by class and gender, and alternative and personal idioms of religious belief. Mexico City and Istanbul, respectively, will accommodate them happily in their webs of remembrance. Magic, lore, incantation replace orthodox belief and dogma and exorcise the demons of religious cultures that condemned women to a life of insidious cruelty in the shadows. Dina asks for death presents, as she nears the end. While vocal in her criticism of Spanish Catholicism's oppression of women, Teresa embraces its unorthodox retranslations and practices. She performs an exorcism after Alicia is unnerved by the presence of an angry ghost called in during a séance by a couple of Mexican engineers who attempted to entertain the two women.

In one of its roles as a chronicler of cultural history, literature registers the conflicts of emergent, prevailing, and residual values. In rejecting the dictates of institutionalized religion, patriarchal hierarchy, and moral values regulated by male desire, which are all implicated in Turkish and Mexican versions of nationhood, Castillo's and Özakin's respective narrators initiate a search for alternative allegiances. They find them variously in the topography of women's lives and memories, in literature and art, in friendship, in the dynamic ethos of exile, and in the sovereign spaces of the city. Benedict Anderson maintains that "the nation is always conceived as a deep, horizontal comradeship."[18] The symbolic denominators of women's writing in exile remove this notion of nation as fraternity from its simultaneously abstract, fixed, and patriarchal framework and recast it in terms of a changing, re-membering, and concretely personal form of lived history.

Emine Sevgi Özdamar's Magical History Tour in *Life Is a Caravansary*

> Once I had a beautiful fatherland.
> The oak tree
> Grew there so high, violets nodded gently.
> It was a dream.
> It kissed me in German and spoke German.
>
> **Heinrich Heine, "Ich hatte einst ein schönes Vaterland"**

Displacement engenders lacunae that signify missing political, social, and cultural contiguities. The elliptical economy of the lacuna fosters the production of meaning—national, ethnic, racial, gendered—that sets the terms of contesting discourses of the subject, society, history, and memory. In migrancy and exile the resistance of communal memories to the dominant cultural norms is markedly lowered. Nevertheless, art, in a Nietzschean vein, allows those who find themselves in the chaos of ruptured histories to create empowering legacies. Geoffrey Hartman argues convincingly that nationalistic histories or officially sanctioned accounts of the past reduce the wealth of communal memories preserved in legends, poetry, symbols, and rituals. Art provides a counterweight to manufactured and monologic memory:

> [A]rt is often more effective in embodying historically specific ideas than the history-writing on which it may draw. Scientific historical research, however essential it is for its negative virtues

of rectifying error and denouncing falsification, has no positive resource to lessen grief, endow calamity with meaning, foster a vision of the world, or legitimate new groups. But art remains in touch with or revives traditional materials that satisfy our need for community without repressing individualist performance.[19]

The earliest expressions of collective memory are stored in linguistic acts, chants, sagas, and epics.[20] Remnants of community memory are also transmitted in rite and ritual, through a mnemonics of the body.[21] Emine Sevgi Özdamar's critically acclaimed *Das Leben ist eine Karawanserei,*[22] the first work by a non-German author to be distinguished by the Ingeborg Bachmann Prize, is a showcase of linguistic memory as a formative dimension of writing outside the nation. The narrative also moves in a performative syntax of remembrance. Community rites and rituals, the bodily enactment of Arabic prayer, shadow plays, gossip, mantras of the "mad" neighborhood soothsayers, and the nationally broadcast trial of Democratic Party leaders all form a coalition of constructing history. Removing memory from a sole remembering agent and a single medium sets the stage for its multiple performances.

Although some critics feel that *Karawanserei* rests on the laurels of its "exoticism," I believe that the critical acclaim of this book is no accident, for it challenges the conceptual limitations of representations of otherness and a hermeneutics that operates at the level of descriptive interpretation.[23] It is certainly true that the novelty of Özdamar's highly visual and metaphorical language is an important factor in the allure of this book. Roland Barthes once remarked that language and fashion behave in similar ways, since "the novelty of a turn of phrase or of a word always constitutes an emphasis destined to repair the wear in its system."[24] Nevertheless, here the linguistic novelty merely masks a semiotic puzzle that depends for its solution on historical knowledge and theoretical imagination. The title of the book is a Turkish proverb. Caravansaries were large inns built around courtyards to accommodate caravans traveling on the long commerce routes through the Middle East and Asia. The proverb defines an individual life both as a brief sojourn on earth and a station of an infinite journey. It suggests parallels both with Özdamar's life and the history she narrates. Özdamar recalls the concrete history of the decade 1950–1960, the era of Turkey's first serious experiment with democracy and its tragic course, in the aesthetically codified idioms of myth, legend, dream, and madness. The critical trajectory of *Karawanserei,* which maps out a culture of specific signifiers redeemed in the narrative memory of exile, can perhaps be best summed up in three implicit questions: What happens when events are converted into language? How does event as language shape cultural and national memory outside the nation? How can signifying systems of a particular culture be translated into another cultural idiom? The search for answers to these questions defines the quest for understanding the transfiguration of a cultural identity fractured in rites of passage. A self-declared novel, *Karawanserei* interweaves an autobiographical tale with the complex history of Ottoman-Turkish culture. Through the uncensoring eyes and the innocent voice of a child narrator, the novel restores for the second generation of Turks living in Germany the history of their now foreign homeland.

The narrator tells her own story in the context of the history of the young Turkish republic, where private and public ordeals and different cultural idioms and generational terms intersect. In this attempt, the book portrays how present relations of continuity and rupture with a recalled past inform a community sensibility in exile. By employing all signifying systems that constitute a specific culture, such as proverbs, fairy tales, children's games, rumor, superstition, ritual, rites of passage, and folk remedies for individual and collective mental imbalance, the narrator tells a magical history to ease the pain inflicted by the upheavals of modern times. Early in the book, the last century of the Ottoman Empire is visually enacted on a carpet that the beard of the narrator's grandfather weaves itself into: "Grandfather spoke, and his unshaven beard grew on his face, and the beard began to weave itself into a carpet."[25] Here, in a long chain of signification, theme and structure merge and the narrator interweaves the woof of her grandfather's memories with the warp of official versions of history. On this carpet that comes into being as a structure of the narrative, the story of the events that led to the demise of the Ottoman Empire, the despotic reign of Abdülhamit, the Young Turks, Bismarck's building of the Bagdad railway, the Ottoman Empire's entry into the war on Germany's side, the partition of the empire among the allies, and Kemal Atatürk's successful guerrilla war that led to the independence of the occupied Anatolian homeland unfold as the grandfather tells (his)story for three days and nights. The story turns into a framing metaphor of the novel itself, which mimics the text(ure) of the narrating carpet. In this dialectic of text and image, the stills of history are translated into words, and words translate ritual and history into systems of signification.

The major focus of Özdamar's work is language as rite, ritual, mode of survival, and zone of comfort in an inhospitable environment. This is not surprising, since the Turkish culture of Germany can only be constituted in the unity of its common language. The factions that characterize politics, national sentiment, religion, social class, and education have migrated alongside the population from the Turkish homeland to the foreign land, where they have become more pronounced and fractured. As a palimpsest of archaic, forgotten, and modern signifying practices, such as homilies, litanies, ancient curses, and politicians' promises, *Karawanserei* undertakes a project of linguistic remembrance. The narrative texture is woven of highly idiomatic and metaphorical Turkish expressions and colloquialisms that appear in deadpan German translation. A colorful Turkish idiom, *içgüveysinden hallice*, which can roughly be translated into English as "things could be worse," appears with increasing frequency in the book. As the narrator relates the steady progression of economic and political difficulties, a growing number of characters respond to questions about how they are doing with "slightly better than a son-in-law who has to live with his in-laws" [mir geht's ein bißchen besser als einem Schwiegersohn, der bei seinen Schwiegereltern leben muß]. The expression expands in translation, for this tongue-in-cheek translation signifies a space of untranslatability, and the translation becomes a strange explication. The Turkish signifier itself, however, coincides easily with its signified, which, in this case, is both a culture-specific and culturally disempowering notion. At the time of Özdamar's story, it functions as a convenient metaphor for the social blows suffered by the working classes in Turkey and their growing sense of resignation. The text requires a shift from a descriptive to a transitive understanding of cultural practice. The narrative negotiates between linguistic and translinguistic markers, between word and gesture, myth and memory.

Since the "conservation of remembrance," as a transmission of culture to children in the form of narratives (folktales, fairy tales, family anecdotes), is usually seen as part of women's labor and women are managers of the " 'iconothèque' of family memory,"[26] many women writers in diaspora are firmly committed to preserving the art of storytelling. Their work assumes the guardianship of personal and communal stories that face the danger of fading into oblivion in the shuffle of history. Noting that words have no childhood in the foreign language (*M*, 42), Özdamar appropriates the foreign idiom and makes it conform to memories of childhood, origins, and homelands. Like many a bilingual writer Özdamar re-members the mother tongue in translation. "Through that language, encountered at mother's knee and parted with only at the grave," as Anderson writes in *Imagined Communities*, "pasts are restored, fellowships are imagined, and futures dreamed."[27]

Özdamar rewrites the memory of the nation outside the nation by sketching a vast textual landscape where personal and confessional stories and collective memory enter a mutually informing dialogue. *Karawanserei* portrays women as they carry the burden of many lives and become either consciously or unwittingly agents of inevitable political transformation. In their voices, songs, tales, and litanies, women reinvent cultural traditions whose modernized spirituality can absorb the shocks of modernity. The most caustic criticisms of the corrupt regime come out of the mouths of the supposedly mad women of the community in metaphors of immediate impact. "The Democrats have buried us under a mountain of American debts," says one of them; "as we say, whoever steals a minaret should also sew a cover for it in order to conceal it. The Democrats have stolen the minaret, but they have no cover to hide it."[28] The narrator's mother has to live with the tragic past of her own mother, who was tortured to death by her husband, a rich landlord of the provinces, a despot with several wives, the form of polygamy sanctioned by Islamic but not secular law. A woman of immense wisdom, the mother of the narrator and her three siblings is a proud heiress of Atatürk's reforms. Her fierce loyalty to Atatürk's political party, Cumhuriyet Halk Partisi (People's Republican Party), turns her into a formidable critic of the American-backed Demokrat Partisi (Democratic Party), the first party to come to power through popular vote in 1950 after the introduction of the multiparty system in 1946. The complicity of this party in delivering Turkey into the hands of American capitalism and imperialism in the fifties, exploitation of the most archaic remnants of Islam for popular votes, rigging of elections, corruption of party officials, buying district votes in bulk, in short, the troubled history of Turkey's first and most significant experiment with democracy, is told in the silently resistant voice of the mother through the words of the innocent child narrator. The mother is a skillful midwife in the delivery of the former culture to the next generation. She is aware of the difficulties her cultural legacy poses for women. Her pedagogical instinct guides her to value the practical aspects and wisdom of tradition and to translate them into the terms of the next generation. Acutely aware of the pain their patriarchal culture will inflict on her daughters, she tries to ease their burden by leavening her religious instruction with folkloristic wisdom, homespun witticism, and gut instinct.

In "Großvaterzunge," Özdamar had implicitly criticized Kemalist reforms for erasing all traces of the Islamic Ottoman culture, thus creating a vacuum where modern Turks struggle to define a cultural identity. In order to found a new nation-state from the multinational, multiethnic, multireligious, multilingual shards of an imperial mosaic, Atatürk scripted a series of Westernization reforms, a discourse of progress that entailed a radical translation from the *alaturka* (Turkish) to the *alafranga* (Frankish) way of life. In a comprehensive work of critical anthropology, *Türk Kimliği: Kültür Tarihinin Kaynakları* (*Turkish identity: Sources of cultural history*), Turkish anthropologist and historian Bozkurt Güvenç observes that "Turks, as the well-known Turkish expresssion goes, have not been able to please either Moses or Jesus, meaning they have not been able to win friends either home or abroad."[29] After the dissolution of the Ottoman Empire and the victory of the guerrilla war of independence fought both against the Ottoman rulers and the Western powers, Atatürk founded a secular (laicist) nation-state, the Republic of Turkey. Güvenç states that when the heirs of the defeated Ottoman state were faced with the options of assuming an Ottoman, Islamic, or Anatolian identity, they chose to be Turks. This was a historical decision driven by a strong identification with the mother tongue. Güvenç deems this as the only viable choice. However, as he sees it, today Turks cannot understand, accept, and incorporate the diverse viewpoints of their heteregenous society, for they have cut themselves off from their own cultural history. This cultural rupture, it has often been asserted, has led to an easy exploitation of religious sentiment by the Democratic Party and other reactionary parties of Turkey's fragile democracy and paved the way to a fundamentalist backlash.

Özdamar's narrator relativizes this view of cultural rupture by showing how, in the lives of her family and community, the practice of Islam has been tempered by superstition, iconoclastic humor, and early Islamic mysticism. One of the great insights of Özdamar's story is the portrayal of Islam with a Turkish accent and of Islamic customs in Turkish costumes. A nomadic people of the Central Asian steppes, the pre-Islamic Turks practiced various shamanistic religions. Furthermore, their social structure was not patriarchal by any measure. Orthodox Islamic practice could never be properly hooked up with this nomadic history. Thus, shrines of holy men and women believed to have performed miracles, blue stones with images of an eye against the evil eye, healing rituals performed by religious men, are part and parcel of everyday practices in *Karawanserei*. The Turkish accent of Islamic practice becomes quite literal when the narrator reproduces her grandmother's Arabic prayers in phonetic Turkish transliteration:

> *Bismillâhirrahmanirrahim. Kül hüvallahü ehad. Allahüssamed.*
> *Lem yelid velem yüled. Velem yekûn lehu küfüven ehad. Amin.*

>As the letters emerging from my grandmother's mouth turned
>into a beautiful sound and a beautiful picture in the sky above
>the cemetery, she blew out her breath, turning her head right
>and left. "The dead need it." I saw the letters: many looked like a
>bird, others like a heart with an arrow through it, still others like
>a caravan.[30]

This passage is a condensed archive of cultural memory, a site of multiple translations, and a sign of longing for a lost alphabet. Although the Koran was translated into Turkish and printed in the Roman alphabet, the language of Islamic prayer remained Arabic. The child narrator can only hear the sounds of Arabic pronounced as if it were Turkish, reproduces them in Turkish transliteration, but imagines the very elaborate picturelike Arabic calligraphy she remembers from the pages of the Koran turning into a parade of images.

In the course of the story, the narrator's family moves from the country to the city and from city to city in search of livelihood. These moves parallel the declining fortunes of a diminishing middle class during the 1950s. One of the moves takes the form of a sudden levitation, and this heavily layered semiotic move corresponds in historical time to the aftermath of the military takeover of 1960. At a family picnic on the grounds of a cemetery, a storm breaks out and the girl and her family are hurled into the sky. During the long flight, she sees her other self in the cemetery, running after the newspapers blown away by the wind and her flying self next to the jets of the air forces that participated in the military coup. She tries to shout to the pilots to tell them that her family had always voted for the People's Republican Party. But nobody hears her. At the end of a long and lonely night of flight, she finds herself in another city with her family. At this juncture, the narrative operates in the fantastic mode. It invokes the lost spiritual aura of Anatolian shamanistic and mystic rituals that are here reclaimed and restored to their potent symbolic meanings. Like the Mevlevi dervishes, who leave their bodily domain in ritual and sacred dance, the narrator reaches out for a state of transcendence. In his *Six Memos for the Next Millennium,* Calvino contextualizes this flight characteristic of magical realism in the history of its earlier cultural expressions:

>I am accustomed to consider literature a search for knowledge.
>In order to move onto existential ground, I have to think of liter-
>ature as extended to anthropology and ethnology and
>mythology. Faced with the precarious existence of tribal life—
>drought, sickness, evil influences—the shaman responded by rid-

ding his body of weight and flying to another world, another level of perception, where he could find the strength to change the face of reality. In centuries and civilizations closer to us, in villages where the women bore most of the weight of a constricted life, witches flew by night on broomsticks or even on lighter vehicles such as ears of wheat or pieces of straw. Before being codified by the Inquisition, these visions were part of the folk imagination, or we might even say of lived experience. I find it a steady feature in anthropology, this link between the levitation desired and the privation actually suffered. It is this anthropological device that literature perpetuates.[31]

This dialectic of "the levitation desired and the privation actually suffered" is typical of the inhabitants of shifting borders and geographies. For Özdamar, memory is not a work of mourning. Its texts cross borders, fly over barriers, from fiction to metafiction, from solemn ritual to the Bakhtinian carnivalesque, from one language to another. Signs detach themselves from their first-order signification and enter a progressive signifying chain. This semiotic project complicates the question of translatability between different cultural discourses. In a review in *The European*, Arno Widmann, a critic for the *Frankfurter Allgemeine*, remarks that readers' problems in understanding Özdamar may have been the result of her "grammarless flood of Oriental images."[32] This is a rather exaggerated claim, since Özdamar's stream-of-consciousness style is meticulously amended by editors, and one is hard pressed to find grammatical mistakes. What the critic fails to see is that although Özdamar writes in German, her idiom retains its unmistakably Turkish memory, embodying both its rhetorical outbursts and its silences. This writing demonstrates that the lived cultural, social, and moral history of a people often remains embedded in an irreducible untranslatibility. The memory of the (m)other tongue will not be erased and transfigures its new medium. A critical appreciation of bilingual texts calls for an understanding of the experiences of people whose reality is determined by different language acts and by their particular relation to a reconstructed past. As the Spanish critic Juan Goytisolo observed, Özdamar "doesn't package Turkey in German for Germans from a facile and picturesque 'orientalist' perspective; via her own hybrid and complex language, she relates the vicissitudes of modern Turkey first for her German-speaking compatriots and second for Germans."[33]

Many Turkish-German women writers like Özakin and Özdamar are aware that exile can foster a sense of exaggerated nationalism, ethnicity, and religion among their compatriots. Edward Said once noted that since exile is a disrupted state of existence, exiles often aspire to reconstruct groups and institutions symbolic of national solidarity and association. Their search for the continuity of links "can lead exiles to reconstitute their broken lives in narrative form, usually by choosing to see themselves as part of a triumphant ideology or restored people."[34] Özdamar's kaleidoscopic narratives, which mimic the configurations of dream and memory, resist the notion of an idealized Turkish history and unifying allegories of roots, home, and heritage. The literary imagination prevents the transformation of cultural memory into doctrinaire rhetoric. Özdamar's narrator parodies official versions of an invented glorious Pan-Turkic history, traced back to the very beginnings of time in the vast Asian steppes, that she read in school textbooks. In the innocent language of childhood, she can also question religious fictions in a disarming manner: "We had religion lessons at school, and the teacher told us that Allah can see everybody and everything at the same time," she remembers. "I couldn't understand that, it was very difficult for me." She is mystified by religious dogma and tries to test the truth of the concept of an omniscient Allah by cursing him and provoking him to punish her: "Allah, I shit on your mouth with the devil."[35] Criticism, parody, satire, and irreverence bordering on sacrilege often put the writer at odds with many of his or her compatriots who cling to notions of a morally superior and whole culture they have left behind. The writer of the diaspora can only feel at home in the alternative space of writing and willed memory.[36] This writing is hyphenated in time. It is suspended between histories and geographies. It resists both the temptation for nostalgia and a false sense of assimilation. All traces of nostalgia are negotiated by a form of parody that resembles a palimpsest of texts from the writer's many histories (and stories). The renegotiated convention of parody orders experience beyond lived temporality where separate times coincide and memory functions diachronically as well as synchronically.

In the geographical and temporal space afforded by exile, Özdamar attempts to understand a culture that is gradually disappearing into forgetfulness through the medium of the mother tongue and to rewrite the (hi)story of the motherland—as a form of countermemory to official history. Many Turkish writers of Germany are cognizant of their particular subject positions as secular or religious Turks, Alevis, or Kurds. Nevertheless, as memoirists of collective voices, they allow others to speak through their various narrative frames and negotiate conflicting viewpoints by positioning them in larger historical and allegorical contexts. Özdamar writes comfortably about her Kurdish background and Islamic upbringing, her

grandfather's open and vocal attacks on Atatürk, and her own radical femi-
nization, liberation, and politicization. *Karawanserei*'s narrative voices relate Turkish fortunes during the decade-long Democratic Party regime
through the direct and immediate experiences of the common people, thus
offering us a real segment of history in its hitherto untold version. In the
end, *Karawanserei* is not a story about exile but about conditions that
necessitate exile. It is not a search for a new national or ethnic identity but
a resistance against cultural amnesia that denies the historical legitimacy
of different identities. It is about the power and endurance of communal
and cultural memory as an antidote against censored history. It is a personal story firmly embedded in social history, a gem of the genre I term
"autobiography as unauthorized biography of the nation."

Pedagogical Gains

> Writing in a foreign language, not in either of the tongues of
> my native country—the Berber of the Dahra mountains or
> the Arabic of the town where I was born—writing has
> brought me to the cries of the women silently rebelling in
> my youth, to my own true origins.
>
> Writing does not silence the voice, but awakens it, above
> all to resurrect so many vanished sisters.
>
> **Assia Djebar,** *Fantasia: An Algerian Cavalcade*

> This idea imposes itself as I write it: every language should
> be bilingual! The asymmetry of body and language, of speech
> and writing   at the threshold of the untranslatable.
>
> From that moment, the scenario of the doubles was cre-
> ated. One word: now two: it's already a story. Speaking to
> you in your own language, I am yourself without really being
> you, fading away in the tracks you leave. Bilingual, I am hence-
> forth free to be entirely so and on my own behalf.
>
> **Abdelkebir Khatibi,** *Love in Two Languages*

The transnational and "bilingual" narratives of the present study foster an
awareness of the contingencies of power structures and value systems in
history. Consequently, they guide the reader away from narrowly defined
or unreflected positions of interpretation. "As other histories emerge from
the archaeology of modernity to disturb the monologue of History," writes
Iain Chambers, "we are reminded of the multiple rhythms of life that have
been written out and forgotten."[1] Benjamin's reflections on history suggest

that the narratives of the powerful are remembered as history, but those of the disenfranchised need to be "wrested away" as memory from the discourse of historical progress. When, in the name of progress, its opponents regarded Fascism as a historical norm, they also granted it its great historical opportunity."[2] Those written out of history find in communal memory a sense of solidarity and identity, a witness to their past, and a (pre)script(ion) for redemption. "[O]nly a redeemed humanity has access to the fullness of its past," writes Benjamin. "In other words, only for a redeemed human race has its past become citable in all its moments."[3] Remembering becomes a form of resistance to the exclusion from history. And literature becomes a conduit of memory, the topos of subjective and historical agency in a time of emotional loss.

It is a truism born of the idea of paradigm shift that when the present changes, so does the past. When a new structure of knowledge emerges, our understanding of the past often undergoes a radical revision. As literature, history, and cultural anthropology programs include more and more emerging literary voices from lesser-known cultures, and "cultural studies" continues to cohabit with national literatures in language and literature departments, literary criticism faces the task of imagining the historical and conceptual coordinates of a dialogue with diasporic, migrant, ethnic cultures. The invasion of literature departments by cultural studies happened not because literature professors wanted to reinvent themselves as anthropologists or art historians or film critics (although it certainly seemed that way at times), but because the shape and the color of the world we live in has been changing very radically for the past two decades. Anthony Easthope argues that cultural study, unlike literary study, cannot assume the centrality of its subject, and, because it relinquishes a unified representational matrix, it "must work across a *non-correspondent* series of conceptualisations." This "requires methods and terms of analysis brought together *unevenly*" from such fields as semiology, sociology, philosophy, historical materialism, and psychoanalysis that question and relativize each other, thus allowing for a self-reflexive position.[4]

The theory debates of the poststructuralist era paved the way to a radical expansion of the field of literary criticism by illustrating that language and other cultural sign systems are inflected by gender, race, class, and ethnicity. When the idea of a unified, disinterested speaking subject thus became untenable, the border between literary study and the study of culture as a signifying system could no longer be defended. Literature would henceforth be regarded as one signifying system among others. The crises and fortunes of history and culture are inscribed in the texts of everyday life, such as journals, diaries, political pamphlets, advertisements, billboards, theme parks, or memorial sites. Cultural studies situates itself at the nexus of theoretical grounding, historical information, and material artifacts. It calls for a critical understanding of the operations of language, its cultural mood and voice, and its accents and cadences of identity, power, mastery, and loss. This synchronic procedure has to be complemented by a diachronic one that traces the grammar of a particular sociocultural history.

The study of cultural memory through literary and autobiographical texts inevitably moves into areas of inquiry in the domain of several other disciplines, such as philosophy, history, art history, anthropology, ethnography, and performance studies. An investigation of cultural memory in the bodily practices and rituals of a community, for example, will open up a field of ethnographic references and more. A community remembers the history of its cultural practices not only in books but in narratives that are performed in vocal, bodily, and scriptural modes. In *How Societies Remember*, a study that elaborates on the insights of Maurice Halbwachs's groundbreaking work on collective memory, Paul Connerton emphasizes the role of ritual and performance in communal acts of remembering. Connerton argues that the recollected images and knowledge of a society's past are preserved and conveyed by ritual performances. Performative memory, in turn, manifests itself in bodily practices. Rite and ritual are further characterized by a "rhetoric of re-enactment" inscribed in the verbal and textual traditions of a given culture.[5] Writers of the diaspora are particularly sensitized to forms of symbolic re membering in the body and the bodily practices of their communities.[6] "The body manifests the stigmata of past experience and also gives rise to desires, failing, and errors," writes Foucault in his analysis of Nietzsche's concept of genealogy. For Foucault, the body represents "the inscribed surface of events," and genealogy, "as an analysis of descent, is . . . situated within the articulation of the body and history. Its task is to expose a body totally imprinted by history and the process of history's destruction of the body."[7] Foucault's critical insight gains in concreteness and appreciation in the classroom, when read next to texts such as *Borderlands* and *Mother Tongue*, where women's bodies are literally embodied memories, upon which cultural, social, and moral values are inscribed.[8]

For Nietzsche genealogy could only be understood through philology, as a line(age) traced in and by language. Genealogy, as philology, requires constant rigor. However, language, the subject of philology, is not constant; its truth is subject to the vicissitudes of history. Genealogy "operates on a field of entangled and confused parchments, on documents that have been scratched over and recopied many times."[9] In other words, genealogy is a kind of palimpsest, and palimpsest is an image often invoked to define memory. The narratives of this study provide us with a critical genealogy of diverse cultures, for they draw upon a vast accumulation of linguistic, literary, and mythological traditions, "record the singularity of events outside of any monotonous finality," and look for these events in unlikely places that are considered "without history—in sentiments, love, conscience, instincts."[10]

Literary texts, autobiographical narratives, and "bilingual" texts are increasingly studied in political science, history, and anthropology courses and provide a countermemory to ethnocentric epistemologies that quite often take as their point of reference culturally biased and methodologically questionable models. Modern cultural anthropology is undergoing a rigorous critique of its long-standing habit of assigning its object—the "other"—to an immutable past. This intellectual colonization of others' histories and memories has come under attack most eloquently by Johannes Fabian. Fabian challenges anthropology's denial of coevalness to its "primitive" other. He maintains that anthropology, which came into being as an academic field of investigation with the rise of colonialism, "is a discourse whose referent has been removed from the present of the speaking/writing subject."[11]

The critical stance of modern ethnography, on the other hand, "derives from the fact that it makes its own contextual grounding part of the question."[12] It engages in a historically informed critique of anthropological practice. Stephen Tyler sees the text of postmodern ethnography as self-consciously incomplete, and, taking his cue from literary hermeneutics, he reconceptualizes the ethnographic project as a dialogue. In fact, Tyler's view of postmodern ethnography can hardly be differentiated from concepts of poststructuralist literary criticism. Postmodern ethnography does not aspire to any form of "universal knowledge" (131), is polyphonic (126), is "neither an object to be represented nor a representation of an object" (131), represents a "dispersed authorship" mirroring the postmodern "dispersed self," and rejects narrative wholeness. However, it is not a fiction, "for the idea of fiction entails a locus of judgment outside the fiction, whereas an ethnography weaves a locus of judgment within itself" (139). In the self-inflicted fragmentation of postmodern ethnography, in its mode of evocation (123) as opposed to representation, in dialogic moments, and in multivoiced speech, in short, in "the rhetoric of ethnography," Tyler locates an "ethical" (122) purpose. The features Tyler names are commensurate with a mode of writing that does not aim for empirical results or a prescriptive understanding of things (e.g., literary texts). I do not think, however, that literary texts can be pressed into the service of a discourse that is expected to form "a locus of judgment within itself" (ethnography). Here literary or fictionalized texts, burdened neither by empirical ambition nor historical facticity, can complement the ethnographic project. Cultural autobiographies and autoethnographies can accommodate a very wide range of voices, experiences, and stories. Transnational literatures fill in the glaring gaps of our understanding of a culturally very complex world. In their investigation of many pasts, they restore missing volumes of literary and cultural heritages to our intellectual history. What was unspoken, erased, repressed comes back to life in memorial constructions of cultural historical loss.

Another field of inquiry opened up by transnational and "bilingual" literary models is translation. A good translation is based not only on a thorough historical and contemporary knowledge of at least two languages (or systems) but also on an interactive relationship of theory and practice. The process of translation is complicated by the respective subject positions of the translators. In "Die Aufgabe des Übersetzers," Benjamin cites the work of Rudolf Pannwitz, whose views on translation he considers along with Goethe's notes to his *Divan* to be possibly the best commentary on the theory of translation to come out of Germany. Pannwitz, like Benjamin himself, is critical of translations that appropriate the soul of another language and subject it to the rule of the language into which it is translated, instead of equalizing the expressive modalities of the two: "Our translations, even the best ones, proceed from a false premise; they want to turn Hindi, Greek, English into German, instead of turning German into Hindi, Greek, English. These translations show a far greater reverence for the usage of their own language than for the spirit of foreign works."[13] In this instance, the fundamental error of the translator is that he is fixated on the arbitrarily defined higher status of his own language. Translation should be neither a full linguistic reconstruction nor an appropriation. Rather, it should incorporate the original language's mode of signification. Both the original and the translation should be recognizable "as fragments of a larger language" [als Bruchstück einer größeren Sprache] (59). Translation is a mode of signification, and this "larger language" denotes the realm of the translatability of languages. The law of the genre of translation is inscribed in the translatability of the original. "The question regarding the translatability of a work has a dual meaning," states Benjamin. "Either: will it find its qualified translator among the totality of its readers? Or, more to the point, does its nature lend itself to translation, and, therefore, call for it in keeping with the significance of the genre?" (50–51). Benjamin attributes a sense of the sacred to the space of translatability. He maintains that one can speak of an unforgettable life or moment that, though it may have been forgotten by all human beings, lives on in "God's memory" [Gedenken Gottes]. By the same token, the translatability of all verbal creations holds the promise of being fulfilled, even if they prove to be untranslatable by human beings (51).

The space of translatability gains a secular significance as the realm of the generative and equalizing power of human language, where languages are free from rankings of status: "Ultimately, translation is the appropriate expression of the deepest relationship languages share. It cannot possibly reveal (*offenbaren*) this concealed relationship itself, nor produce (*herstellen*) it, but it can represent or embody (*darstellen*) it by realizing it in its embryonic or intensive form" (52–53). Thus, translation comes into being as the second life of the original and turns into the promise of its numerous re-creations (51). In this sense, the act of translation may be said to correspond to the transmission of cultural and linguistic memory. By translating and incorporating into a second language an unknown or forgotten literary idiom, cultural semiotic, or lyric tradition, transnational works grant the original "text" an afterlife.[14] The genre of "bilingual" writing rests on an implicit translation that equally validates and celebrates the languages it works with. The most important implication of Benjamin's concept of translation for transnational, diasporic literatures is that translation and memory participate in the same structural mode. They are both structures of postponement, reconfigured from shards of a prior structure in a temporal (historical) continuum. As a form of referral, replication, supplementation, and ellipsis, translation can both perform and disrupt the work of cultural memory with which it is intertwined.

In the postnational, postindustrial, and postdisciplinary world, culture can no longer be understood as a fundamental model but rather as an interaction of cultures and can perhaps speak only as translation. Is a comprehensive theory of cultural translation possible or desirable? Since cultural translation is a process rather than a product, it may well resist subjection to grids of intelligibility and academically sanctioned philosophical forms. In *The Other Heading*, Jacques Derrida poses the critical question of regulative idiom and translation, a question that becomes highly charged in a multicultural world:

What philosophy of translation will dominate in Europe? In a Europe that from now on should avoid both the nationalistic tensions of linguistic difference and the violent homogenization of languages through the neutrality of a translating medium that would claim to be transparent, metalinguistic, and universal?[15]

In order to transcend both the anxiety of linguistic difference and the erasure of linguistic specificity, we need to acquire fluency in a bilingual and bicultural idiom. Tales of diaspora, exile, and migration cultivate an appreciation for the translatability of languages and cultures as well as for the untranslatability of certain forms of cultural specificity. College courses increasingly include multicultural and postcolonial texts from all over the world, and there is a growing body of scholarship on emergent and ethnic literatures. Linguistic difference and linguistic diversity are a major focus of these literatures. However, current scholarship tends to ignore the issue of linguistic difference and cultural translatability, although it remains sensitive to other forms of difference—race, ethnicity, gender, and, to a lesser degree, class. It is clearly not feasible to acquire fluency in several languages, and there is nothing wrong with relying on translations. We need to bear in mind, however, that if our reception of transnational, emergent, diasporic literatures is mediated only through English, not only linguistic but also cultural differences and specificities will be lost in translation. And our newly developed transnational, postcolonial literature courses will not be very different from the traditional World Literature in English Translation course.

Our curriculum needs to reflect the crossroads, crises, and challenges that inform every aspect of our contemporary culture. The first effort in this endeavor would be a critical engagement with the literary and artistic productions of underrepresented, lesser-known cultures. This involves "listening" to languages that go into the production of written texts. Although written in a language not the writer's own, the texts of this study resonate with the memory of their first language, "the mother tongue." As a form of translation, this *bilingue* writing "gives voice to the intentio of the original not as reproduction but as harmony, as a complement to the language in which it speaks, as its own form of intentio."[16] Although Benjamin sees the "pure language" of translation as an arbiter between languages (59), diasporic texts sometimes come with a more sobering message: that other worlds are not necessarily transparent in translation, that there are spaces of untranslatability between languages, cultures, and texts, that these spaces define and mark the silences and pathos of exile, and that the ideality of a unifying language does not conform to the reality of a world where many are dispossessed of the hospitable space of their own idiom.

The emerging body of nonterritorial, postnational literary paradigms of a world on the move offer a multistage learning process. They not only reclaim and present the neglected chapters of a larger global cultural past we can no longer afford to ignore, but they also imagine forms of communities not bound by conventional commonalities, those of territory, history, language, and religion. They demonstrate the fallibility of politically endorsed identities and resist classification along unidimensional lines of nationality, ethnicity, gender, and class. At the end of "Un Tapiz: The Poetics of Concientización," which concludes with an interpretation of Anzaldúa's *Borderlands*, Cherríe Moraga's *Loving in the War Years*, and her own *The Mixquiahuala Letters*, Ana Castillo notes:

> It may be said (and indeed, it has) that neither the character of Teresa, nor the works of Anzaldúa and Moraga are representative of the thoughts or lives of the majority of women. Yet in the history of civilization, when can it be claimed that a poet is the typical citizen marching in step with the times? Poets and artists are dreamers who weave stories out of their dreams, which *are* reflective of their times, but which most people do not, cannot, or refuse to see during their times. (*MD*, 178–79)

The works of Castillo, Anzaldúa, Kingston, Özdamar, Moníková, or Danticat may not be "representative of the thoughts or lives of the majority of women." But they are representative of the destinies of women and men who have lost their footing in history, their place in geography, and their families to persecution in any form.

Writers who have become chroniclers and agents of the modern history of migrations and displacements fortify us with insights about our own culture(s) and the means to turn lamentations of loss into statements of empowerment. They transform the losses sustained in exile into a lyric pathos of survival and a somber celebration of linguistic mastery. They establish verbal and cultural bi- and multilingualism as the first prerequisite of emphatic identification with loss and diasporic pathos. Khatibi reflects eloquently on the erosion of prejudice and the engendering of love, wisdom, and transcendence in the meeting of languages:

> A foreigner, I must become attached to everything which exists on and under the earth. Language belongs to no one, it belongs

to no one and I know nothing about anyone. In my mother tongue, didn't I grow up as an adopted child? From one adoption to another, I thought I was language's own child.

Bi-lingue? My luck, my own individual abyss and my lovely amnesiac energy. An energy I don't experience as deficiency, curiously enough. Rather, it's my third ear.[17]

The third ear expands our capacity for hearing the diverse accents of idiom, history, memory, and identity. This *amour bilingue* or *multilingue* transcends the limitations of hyphenation, hybridity, and being in love with an arbitrary vision of identity. It complements the possibilities of the languages it participates in and outlines a grammar of new discourses of community and culture beyond territorial borders.

Chapter I

1. Michel-Rolph Trouillot, *Silencing the Past: Power and the Production of History* (Boston: Beacon Press, 1995), maintains that histories can be silenced through unequal access to means of historical production. Silences and erasure can inform historical writing at "four crucial moments: the moment of fact creation (the making of *sources*); the moment of fact assembly (the making of *archives*); the moment fact retrieval (the making of *narratives*); and the moment of retrospective significance (the making of *history* in the final instance)" (26). Trouillot cites the example of the silencing of the Haitian revolution by Western historiography as an instance of the "uneven power in the production of sources, archives, and narratives" (27).

2. Arjun Appadurai, *Modernity at Large: Cultural Dimensions of Modernization* (Minneapolis: University of Minnesota Press, 1996), 60.

3. Guillermo Gómez-Peña, *Warrior for Gringostroika* (Saint Paul, Minn.: Graywolf Press, 1993), 47.

4. Emily Apter, "Comparative Exile: Competing Margins in the History of Comparative Literature," in *Comparative Literature in the Age of Multiculturalism*, ed. Charles Bernheimer (Baltimore: Johns Hopkins University Press, 1995), 86.

5. Homi K. Bhabha, "DissemiNation: Time, Narrative, and the Margins of Modern Nation," in *Nation and Narration*, ed. Homi K. Bhabha (London: Routledge, 1990), 291.

6. Ibid., 307.

7. Hans-Georg Gadamer, *Wahrheit und Methode. Grundzüge einer philosophischen Hermeneutik* (Truth and method. Foundations of a philosopical hermeneutics) (Tübingen: J. C. B. Mohr [Paul Siebeck], 1960), 426.

8. Emmanuel Lévinas, *Entre nous: On Thinking-of-the-Other*, trans. Michael B. Smith and Barbara Harshav (New York: Columbia University Press, 1998), 3.

9. Iain Chambers, *Migrancy, Culture, Identity* (London: Routledge, 1994), 128.

10. Gómez-Peña, *Warrior for Gringostroika*, 49.

11. Appadurai, *Modernity at Large*, 49.

12. For a very fine introduction to italophone writers see Graziella Parati, "Looking through Non-Western Eyes: Immigrant Women's Autobiographical Narratives in Italian," in *Writing New Identities: Gender, Nation, and Immigration in Contemporary Europe*, ed. Gisela Brinker-Gabler and Sidonie Smith (Minneapolis: University of Minnesota Press, 1997), 118–42.

13. Hélène Cixous, *Three Steps on the Ladder of Writing*, trans. Sarah Cornell and Susan Sellers (New York: Columbia University Press, 1993), 20.

14. Etienne Balibar, "The Nation Form: History and Ideology," trans. Chris Turner, in Etienne Balibar and Immanuel Wallerstein, *Race, Nation, Class: Ambiguous Identities* (London: Verso, 1991), 97.

15. Appadurai, *Modernity at Large*, 164.

16. Rosario Ferré, *The Youngest Doll* (Lincoln: University of Nebraska Press, 1991), 155.

17. Cathy N. Davidson, "Immigrant Writing," in *The Oxford Companion to Women's Writing in the United States*, ed. Cathy N. Davidson and Linda Wagner-Martin (New York: Oxford University Press, 1995), 417.

18. Gérard Chaliand and Jean Pierre Rageau, *The Penguin Atlas of Diasporas*, trans. A. M. Barrett (New York: Viking, 1995), xiv.

19. Robin Cohen, *Global Diasporas: An Introduction* (London: UCL [University College London] Press, 1997), 23.

20. Ibid., 176.

21. R. B. Kitaj, *First Diasporist Manifesto* (New York: Thames and Hudson, 1989), 29–30.

22. Salman Rushdie, *Imaginary Homelands: Essays and Criticism, 1981–1991* (London: Penguin/Granta, 1991), 20.

23. Edward W. Said, *Culture and Imperialism* (New York: Alfred A. Knopf, 1993), 66.

24. Edward W. Said, "The Mind of Winter: Reflections on Life in Exile," *Harper's* 269, no. 1612 (1984): 55.

25. Rushdie, *Imaginary Homelands*, 124–25.

26. See Gustavo Pérez Firmat, *Life-on-the-Hyphen: The Cuban-American Way* (Austin: University of Texas Press, 1994).

27. Yurij Lotman and B. A. Uspensky, "On the Semiotic Mechanism of Culture," trans. George Mihaychuk, *New Literary History* 9 (1978): 213.

28. Richard Terdiman, *Present Past: Modernity and the Memory Crisis* (Ithaca: Cornell University Press, 1993), 70.

29. Lotman and Uspensky, "Semiotic Mechanism of Culture," 214.

30. Maurice Halbwachs, *On Collective Memory*, ed. and trans. Lewis A. Coser (Chicago: University of Chicago Press, 1992), 51.

31. George E. Marcus and Michael M. J. Fischer, *Anthropology as Cultural Critique: An Experimental Moment in the Human Sciences* (Chicago: University of Chicago Press, 1986), 139.

32. Caren Kaplan, "Resisting Autobiography: Out-Law Genres and Transnational Feminist Subjects," in *De/Colonizing the Subject: The Politics of Gender in Women's Autobiography*, ed. Sidonie Smith and Julia Watson (Minneapolis: University of Minnesota Press, 1992), 115–38.

33. Teresa McKenna, *Migrant Song: Politics and Process in Contemporary Chicano Literature* (Austin: University of Texas Press, 1997), 105.

34. This term is used by Chicano critic Juan Bruce-Novoa to describe the typical Chicano speech where not only words from both English and Spanish are juxtaposed or mixed codes are used but also grammatical patterns are subtly merged and idioms cross-culturally employed. See Juan Bruce-Novoa, *Retrospace: Collected Essays on Chicano Literature* (Houston: Arte Publico Press, 1990), 50.

Chapter 2

1. Gilles Deleuze and Félix Guattari, *Kafka: Toward a Minor Literature*, trans. Dona Polan (Minneapolis: University of Minnnesota Press, 1986), 19

2. Deleuze and Guattari's source of the term "minor literature" is an entry in Kafka's diaries on *kleine Literaturen* (small literatures). These literatures, such as Jewish literature written in Warsaw or contemporary Czech literature, represent a specific form of national consciousness. They are marked by a propensity for symbolic expression and a resistance to restrictive principles that imply an alternative, anti-establishment aesthetics. See Ülker Gökberk, "Understanding Alterity: *Ausländerliteratur* between Relativism and Universalism," in *Theoretical Issues in Literary History*, ed. David Perkins (Cambridge, Mass.: Harvard University Press, 1991), 170–72. "Minor literature" is one of the categories Gökberk uses productively in profiling the literature of non-German writers writing in Germany today.

3. Deleuze and Guattari, *Kafka*, 18.

4. Novalis (Friedrich von Hardenberg), *Schriften*, ed. Paul Kluckhohn and Richard Samuel, 4 vols. (Stuttgart: Kohlhammer, 1960), 3:429–30, no. 820.

5. Sigmund Freud, "Das Unheimliche," in *Gesammelte Werke*, ed. Anna Freud et al., 18 vols. (London: Imago, 1940–52), 12:235.

6. Julia Kristeva, *Strangers to Ourselves*, trans. Leon S. Roudiez (New York: Columbia University Press, 1991), 191.

7. Ibid., 192.

8. Deleuze and Guattari, *Kafka*, 16.

9. Georg Lukács, *Wider den mißverstandenen Realismus* (Hamburg: Claasen, 1958), 87, 56. Furthermore, Lukács sees in Kafka's "wonderfully expressive details" a stylized timelessness. Such details do not represent, as they do in realism, "the axes of the transformations and conflicts of their own existence" but are "the ciphers of the unfathomable beyond" (87–88).

10. Deleuze and Guattari, *Kafka*, 17.

11. Appadurai, *Modernity at Large*, 56.

12. Deleuze and Guattari, *Kafka*, 26–27.

13. Ibid., 26.

14. Friedrich Nietzsche, "Vom Nutzen und Nachteil der Historie für das Leben," in *Werke*, ed. Karl Schlechta, 3 vols. (Munich: Carl Hanser, 1956), 1:219.

15. Paul de Man, "Literary History and Literary Modernity," in *Blindness and Insight: Essays in the Rhetoric of Contemporary Criticism*, 2d ed. (Minneapolis: University of Minnesota Press, 1983), 148.

16. Nietzsche, "Vom Nutzen und Nachteil," 261.

17. Jorge Luis Borges, "Funes the Memorius," trans. James E. Irby, in *Labyrinths*, ed. Donald A. Yates and James E. Irby (New York: New Directions, 1962), 65.

18. Walter Benjamin, "Über den Begriff der Geschichte," in *Illuminationen* (Frankfurt am Main: Suhrkamp, 1977), 253.

19. Terdiman, *Present Past*, 240.

20. Freud, "Konstruktionen in der Analyse," in *Gesammelte Werke*, 16:44.

21. Kristeva, *Strangers to Ourselves*, 192.

22. Paul Ricoeur, "Psychoanalysis and the Movement of Contemporary Culture," trans. Willis Domingo, in *The Conflict of Interpretations*, ed. Don Ihde (Evanston: Northwestern University Press, 1974), 134.

23. Jacques Le Goff, *History and Memory*, trans. Steven Rendall and Elizabeth Claman (New York: Columbia University Press, 1992), xi.

24. Geoffrey H. Hartman, "Public Memory and Its Discontents," *Raritan* 13, no. 4 (1994): 24–40, 27.

25. See, for example, Saul Friedländer, *Memory, History, and the Extermination of the Jews of Europe* (Bloomington: Indiana University Press, 1993); Geoffrey Hartman, ed., *Bitburg in Moral and Political Perspective* (Bloomington: Indiana University Press, 1986), and ed., *Holocaust Remembrance: The Shapes of Memory* (Cambridge, Mass.: Blackwell, 1994); Lawrence L. Langer, *Holocaust Testimonies: The Ruins of Memory* (New Haven: Yale University Press, 1991), and *Preempting the Holocaust* (New Haven: Yale University Press, 1998), James Young, *The Texture of Memory: Holocaust Memorials and Meaning* (New Haven: Yale University Press, 1993), and *The Art of Memory: Holocaust Memorials in History* (New York: Prestel-Verlag, 1994); and Barbie Zelizer, *Remembering to Forget: Holocaust Memory through the Camera's Eye* (Chicago: University of Chicago Press, 1998). Geoffrey Hartman is project director of the Fortunoff Video Archive for Holocaust Testimonies.

26. Andreas Huyssen, *Twilight Memories: Marking Time in a Culture of Amnesia* (New York: Routledge, 1995), 7.

27. The English translation of *Erzähler der Nacht* was published in 1993 in the United States with the title *Damascus Nights*, trans. Philip Boehm (New York: Farrar, Straus and Giroux).

28. See Rafik Schami, *Damals dort und heute hier. Über Fremdsein* (Then there and now here. On being foreign), interviews with Erich Jooß, ed. Erich Jooß (Freiburg: Herder, 1998), 116. Quotations from Schami are cited in the text with the abbreviations listed: *D: Damals dort und heute hier; EN: Erzähler der Nacht* (Weinheim: Beltz & Geldberg, 1989; Munich: dtv, 1994).

29. Benjamin, "Der Erzähler," in *Illuminationen*, 388.

30. Ibid., 393.

31. Jorge Luis Borges, "The Thousand and One Nights," in *Seven Nights*, trans. Eliot Weinberger (New York: New Directions, 1984), 49.

32. Ibid., 50.

33. A recent excellent book by Virginia Danielson, *The Voice of Egypt: Umm Kulthum, Arabic Song, and Egyptian Society* (Chicago: University of Chicago Press, 1997), interweaves the history of modern Egypt with the life and art of Umm Kulthum. Here a musician's biography holds up the mirror to the cultural history of a particular time and place. My understanding of Kulthum's unique position in Arab culture is much indebted to this book.

34. Danielson, *The Voice of Egypt*, 186.

35. Malcolm Bradbury, "The Man with a Story for Everything," review of *Damascus Nights*, by Rafik Schami, *New York Times Book Review*, November 7, 1993, 13. Bradbury finds Schami's tale "timely and timeless" (13). Although Bradbury offers a positive and fairly balanced view of the novel, he misses or glosses over the power of community memory in tranlating history. Consequently, he interprets Schami's allegory of history as a mode of self-exoticization: "The 'Orient' is here seen not in its full political density and danger, rather in a kind of eternal haze" (13). This view is contradicted in Iman O. Khalil, "Narrative Strategies as Cultural Vehicles: On Rafik Schami's *Erzähler der Nacht*," in *The German Mosaic: Cultural and Linguistic Divesity in Society*, ed. Carol Aisha Blackshire-Belay (Westport, Conn.: Greenwood Press, 1994), 217–24. Khalil argues that Schami presents a vivid picture of the diversity of the Arab world that challenges the West's clichéd perceptions of the Orient.

36. Douglas Jehl, "Breathing Life into Folklore of a Golden Arab Past," *New York Times*, September 16, 1999, A4 (YNE), International section.

37. Gadamer, *Wahrheit und Methode*, 367.

38. Hélène Cixous, interview with Mireille Calle-Gruber, in Hélène Cixous and Mireille Calle-Gruber, *Rootprints: Memory and Life Writing*, trans. Eric Prenowitz (London: Routledge, 1997), 48.

39. Antonio Benítez-Rojo, *The Repeating Island: The Caribbean and the Postmodern Perspective*, 2d ed., trans. James E. Maraniss (Durham: Duke University Press, 1996), 11.

40. Oliver Sacks, *The Island of the Colorblind* (New York: Vintage, 1997), 4.

41. Quoted in Renee H. Shea, "Traveling Worlds with Edwidge Danticat," *Poets and Writers* 25, no. 1 (1997): 51.

42. Edwidge Danticat, *Breath, Eyes, Memory* (New York: Soho Press, 1994; rpt. New York: Vintage, 1995) 179–80.

43. Ferré, *The Youngest Doll*, 163.

44. Trouillot, *Silencing the Past*, 31.

45. Ibid., 32.

46. The last of these military coups ousted Jean-Bertrand Aristide, who had been elected president in 1991. American intervention restored the Aristide presi-

dency, and the former dissident priest served out his original term—six years—in office. At the time of this writing, Rene Preval is the popularly elected president of Haiti.

47. Danticat, *Breath, Eyes, Memory*, 54.

48. Carol A. Padden, "Folk Explanation in Language Survival," in *Collective Remembering*, ed. David Middleton and Derek Edwards (London: Sage, 1990), 201.

49. Quoted in Shea, "Traveling Worlds," 48.

50. Trouillot, *Silencing the Past*, 55.

51. Shea, "Traveling Worlds," 49.

52. Rosario Ferré, *The House on the Lagoon* (New York: Farrar, Straus and Giroux, 1995), 330.

53. Ferré, *The Youngest Doll*, 155.

54. Ferré, *House on the Lagoon*, 133.

55. John Berger, "Rumour," preface to Latife Tekin, *Berji Kristin: Tales from the Garbage Hills*, trans. Ruth Christie and Saliha Paker (London: Marion Boyars, 1993), 7.

56. Ferré, *House on the Lagoon*, 190.

57. Michel de Certeau, *Heterologies: Discourse on the Other*, trans. Brian Massumi (Minneapolis: University of Minnesota Press, 1986), 200.

58. Novalis, *Heinrich von Ofterdingen*, in *Schriften*, 1:259.

59. De Certeau, *Heterologies*, 202–03.

60. Ferré, *House on the Lagoon*, 386.

61. David Middleton and Derek Edwards, introduction to *Collective Remembering*, 9.

62. De Certeau, *The Practice of Everyday Life*, trans. Steven Rendall (Berkeley and Los Angeles: University of California Press, 1984), 87.

63. Cristina Garcia, *Dreaming in Cuban* (New York: Alfred A. Knopf, 1992), 99.

64. Ferré, *House on the Lagoon*, 330.

65. De Certeau, *Practice of Everyday Life*, 87–88.

Chapter 3

1. In addition to the autobiographical works discussed in this study, Sara Suleri's *Meatless Days* (Chicago: University of Chicago Press, 1989); Meena Alexander's *Fault Lines: A Memoir* (New York: Feminist Press at the City University of New York, 1993); and most recently, Edward Said's *Out of Place: A Memoir* (New York: Alfred A. Knopf, 1999) are memoirs of great poetic and philosophical depth. They offer novel critical insights into issues of language and identity, migration and memory, and social constructions of gender and ethnicity.

2. See, for example, Françoise Lionnet, *Autobiographical Voices: Race, Gender, Self-Portraiture* (Ithaca: Cornell University Press, 1989); and Michael M. J. Fischer, "Autobiographical Voices (1, 2, 3) and Mosaic Memory: Experimental Sondages in the (Post)modern World," in *Autobiography and Postmodernism*, ed. Kathleen Ashley,

Leigh Gilmore, and Gerald Peters (Amherst: University of Massachusetts Press, 1994), 79–129.

3. Fischer, "Autobiographical Voices," 79.

4. Michael M. J. Fischer, "Ethnicity and Postmodern Arts of Memory," in *Writing Culture: The Politics and Poetics of Ethnography,* ed. James Clifford and George E. Marcus (Berkeley and Los Angeles: University of California Press, 1986), 195–96.

5. Lionnet, *Autobiographical Voices,* 29.

6. Fischer, "Autobiographical Voices," 80–82.

7. Kristeva, *Strangers to Ourselves,* 29.

8. William C. Spengemann, *The Forms of Autobiography: Episodes in the History of the Literary Genre* (New Haven: Yale University Press, 1980), xvi.

9. In "Maxine Hong Kingston," the introduction to his interview with Maxine Hong Kingston in *A World of Ideas II: Public Opinions from Private Citizens* (New York: Doubleday, 1990), Bill Moyers writes that Kingston's two memoirs *The Woman Warrior* and *China Men* "are the most widely taught books by a living American author on college campuses today" (11). In 1991, the Modern Language Association of America published in its Approaches to Teaching World Literature series *Approaches to Teaching Kingston's "The Woman Warrior,"* ed. Shirley Geok-lin Lim (New York: Modern Language Association), a valuable collection of essays by prominent American and Chinese-American critics.

10. In my endeavors to understand the purpose and function of historical knowledge in individual lives and to grasp the subtle interplay and complex negotiations between history and memory, I have benefited much from Bernard Lewis's 1974 lectures delivered at Yeshiva Universtiy and published under the title *History—Remembered, Recovered, Invented* (Princeton: Princeton University Press, 1975).

11. "Literary history is the great morgue where everyone seeks out the dead one they love or are related to." Heinrich Heine, *Die romantische Schule, Säkularausgabe,* ed. Die nationalen Forschungs- und Gedenkstättten der klassischen deutschen Literatur in Weimar and Centre National de la Recherche (Berlin: Akademie Verlag; Paris: Editions du CNRS, 1972), 8:18.

12. Joan Lidoff, "Autobiography in a Different Voice: *The Woman Warrior* and the Question of Genre," in Lim, *Approaches to Teaching,* 117.

13. Maxine Hong Kingston, *The Woman Warrior: Memoirs of a Girlhood among Ghosts* (New York: Alfred A. Knopf, 1976; New York: Vintage, 1989), 46.

14. Quoted in Moyers, "Maxine Hong Kingston," 11.

15. Kingston, *The Woman Warrior,* 3.

16. Maxine Hong Kingston, *China Men* (New York: Alfred A. Knopf, 1977; New York: Vintage, 1989), 17–21.

17. Quoted in Moyers, "Maxine Hong Kingston," 17.

18. Cynthia Sau-ling Wong, "Autobiography as Guided Chinatown Tour? Maxine Hong Kingston's *The Woman Warrior* and Chinese-American Autobiographical Controversy," in *Multicultural Autobiography: American Lives,* ed. James Robert Payne (Knoxville: University of Tennessee Press, 1992), 248.

19. Ibid., 252–53.

20. Ibid., 253.

21. Thomas J. Ferraro, *Ethnic Passages: Literary Immigrants in Twentieth-Century America* (Chicago: University of Chicago Press, 1993), 167–68.

22. Sau-ling Cynthia Wong, "Kingston's Handling of Traditional Chinese Sources," in Lim, *Approaches to Teaching*, 26–27.

23. Kingston, *The Woman Warrior*, 185.

24. Fischer, "Ethnicity," 195.

25. Ferraro, *Ethnic Passages*, 180.

26. Kingston, *The Woman Warrior*, 209.

27. Oscar Hijuelos, *Our House in the Last World* (New York: Persea Books, 1983), 168.

28. In another Cuban-American novel, Cristina Garcia's above-mentioned *Dreaming in Cuban*, the narrator's mother, Lourdes, frequently confers in her New York exile with the ghost of her departed father. The pursuance of the narrator's aunt Moon Orchid by ghosts in *The Woman Warrior* is mentioned in the discussion of Kingston's memoir in this chapter.

29. Freud, "Erinnern, Wiederholen, Durcharbeiten," in *Gesammelte Werke*, 10:127.

30. Hijuelos, *Our House*, 215.

31. Cixous, in Cixous and Calle-Gruber, *Rootprints*, 43.

32. Hijuelos, *Our House*, 88–89.

33. Paul John Eakin, *Fictions in Autobiography: Studies in the Act of Self-Invention* (Princeton: Princeton University Press, 1985), 7.

34. De Man, "Autobiography as De-facement," in *The Rhetoric of Romanticism* (New York: Columbia University Press, 1984), 68–69.

35. In a short essay on *Pavane*, Josef A. Modzelewski unpacks the various allusions for the reader: "The title *Pavane für eine verstorbene Infantin* . . . recalls the famous piano composition by the great French composer, Maurice Ravel, *Pavane pour une infante défunte*, a piece which contains elements of dance and sadness. . . . [T]he cover of the book . . . is a black and white negative reproduction of the renowned painting by Diego Velázquez, *Las Meninas*." Modzelewski argues that although Moníková's book is full of direct and veiled allusions to great works of art, it "does not satisfy the awakened hunger for greatness. On the contrary, it provokes at times even a feeling of distaste" (22). He finds the tone of the book oppressive and disturbing, and, referring to another critic W. Iggers, who saw no unifying theme in the book, Modzelewski surmises that Iggers was probably too disturbed by the book to find a binding theme (24). Modzelewski also reads *Pavane* as Moníková's autobiography in German exile, as her "exorcism of her own oppression and displacement in West Germany—her literary catharsis" (30) (Josef A. Modzelewski, "Libuše's Success and Francine's Bitterness: Libuše Moníková and Her Protagonist in *Pavane für eine verstorbene Infantin*," in Blackshire-Belay, *The German Mosaic*, 21–31).

36. Libuše Moníková, *Pavane für eine verstorbene Infantin* (Berlin: Rotbuch, 1983), 18.

37. Freud, "Trauer und Melancholie," in *Gesammelte Werke*, 10:429.

38. Moníková, *Pavane*, 134.

39. Calle-Gruber, in Cixous and Calle-Gruber, *Rootprints*, 168.

40. Moníková, *Pavane*, 9.

41. Eakin, *Fictions in Autobiography*, 9.

42. Richard Rodriguez, for example, calls his autobiography, *The Hunger of Memory: The Education of Richard Rodriguez* (Boston: David R. Godine, 1982), "a book about language." He declares with passion that he writes about poetry, "the new Roman Catholic liturgy; learning to read; writing; political terminology. Language has been the great subject of my life. In college and graduate school, I was registered as an 'English major.' But well before then, from my first day of school, I was a student of language. Obsessed by the way it developed my public identity" (7).

43. Eva Hoffman, *Lost in Translation: A Life in a New Language* (New York: E. P. Dutton, 1989; New York: Penguin, 1990), 191.

44. Rushdie, *Imaginary Homelands*, 17.

45. Hoffman, *Lost in Translation*, 231–32.

46. Abdelkebir Khatibi, *Love in Two Languages*, trans. Richard Howard (Minneapolis: University of Minnesota Press, 1990), 108.

47. Hoffman, *Lost in Translation*, 275.

48. Danuta Zadworna Fjellestad, " 'The Insertion of the Self into the Space of Borderless Possibility: Eva Hoffman's Exiled Body," *MELUS* 20, no. 2 (1995): 143.

49. Hoffman, *Lost in Translation*, 275.

50. Fjellestad, "Insertion of the Self," 143

51. Hoffman, *Lost in Translation*, 280.

52. Fischer, "Ethnicity," 210.

53. Hoffman, *Lost in Translation*, 242.

54. Eakin, *Fictions in Autobiography*, 5.

55. William Boelhower, *Through a Glass Darkly: Ethnic Semiosis in American Literature* (New York: Oxford University Press, 1987), 140.

56. Lidoff, "Autobiography in Different Voice," 117–18.

57. Fischer, "Ethnicity," 198.

58. Kaplan, "Resisting Autobiography," 134.

Chapter 4

1. For a critical history of the Turkish migrant experience in Germany from political, anthropological, and cultural perspectives, see the essays by Azade Seyhan, Dietrich Thränhardt, Ruth Mandel, Heidrun Suhr, Arlene Akiko Teraoka, and Anna K. Kuhn in the special issue "Minorities in German Culture," *New German Critique* 46 (winter 1989).

2. Özdamar, "Schwarzauge und Sein Esel," *Die Zeit*, March 9, 1993, 21.

3. Özdamar, *Mutterzunge* (Berlin: Rotbuch, 1990), 80. Subsequent references are given in the text with the abbreviation *M*. The English translation of *Mutterzunge*, Özdamar's first book, was enthusiastically reviewed by Charlotte Innes in the *New York Times Book Review*, September 25, 1994, 1.

4. Bruce-Novoa, *Retrospace*, 58.

5. Ana Castillo, *Massacre of the Dreamers: Essays on Xicanisma* (Albuquerque: University of New Mexico Press, 1994), 21. Subsequent references are given in the text with the abbreviation *MD*.

6. Gómez-Peña, "Bilingualism, Biculturalism, and Borders," interview by Coco Fusco, in Coco Fusco, *English is Broken Here: Notes on Cultural Fusion in the Americas* (New York: New Press, 1995), 153.

7. Ibid., 156.

8. Renato Rosaldo, *Culture and Truth: The Remaking of Social Analysis* (Boston: Beacon, 1989), 163.

9. Ibid., 161.

10. Le Goff, *History and Memory*, 54.

11. For a brief discussion of this association see Bruce-Novoa, *Retrospace*, 57–58.

12. Ibid., 58.

13. Le Goff, *History and Memory*, 54.

14. See, for example, Angie Chabram Dernersesian, " 'Chicana! Rican? No, Chicana-Riqueña!' Refashioning the Transnational Connection," in *Multiculturalism: A Critical Reader*, ed. David Theo Goldberg (Oxford: Blackwell, 1994).

15. Gómez-Peña, "Bilingualism, Biculturalism, and Borders," 157.

16. Bruce-Novoa, *Retrospace*, 50.

17. Gómez-Peña, "Bilingualism, Biculturalism, and Borders," 157.

18. Sandra Cisneros, interview by Feroza Jussawalla, in *Interviews with Writers of the Postcolonial World*, ed. Feroza Jussawalla and Reed Way Dasenbrock (Jackson: University Press of Mississippi, 1992), 288.

19. Gloria Anzaldúa, *Borderlands/La Frontera: The New Mestiza* (San Francisco: Aunt Lute Books, 1987), 18.

20. Full translation: "Then the interpreter came. He spoke to the foreman. Told him this guy lost his income tax form. The tax office said this was really bad. There is no form. It's a mess. You can't get child credit or whatever. No way! No residence permit either. The immigration police won't give it. The housing office says no, too. The employment office didn't give a permit either. I am sending the boy to vocational school. This is really shit. Did you get a sick report?"

21. Vowel harmoy is a phonetic assimilation of the vowels in a word or suffix, so as to harmonize with the vowels in neighboring words. For example, front and back vowels and rounded and unrounded ones change to conform to one group, for example, either back or front. In Turkish, vowels of any suffix designating case or functioning as a preposition or (adverbial) particle conform to the vowel category of the preceding word.

22. For example, "El famoso gaitero, un maravedi porque empiece y diez porce acabe" [Give the famous (windpipe) player five coins to play and ten coins to stop]; "Beş para ver oynasın, on para ver susmaz" [Give him five coins to play, give him ten coins (to stop), but he won't stop]. Or, "Donde una puerta se sierra, otra se abre" [Wherever a door closes, another opens]; "Bir kapıyı kapayan Allah öbürünü açar" [When God closes one door, he opens another one].

23. "Mexicans have traditionally been seen as extremely oral; Chicanos, having a culture of resistance and not a culture of affirmation like the Mexicans, have developed an extremely minimal, direct, and confrontational way of relating intellectually . . . . I think that Mexicans find Chicano literature very simplistic. Chicanos find Mexican literature extremely coded, extremely intellectual" (Gómez-Peña, "Bilingualism, Biculturalism, and Borders," 152–53).

24. Linda Hutcheon, *A Theory of Parody: The Teachings of Twentieth-Century Art Forms* (New York: Methuen, 1985), 30.

25. Alvina A. Quintana, "Ana Castillo's *The Mixquiahuala Letters*: The Novelist as Ethnographer," in *Criticism in the Borderlands: Studies in Chicano Literature, Culture, and Ideology*, ed. Héctor Calderón and José David Saldívar (Durham: Duke University Press, 1991), 80.

26. Hutcheon, *A Theory of Parody*, 53–54.

27. Ana Castillo, *So Far from God* (New York: W. W. Norton, 1993), 25.

28. Marc Zimmerman, *U.S. Latino Literature: An Essay and Annotated Bibliography* (Chicago: MARCH/Abrazo Press, 1992), 27.

29. Bruce-Novoa, *Retrospace*, 118.

30. Zimmerman, *U.S. Latino Literature*, 24.

31. "Even as Chicano literature developed throughout the 1960s and 1970s and on into the 1980s, even as new Chicano writers showed new levels of sophistication, left older modes of protest and incorporated new Latin American and U.S. models as the bases for their developing work, the *Aztlán* myth or one of its variations as a 'sacred space' would still tend to characterize Chicano literature and serve as its paradigm, only to be eroded by the more secular, rationalist and feminist trends that would emerge increasingly in the 1980s as a literature of settlement and acculturation began to displace the older cultural model for many writers" (Zimmerman, *U.S. Latino Literature*, 23).

32. Bruce-Novoa, *Retrospace*, 165.

33. Ramón Saldívar, *Chicano Narrative: The Dialectics of Difference* (Madison: University of Wisconsin Press, 1990).

34. Zimmerman, *U.S. Latino Literature*, 27.

35. Anzaldúa, *Borderlands*, 3.

36. Mikhail M. Bakhtin, *The Dialogic Imagination*, trans. Caryl Emerson and Michael Holquist, ed. Michael Holquist (Austin: University of Texas Press, 1981), 323–24.

37. Anzaldúa, *Borderlands*, preface.

38. Bakhtin, *The Dialogic Imagination*, 263.

39. Anzaldúa, *Borderlands*, 59.

40. Gómez-Peña, "Documented/Undocumented," trans. Rubén Martínez, in *The Graywolf Annual Five: Multicultural Literacy*, ed. Rick Simonson and Scott Walker (Saint Paul, Minn.: Graywolf Press, 1988), 130.

41. In German, the word *Zunge* (tongue), unlike in Turkish and English, does not have the extra signified "language."

42. Gómez-Peña, "Bilingualism, Biculturalism, and Borderlands," 152.

43. Roland Barthes, *New Critical Essays*, trans. Richard Howard (New York: Hill and Wang, 1980), 116.

44. Anzaldúa, *Borderlands*, 78.

45. Ibid., 2–3.

Chapter 5

1. Catherine Belsey, "History at the Level of the Signifier," paper presented at the conference "Crossroads in Cultural Studies," Tampere, Finland, June 30, 1998, photocopy, 1.

2. Kristeva, *New Maladies of the Soul*, trans. Ross Guberman (New York: Columbia University Press, 1995), 202.

3. Ibid., 208.

4. Friedrich Schlegel, *Kritische Ausgabe*, ed. Ernest Behler (Paderborn: Schöningh, 1967), 2:182.

5. Ana Castillo, "My Mother's Mexico," in *Latina: Women's Voices from the Borderlands*, ed. Lillian Castillo-Speed (New York: Touchstone), 30.

6. Ibid., 36.

7. Ana Castillo, *The Mixquiahuala Letters* (Binghamton, N.Y.: Bilingual Press/Editorial Bilingüe, 1986). Subsequent references are given in the text, abbreviated *ML*.

8. Stephen A. Tyler, "Post-modern Ethnography: From Document of the Occult to Occult Document," Clifford and Marcus in *Writing Culture*, 138.

9. In one of the *Athäneum* fragments, Friedrich Schlegel names two types of writers who work into the structure of the text two very different implied readers:

> The analytic writer observes the reader as he is; he then makes his calculations and sets up his machines in order to make the proper impresssion on him. The synthetic writer constructs and creates a reader as he should be; he doesn't imagine him calm and dead, but alive and responsive. He lets whatever he has created take shape gradually before the reader's eyes, or he urges the reader to discover it himself. He doesn't try to make any particular impression on the reader, but enters with him into the sacred relationship of the most profound symphilosophy or sympoetry. (*Kritische Ausgabe*, 2:161, no. 112)

10. See Ülker Gökberk, "Encounters with the Other in German Cultural Discourse: Intercultural *Germanistik* and Aysel Özakin's Journeys of Exile," in *Other Ger-*

manies: Questioning Identity in Women's Literature and Art, ed. Karen Jankowsky and Carla Love (Albany: State University of New York Press, 1997), 19–55.

11. Aysel Özakin, *Die blaue Maske*, trans. Carl Koß (Hamburg: Sammlung Luchterhand, 1989), 129.

12. G. W. F. Hegel, *Theorie-Werkausgabe*, ed. Eva Moldenhauer and Karl Markus Michel, 20 vols. (Frankfurt am Main: Suhrkamp, 1969–71), 3:591.

13. The novels Özakin, a multilingual writer, wrote in Germany were originally written in Turkish but published in German. Özakin collaborated in the translations by a group of excellent translators. More recently she has written two novels in English (*Faith, Lust and Airconditioning* and *The Tongue of the Mountain*) in England, where she currently resides. These novels have not so far been published in England but were published in German translation in Germany with the titles *Glaube, Liebe, Aircondition. Eine türkische Kindheit* (1991) and *Die Zunge der Berge* (1994).

14. Özakin, *Die blaue Maske*, 166.

15. Pierre Nora, "Between Memory and History: *Les Lieux des Mémoire*," trans. Marc Roudebush in the special issue "Memory and Counter-Memory," ed. Natalie Zemon Davis and Randolph Starn, *Representations* 26 (spring 1989): 7.

16. Özakin, *Die blaue Maske*, 175.

17. Lionnet, *Autobiographical Voices*, 21.

18. Benedict Anderson, *Imagined Communities: Reflections on the Origin and Spread of Nationalism*, 2d ed. (London: Verso, 1991), 7.

19. Hartman, "Public Memory," 31.

20. See Lewis, *History*, 43.

21. See Paul Connerton, *How Societies Remember* (Cambridge: Cambridge University Press, 1989).

22. In addition to the 1991 Ingeborg Bachmann Prize, *Das Leben ist eine Karawanserei* received the Walter Hasenclever Prize in 1993. In 1995, Özdamar was invited to New York University as writer-in-residence. After its publication in Spain by Alfaguara, *Karawanserei* made the International Books of the Year List of the *Times Literary Supplement*, December 2, 1994, 12. See note 33 below. Most recently, Özdamar received the 1999 Chamisso Prize, awarded to the best nonnative writer writing in German. An English translation of *Karawanserei* by Luise von Flotow will be published by Middlesex University Press, London.

23. An account of the debate around the awarding of the Ingeborg Bachmann Prize to Özdamar's book is given in Karen Jankowsky, " 'German' Literature Contested: The 1991 Ingeborg-Bachmann-Prize Debate, 'Cultural Diversity,' and Emine Sevgi Özdamar," *German Quarterly* 70 (summer 1997): 261–76.

24. Roland Barthes, *The Fashion System*, trans. Matthew Ward and Richard Howard (New York: Hill and Wang, 1983), 15.

25. Emine Sevgi Özdamar, *Das Leben ist eine Karawanserei hat zwei Türen aus einer kam ich rein aus der anderen ging ich raus* (Cologne: Kiepenheuer & Witsch, 1992), 38.

26. Le Goff, *History and Memory*, 89–90.

27. Anderson, *Imagined Communities*, 154.

28. Özdamar, *Das Leben ist eine Karawanserei*, 171.

29. Bozkurt Güvenç, *Türk Kimliği: Türk Tarihinin Kaynakları* (Turkish identity: Sources of cultural history) (Istanbul: Remzi Kitabevi, 1996), 331.

30. Özdamar, *Das Leben ist eine Karawanserei*, 18.

31. Italo Calvino, *Six Memos for the Next Millennium*, trans. Patrick Creagh (New York: Vintage, 1993), 26–27.

32. Arno Widman, "Why Don't the Germans Love to Read Their Own New Writers?" *European*, January 28–February 3, 1994, 12.

33. Juan Goytisolo, review of *Life Is a Caravansaray*, by Emine Sevgi Özdamar, *Times Literary Supplement*, December 2, 1994, 12.

34. See Said, "The Mind of Winter," 51. In this achingly insightful essay, Said reflects on the uncanny dialectic between nationalism and exile. "Nationalism is an assertion of belonging to a place, a people, a heritage. It affirms the home created by a community of language, culture, and customs; and by so doing, it fends off the ravages of exile." Said locates reactive features in both nationalism and exile and likens their relationship to "Hegel's dialectic of servant and master, opposites informing and constituting each other"(50).

35. Özdamar, *Das Leben ist eine Karawanserei*, 212.

36. See Alexander, *Fault Lines*. Alexander, an accomplished poet and critic, regards her own writing as a search for a homeland (4). As "a woman cracked by multiple migrations" (3), she finds a safety net only in the stories she tells: "As I make up a katha, a story of my life, the lives before me, around me, weave into a net without which I would drop ceaselessly. They keep me within range of difficult truths, the exhilarating dangers of memory" (5).

Afterword

1. Chambers, *Migrancy, Culture, Identity*, 127.

2. Benjamin, "Begriff der Geschichte," 255.

3. Ibid., 252.

4. Anthony Easthope, *Literary into Cultural Studies* (London: Routledge, 1991), 171.

5. Connerton, *How Societies Remember*, 65.

6. Turkish-German women writers often portray the conflicted self-representations of Turkish women in Germany. For example, women who have never worn headscarves or veils in Turkey revert to this historically distant (and displaced) practice in Germany in order to mark or construct an ethnic identity.

7. Michel Foucault, *Language, Counter Memory, Practice*, ed. Donald F. Bouchard and trans. Donald F. Bouchard and Sherry Simon (Ithaca, N.Y.: Cornell University Press, 1977), 148.

8. See also Assia Djebar, *Fantasia: An Algerian Cavalcade*, trans. Dorothy S. Blair (Portsmouth, N.H.: Heinemann, 1993). Djebar notes that the learning and the recitation of the Koran is linked to the body. Koranic verses written on both sides of

the tablet had to be wiped off once the students could recite them by heart: "We scrubbed the piece of wood thoroughly, just like other people wash their clothes: the time it took to dry seemed to ensure the interval that the memory needed to digest what it had swallowed" (183). Also when reciting the Koran, the reciters sway from side to side.

9. Foucault, *Language, Counter Memory, Practice,* 139.

10. Ibid., 139–40.

11. Johannes Fabian, *Time and the Other: How Anthropology Makes Its Object* (New York: Columbia University Press, 1983), 143. See also Bernard McGrane, *Beyond Anthropology: Society and the Other* (New York: Columbia University Press, 1989).

12. Tyler, "Post-modern Ethnography," 139.

13. Quoted in Benjamin, "Die Aufgabe des Übersetzers," in *Illuminationen,* 61.

14. For example, Yüksel Pazarkaya and Zafer Şenocak, two Turkish poets writing in German, have reintroduced forms of Ottoman court poetry into contemporary German poetry.

15. Jacques Derrida, *The Other Heading: Reflections on Today's Europe,* trans. Pascale-Anne Brault and Michael B. Naas (Blomington: Indiana University Press, 1992), 58.

16. Benjamin, "Die Aufgabe des Übersetzers," 59.

17. Khatibi, *Love in Two Languages,* 4–5.

WORKS CITED

Alexander, Meena. *Fault Lines: A Memoir*. New York: Feminist Press at the City University of New York, 1993.

Anderson, Benedict. *Imagined Communities: Reflections on the Origin and Spread of Nationalism*. 2d ed. London: Verso, 1991.

Anzaldúa, Gloria. *Borderlands/La Frontera: The New Mestiza*. San Francisco: Aunt Lute Books, 1987.

Appadurai, Arjun. *Modernity at Large: Cultural Dimensions of Globalization*. Minneapolis: University of Minnesota Press, 1996.

Apter, Emily. "Comparative Exile: Competing Margins in the History of Comparative Literature." In *Comparative Literature in the Age of Multiculturalism*, ed. Charles Bernheimer, 86–96. Baltimore: Johns Hopkins University Press, 1995.

Bakhtin, Mikhail M. *The Dialogic Imagination*. Trans. Caryl Emerson and Michael Holquist. Ed Michael Holquist. Austin: University of Texas Press, 1981.

Balibar, Etienne. "The Nation Form: History and Ideology." Trans. Chris Turner. In Etienne Balibar and Emmanuel Wallerstein, *Race, Nation, Class: Ambiguous Identities*, 86–106. London: Verso, 1991.

Barthes, Roland. *New Critical Essays*. Trans. Richard Howard. New York: Hill and Wang, 1980.

———. *The Fashion System*. Trans. Matthew Ward and Richard Howard. New York: Hill and Wang, 1983.

Belsey, Catherine. "History at the Level of the Signifier." Paper presented at the conference "Crossroads in Cultural Studies," Tampere, Finland, June 30, 1998. Photocopy.

Benítez-Rojo, Antonio. *The Repeating Island: The Caribbean and the Postmodern Perspective*. 2d ed. Trans. James E. Maraniss. Durham: Duke University Press, 1996.

Benjamin, Walter. *Illuminations*. Trans. Harry Zohn. Ed. Hannah Arendt. New York: Schocken, 1969.

———. "Der Erzähler," In *Illuminationen*, 385–410. Frankfurt am Main: Suhrkamp, 1977.

Benjamin, Walter. "Die Aufgabe des Übersetzers." In *Illuminationen*, 50–62.

———. "Über den Begriff der Geschichte." In *Illuminationen*, 251–61.

Berger, John. "Rumour." Preface to Latife Tekin, *Berji Kristin: Tales from the Garbage Hills*. Trans. Ruth Christie and Saliha Paker, 5–8. London: Marion Boyars, 1993.

Bhabha, Homi K. "DissemiNation: Time, Narrative, and the Margins of Modern Nation." In *Nation and Narration*, ed. Homi K. Bhabha, 291–322. London: Routledge, 1990.

Boelhower, William. *Through a Glass Darkly: Ethnic Semiosis in American Literature*. New York: Oxford University Press, 1987.

Borges, Jorge Luis. "Funes the Memorius." Trans. James E. Irby. In *Labyrinths*, ed. Donald A. Yates and James E. Irby, 59–66. New York: New Directions, 1962.

———. "The Thousand and One Nights." In *Seven Nights*, trans. Eliot Weinberger, 42–57. New York: New Directions, 1984.

Bradbury, Malcolm. "The Man with a Story for Everything." Review of *Damascus Nights*, by Rafik Schami. *New York Times Book Review*, November 7, 1993, 13.

Bruce-Novoa, Juan. *Retrospace: Collected Essays on Chicano Literature*. Houston: Arte Publico Press, 1990.

Calvino, Italo. *Six Memos for the Next Millennium*. Trans. Patrick Creagh. New York: Vintage, 1993.

Castillo, Ana. *The Mixquiahuala Letters*. Binghamton, N.Y.: Bilingual Press/Editorial Bilingüe, 1986; New York: Anchor Books, 1992.

———. *So Far from God*. New York: W.W. Norton, 1993.

———. *Massacre of the Dreamers: Essays on Xicanisma*. Albuquerque: University of New Mexico Press, 1994.

———. "My Mother's Mexico." In *Latina: Women's Voices from the Borderlands*, ed. Lillian Castillo-Speed, 26–36. New York: Touchstone, 1995.

Chabram Dernersesian, Angie. " 'Chicana! Rican? No, Chicana-Riqueña!' Refashioning the Transnational Connection." In *Multiculturalism: A Critical Reader*, ed. David Theo Goldberg, 269–95. Oxford: Blackwell, 1994.

Chaliand, Gérard, and Jean Pierre Rageau. *The Penguin Atlas of Diasporas*. Trans. A.M. Barrett. New York: Viking, 1995.

Chambers, Iain. *Migrancy, Culture, Identity*. London: Routledge, 1994.

Cisneros, Sandra. *The House on Mango Street*. New York: Vintage, 1991.

———. Interview by Feroza Jussawalla. In *Interviews with Writers of the Postcolonial World*, ed. Feroza Jussawalla and Reed Way Dasenbrock, 286–306. Jackson: University Press of Mississippi, 1992.

Cixous, Hélène. *Three Steps on the Ladder of Writing*. Trans. Sarah Cornell and Susan Sellers. New York: Columbia University Press, 1993.

Cixous, Hélène, and Mireille Calle-Gruber. *Rootprints: Memory and Life Writing*. Trans. Eric Prenowitz. London: Routledge, 1997.

Cohen, Robin. 1997. *Global Diasporas: An Introduction.* London: UCL (University College London) Press, 1997.

Connerton, Paul. *How Societies Remember.* Cambridge: Cambridge University Press, 1989.

Danielson, Virginia. *The Voice of Egypt: Umm Kulthum, Arabic Song, and Egyptian Society in the Twentieth Century.* Chicago: The University of Chicago Press, 1997.

Danticat, Edwidge. *Breath, Eyes, Memory.* New York: Soho Press, 1994; New York: Vintage, 1995.

———. *Krik? Krak!* New York: Soho Press, 1995.

Davidson, Cathy N. "Immigrant Writing." In *The Oxford Companion to Women's Writing in the United States,* ed. Cathy N. Davidson and Linda Wagner-Martin, 417. New York: Oxford University Press, 1995.

de Certeau, Michel. *The Practice of Everyday Life.* Trans. Steven Rendall. Berkeley and Los Angeles: University of California Press, 1984.

———. *Heterologies: Discourse on the Other.* Trans. Brian Massumi. Minneapolis: University of Minnesota Press, 1986.

de Man, Paul. 1983. "Literary History and Literary Modernity." In *Blindness and Insight: Essays in the Rhetoric of Contemporary Criticism,* 142–65. 2d ed. Minneapolis: University of Minnesota Press, 1983.

———. "Autobiography as De-facement." In *The Rhetoric of Romanticism,* 67–81. New York: Columbia University Press, 1984.

Deleuze, Gilles, and Félix Guattari. 1986. *Kafka: Toward a Minor Literature.* Trans. Dana Polan. Minneapolis: University of Minnesota Press, 1986.

Derrida, Jacques. *The Other Heading: Reflections on Today's Europe.* Trans. Pascale-Anne Brault and Michael B. Naas. Bloomington: Indiana University Press, 1992.

Djebar, Assia. *Fantasia: An Algerian Cavalcade.* Trans. Dorothy S. Blair. Portsmouth, N.H.: Heinemann, 1993.

Eakin, Paul John. *Fictions in Autobiography: Studies in the Act of Self-Invention.* Princeton: Princeton University Press, 1985.

Easthope, Anthony. *Literary into Cultural Studies.* London: Routledge, 1991.

Fabian, Johannes. *Time and the Other: How Anthropology Makes Its Object.* New York: Columbia University Press, 1983.

Ferraro, Thomas J. *Ethnic Passages: Literary Immigrants in Twentieth-Century America.* Chicago: University of Chicago Press, 1993.

Ferré, Rosario. *The Youngest Doll.* Lincoln: University of Nebraska Press, 1991.

———. *The House on the Lagoon.* New York: Farrar, Straus and Giroux, 1995.

Fischer, Michael, M. J. "Ethnicity and the Postmodern Arts of Memory." In *Writing Culture: The Politics and Poetics of Ethnography,* ed. James Clifford and George E. Marcus, 194–233. Berkeley and Los Angeles: University of California Press, 1986.

———. "Autobiographical Voices (1, 2, 3) and Mosaic Memory: Experimental Sondages in the (Post)modern World." In *Autobiography and Postmodernism,* ed.

Kathleen Ashley, Leigh Gilmore, and Gerald Peters, 79–127. Amherst: University of Massachusetts Press, 1994.

Foucault, Michel. *Language, Counter Memory, Practice.* Ed. Donald F. Bouchard. Trans. Donald F. Bouchard and Sherry Simon. Ithaca, N.Y.: Cornell University Press, 1977.

Freud, Sigmund. "Erinnern, Wiederholen und Durcharbeiten." In *Gesammelte Werke,* ed. Anna Freud et al., 10:126–36. London: Imago, 1940–52.

———. "Trauer und Melancholie." In *Gesammelte Werke,* 10:428–46.

———. "Das Unheimliche." In *Gesammelte Werke,* 12:229–68.

———. "Konstruktionen in der Analyse." In *Gesammelte Werke,* 16:43–56.

———. *The Standard Edition of the Complete Psychological Works.* Ed. and trans. James Strachey. 24 vols. London: Hogarth Press and the Institute of Psychoanalysis, 1953–74.

Friedländer, Saul. *Memory, History, and the Extermination of the Jews of Europe.* Bloomington: Indiana University Press, 1993.

Gadamer, Hans-Georg. *Wahrheit und Methode. Grunzüge einer philosophischen Hermeneutik.* Tübingen: J. C. B. Mohr (Paul Siebeck), 1960.

———. *Truth and Method.* Trans. Joel Weinsheimer and Donald G. Marshall. New York: Continuum, 1996.

Garcia, Cristina. *Dreaming in Cuban.* New York: Alfred A. Knopf, 1993.

Gökberk, Ülker. "Understanding Alterity: *Ausländerliteratur* between Relativism and Universalism." In *Theoretical Issues in Literary History,* ed. David Perkins, 143–72. Cambridge, Mass.: Harvard University Press, 1991.

———. "Encounters with the Other in German Cultural Discourse: Intercultural *Germanistik* and Aysel Özakin's Journeys of Exile." In *Other Germanies: Questioning Identity in Women's Literature and Art,* ed. Karen Jankowsky and Carla Love, 19–55. Albany: State University of New York Press, 1997.

Gómez-Peña, Guillermo. "Documented/Undocumented." Trans. Rubén Martínez. In *The Graywolf Annual Five: Multicultural Literacy,* ed. Rick Simonson and Scott Walker, 127–34. Saint Paul, Minn.: Graywolf Press, 1988.

———. *Warrior for Gringostroika.* Saint Paul, Minn.: Graywolf Press, 1993.

———. "Bilingualism, Biculturalism, and Borders." Interview by Coco Fusco. In Coco Fusco, *English Is Broken Here: Notes on Cultural Fusion in the Americas,* 147–58. New York: New Press, 1995.

Goytisolo, Juan. Review of *Life Is a Caravanserai* by Emine Sevgi Özdamar. *Times Literary Supplement,* December 2, 1994, 12.

Güvenç, Bozkurt. *Türk Kimliği: Kültür Tarihinin Kaynakları.* Istanbul: Remzi Kitabevi, 1996.

Halbwachs, Maurice. *On Collective Memory.* Ed. and trans. Lewis A. Coser. Chicago: University of Chicago Press, 1992.

Hartman, Geoffrey H. "Public Memory and Its Discontents." *Raritan* 13, no. 4 (1994): 24–40.

————, ed. *Bitburg in Moral and Political Perspective.* Bloomington: Indiana University Press, 1986.

————, ed. *Holocaust Remembrance: The Shapes of Memory.* Cambridge, Mass.: Blackwell, 1994.

Hegel, G. W. F. *Theorie-Werkausgabe.* Ed. Eva Moldenhauer and Karl Markus Michel. 20 vols. Frankfurt am Main: Suhrkamp, 1969–71.

Heine, Heinrich. *Die romantische Schule.* In *Säkularausgabe,* 8:7–123. Berlin: Akademie Verlag and Paris: Editions du CNRS, 1972.

Hijuelos, Oscar. *Our House in the Last World.* New York: Persea Books, 1983; New York: Washington Square Press, 1990.

Hoffman, Eva. *Lost in Translation: A Life in a New Language.* New York: E. P. Dutton, 1989; New York: Penguin, 1990.

Hutcheon, Linda. *A Theory of Parody: The Teachings of Twentieth-Century Art Forms.* New York: Methuen, 1985.

Huyssen, Andreas. 1995. *Twilight Memories: Marking Time in a Culture of Amnesia.* New York: Routledge, 1995.

Innes, Charlotte. "Turkish-German Stories." Review of *Mother Tongue* by Emine Sevgi Özdamar. *New York Times Book Review,* September 25, 1994, 1.

Jankowsky, Karen. " 'German' Literature Contested: The 1991 Ingeborg-Bachmann-Prize Debate, 'Cultural Diversity,' and Emine Sevgi Özdamar." *German Quarterly* 70 (summer 1997): 261–76.

Jehl, Douglas. "Breathing Life into Folklore of a Golden Arab Past." *New York Times,* September 16, 1999, International section, A4 (YNE).

Kaplan, Caren. "Resisting Autobiography: Out-Law Genres and Transnational Feminist Subjects." In *De/Colonizing the Subject: The Politics of Gender in Women's Autobiography,* ed. Sidonie Smith and Julia Watson, 115–38. Minneapolis: University of Minnesota Press, 1992.

Khalil, Iman O. "Narrative Strategies as Cultural Vehicles: On Rafik Schami's Novel *Erzähler der Nacht.*" In *The German Mosaic: Cultural and Linguistic Diversity in Society,* ed. Carol Aisha Blackshire-Belay, 217–24. Westport, Conn.: Greenwood Press, 1994.

Khatibi, Abdelkebir. *Love in Two Languages.* Trans. Richard Howard. Minneapolis: University of Minnesota Press, 1990.

Kingston, Maxine Hong. *The Woman Warrior: Memoirs of a Girlhood among Ghosts.* New York: Alfred A. Knopf, 1976; New York: Vintage, 1989.

————. *China Men.* New York: Alfred A. Knopf, 1980.

Kitaj, R. B. *First Diasporist Manifesto.* New York: Thames and Hudson, 1989.

Kristeva, Julia. *Strangers to Ourselves.* Trans. Leon S. Roudiez. New York: Columbia University Press, 1991.

————. *New Maladies of the Soul.* Trans. Ross Guberman. New York: Columbia University Press, 1995.

Langer, Lawrence L. *Holocaust Testimonies: The Ruins of Memory.* New Haven: Yale University Press, 1991.

————. *Preempting the Holocaust*. New Haven: Yale University Press, 1998.

Le Goff, Jacques. *History and Memory*. Trans. Steven Rendall and Elizabeth Claman. New York: Columbia University Press, 1992.

Lévinas, Emmanuel. *Entre nous: On Thinking of the Other*. Trans. Michael B. Smith and Barbara Harshav. New York: Columbia University Press, 1998.

Lewis, Bernard. *History—Remembered, Recovered, Invented*. Princeton: Princeton University Press, 1975.

Lidoff, Joan. "Autobiography in a Different Voice: *The Woman Warrior* and the Question of Genre." In *Approaches to Teaching "The Woman Warrior*," ed. Shirley Geok-lin Lim, 116–20. New York: Modern Language Association, 1991.

Lionnet, Françoise. *Autobiographical Voices: Race, Gender, Self- Portraiture*. Ithaca, N.Y.: Cornell University Press, 1989.

Lotman, Yurij, and B. A. Uspensky. "On the Semiotic Mechanism of Culture." Trans. George Mihaychuk. *New Literary History* 9 (1978): 211–32.

Lúkacs, Georg. *Wider den mißverstandenen Realismus*. Hamburg: Claassen, 1958.

Marcus, George E., and Michael M. J. Fischer. *Anthropology as Cultural Critique: An Experimental Moment in the Human Sciences*. Chicago: University of Chicago Press, 1986.

McGrane, Bernard. *Beyond Anthropology: Society and the Other*. New York: Columbia University Press, 1989.

McKenna, Teresa. *Migrant Song: Politics and Process in Contemporary Chicano Literature*. Austin: University of Texas Press, 1997.

Middleton, David, and Derek Edwards, eds. *Collective Remembering*. London: Sage, 1990.

Modzelewski, Jozef A. "Libuše's Success and Francine's Bitterness: Libuše Moníková and Her Protagonist in *Pavane für eine verstorbene Infantin*." In *The German Mosaic: Cultural and Linguistic Diversity in Society*, ed. Carol Aisha Blackshire-Belay, 21–31. Westport, Conn.: Greenwood Press, 1994.

Moníková, Libuše. *Pavane für eine verstorbene Infantin*. Berlin: Rotbuch, 1983.

Moyers, Bill. "Maxine Hong Kingston." In *A World of Ideas II: Public Opinions from Private Citizens*, 11–18. New York: Doubleday, 1990.

New German Critique. Special issue "Minorities in German Culture." Ed. Russell A. Berman, Azade Seyhan, and Arlene A. Teraoka. Number 46 (spring 1989).

Nietzsche, Friedrich. "Vom Nutzen und Nachteil der Historie für das Leben." In *Werke*, ed. Karl Schlechta, 1:209–85. Munich: Carl Hanser, 1956.

————. *On the Advantage and Disadvantage of History for Life*. Trans. Peter Preuss. Indianapolis: Hackett, 1980.

Nora, Pierre. "Between Memory and History: *Les Lieux de Mémoire*." Trans. Marc Roudebush. *Representations* 26 (spring 1989): 7–25.

Novalis (Friedrich von Hardenberg). *Schriften*. Ed. Paul Kluckhohn and Richard Samuel. 4 vols. Stuttgart: Kohlhammer, 1960.

Özakin, Aysel. *Soll ich hier alt werden? Türkin in Deutschland. Erzählungen*. Trans. H. A. Schmiede. Hamburg: buntbuch-Verlag, 1982.

————. *Mavi Maske.* Istanbul: Can, 1988.

————. *Die blaue Maske.* Trans. Carl Koß. Hamburg: Sammlung Luchterhand, 1991.

————. *Glaube, Liebe Aircondition. Eine türkische Kindheit.* Trans. Cornelia Holfelder-von der Tann. Hamburg: Sammlung Luchterhand, 1991.

————. *Die Zunge der Berge.* Trans. Jeremy Gaines and Klaus Binder. Hamburg: Sammlung Luchterhand, 1994.

Özdamar, Emine Sevgi. *Mutterzunge.* Berlin: Rotbuch Verlag, 1990.

————. *Das Leben ist eine Karawanserei hat zwei Türen aus einer kam ich rein aus der anderen ging ich raus.* Cologne: Kiepenheuer & Witsch, 1992.

————. "Schwarzauge und sein Esel." *Die Zeit,* March 9, 1993, 21.

————. *Mother Tongue.* Trans. Craig Thomas. Toronto: Coach House Press, 1994.

Padden, Carol A. "Folk Explanation in Language Survival." In *Collective Remembering,* ed. David Middleton and Derek Edwards, 190–202. London: Sage, 1990.

Parati, Graziella. "Looking through Non-Western Eyes: Immigrant Women's Autobiographical Narratives in Italian." In *Writing New Identities: Gender, Nation, and Immigration in Contemporary Europe,* ed. Gisela Brinker-Gabler and Sidonie Smith, 118–42. Minneapolis: University of Minnesota Press, 1997.

Pérez Firmat, Gustavo. *Life-on-the-Hyphen: The Cuban-American Way.* Austin: University of Texas Press, 1994.

Quintana, Alvina E. "Ana Castillo's *The Mixquiahuala Letters*: The Novelist as Ethnographer." In *Criticism in the Borderlands: Studies in Chicano Literature, Culture, and Ideology,* ed. Héctor Calderón and José David Saldívar, 72–83. Durham: Duke University Press, 1991.

Ricoeur, Paul. "Psychoanalysis and the Movement of Contemporary Culture." Trans. Willis Domingo. In *The Conflict of Interpretations,* ed. Dan Ihde, 121–59. Evanston: Northwestern University Press, 1974.

Rodriguez, Richard. *Hunger of Memory: The Autobiography of Richard Rodriguez.* Boston: David R. Godine, 1982.

Rosaldo, Renato. *Culture and Truth: The Remaking of Social Analysis.* Boston: Beacon Press, 1989.

Rushdie, Salman. *Imaginary Homelands: Essays and Criticism, 1981–1991.* London: Penguin/Granta, 1991.

Sacks, Oliver. *The Island of the Colorblind.* New York: Vintage, 1997.

Said, Edward W. "The Mind of Winter: Reflections on Life in Exile." *Harper's* 269, no. 1612 (1984): 49–55.

————. *Culture and Imperialism.* New York: Alfred A. Knopf, 1993.

————. *Out of Place: A Memoir.* New York: Alfred A. Knopf, 1999.

Saldívar, Ramón. *Chicano Narrative: The Dialectics of Difference.* Madison: University of Wisconsin Press, 1990.

Schami, Rafik. *Erzähler der Nacht.* Weinheim: Beltz & Geldberg, 1989; Munich: dtv, 1994.

————. *Damascus Nights.* Trans. Philip Boehm. New York: Farrar, Straus and Giroux, 1993.

Schami, Rafik. *Damals dort und heute hier. Über Fremdsein.* Ed. Erich Jooß. Freiburg: Herder, 1998.

Schlegel, Friedrich. *Kritische Ausgabe.* Ed. Ernst Behler. Vol. 2. Paderborn: Schöningh, 1967.

Shea, Renee H. "Traveling Worlds with Edwidge Danticat." In *Poets and Writers* 25, no. 1(1997): 42–51.

Spengemann, William C. *The Forms of Autobiography: Episodes in the History of the Literary Genre.* New Haven: Yale University Press, 1980.

Suleri, Sara. *Meatless Days.* Chicago: University of Chicago Press, 1989.

Terdiman, Richard. *Present Past: Modernity and the Memory Crisis.* Ithaca, N.Y.: Cornell University Press, 1993.

Trouillot, Michel-Rolph. *Silencing the Past: Power and the Production of History.* Boston: Beacon Press, 1995.

Tyler, Stephen A. "Post-modern Ethnography: From Document of the Occult to Occult Document." In *Writing Culture: The Politics and Poetics of Ethnography,* ed. James Clifford and George E. Marcus, 122–40. Berkeley and Los Angeles: University of California Press, 1986.

Widmann, Arno. "Why Don't the Germans Love to Read Their Own New Writers?" *European,* January 28–February 3, 1994, 12–13.

Wong, Sau-ling Cynthia. "Kingston's Handling of Traditional Chinese Sources." In *Approaches to Teaching "The Woman Warrior."* ed. Shirley Geok-lin Lim, 26–36. New York: Modern Language Association, 1991.

———. "Autobiography as Guided Chinatown Tour? Maxine Hong Kingston's *The Woman Warrior* and Chinese-American Autobiographical Controversy." In *Multicultural Autobiography: American Lives,* ed. James Robert Payne, 248–79. Knoxville: University of Tennessee Press, 1992.

Young, James. *The Texture of Memory: Holocaust Memorials and Meaning.* New Haven: Yale University Press, 1993.

———. *The Art of Memory: Holocaust Memorials in History.* New York: Prestel-Verlag, 1994.

Zadworna Fjellestad, Danuta. " 'The Insertion of the Self into the Space of Borderless Possibility': Eva Hoffman's Exiled Body." *MELUS* 20 (summer 1995): 133–47.

Zelizer, Barbie. *Remembering to Forget: Holocaust Memory through the Camera's Eye.* Chicago: University of Chicago Press, 1998.

Zimmerman, Marc. *U.S. Latino Literature: An Essay and Annotated Bibliography.* Chicago: MARCH/Abrazo Press, 1992.

Halbwachs, Maurice, 17, 153

Hartman, Geoffrey, 141; on technology and memory, 39, 40; works on the Holocaust, 164n24;

Hassan, Ihab, *Out of Egypt*, 93

Hegel, G.W.F., 49, *Die Phänomenologie des Geistes* (Phenomenology of the Spirit), 134

Heine, Heinrich, 42–43, 70

hermeneutics, 142; of culture, 38; literary, 154, Romantic, 132. *See also* Gadamer; Ricoeur

Herodotus, *Histories*, 41

heteroglossia, 116–17. *See also* Bakhtin

Hijuelos, Oscar, 8, 18, 68, 69, 70; *Our House in the Last World*, 78–82

historiography, 57, 60–61, 62, 65, 161n1; critical, 38; poetic, 63

history: in Benjamin, 34–35, 131, 151–52; censored, 150; and memory, 31, 33–35, 38–40, 61, 62;

Hoffman, Eva, 10, 18, 68, 69, 70; *Lost in Translation*, 88–94

Hoffmann, E.T.A., *Der Sandmann* (The Sandman), 25

Holocaust, 39, 40, 92; books on memory of, 164n24

Hutcheon, Linda, on parody, 111

Huyssen, Andreas, *Twilight Memories*, 40

hybridity, 5, 121, 159; cultural, 51

hyphen, 15, 76, 78

hyphenation, 71, 159

identity: collective, 28, 95; cultural, 12, 66, 69, 122, 126, 127, 130, 136, 137, 143, 145; ethnic, 51, 66, 111, 150; national, 20, 28, 51, 68, 126, 150

interlinguality (interlingualism), 19, 107, 108, 163n34. *See also* Bruce-Novoa

island(s): cultures of, 18, 29, 50, 62; memories of, 50–64

Jooß, Erich, interview with Rafik Schami, 41, 47–48

Kafka, Franz, 18; in Gilles Deleuze and Félix Guattari's *Kafka: Toward a Minor Literature*, 23–24, 27–28; in Libuše Moníková's *Pavane für eine verstorbene Infantin*, 84, 85, 86–87

Kalevala, 8

Kant, Immanuel, 24

Kaplan, Caren: on autobiography, 18; "Resisting Autobiography: Out-Law Genres and Transnational Feminist Subjects," 95, 96

Kassem, Abd al-Karim, 46

Khalil, Iman O., 165n35

Khatibi, Abdelkebir, 8, 158; *Love in Two Languages*, 91, 96

Kingston, Maxine Hong, 18, 68, 69, 70, 88, 158; *China Men*, 72; on ghosts and the fantastic, 94; *The Woman Warrior*, 66, 69–78, 82, 88, 93, 94, 95

Kipling, Rudyard, 14

Kitaj, R.B., *First Diasporist Manifesto*, 12

Kristeva, Julia, 18, 26, 130; on the foreigner, 69; on psychoanalysis, 38; on symbolic denominators of memory, 128–29

Kulthum, Umm, 45

labor migration: Mexican, 19, 104–6, 126; Turkish, 19, 99–101, 102, 104–6, 111, 112, 126

Laclos, Choderlos de, *Les liaisons dangereuses*, 60

Le Goff, Jacques, *History and Memory*, 38–39, 104

Lévinas, Emmanuel, 6

Lewis, Bernard, 167n10, 173n20

Lidoff, Joan, on Kingston's *Warrior Woman*, 70, 71

Lionnet, Françoise, 67, 173n17

literature(s), diasporic, exilic, transnational (definitions of), 9–13

loss, 9, 16, 19, 28, 47, 65, 70, 82, 84, 86, 91, 114, 126, 139, 152, 153, 158; psychology of, 13

Lotman, Yurij, and B.A. Uspensky, on culture, 15, 16

Lukács, Georg, 28, 102, 163n9

Maalouf, Amin, 8

Marcus, George E., and Michael M.J. Fischer. *See* Fischer

Marx, Karl, 101, 112

McKenna, Teresa, 19

MELUS (*Multiethnic Literatures of the United States*), 9

memory: ancestral, 20, 94, 103; collective, 8, 11, 12, 13, 37, 38, 39, 51, 60, 107, 117, 128, 138, 142, 145, 153; communal, 13, 40, 73, 74, 126, 141, 150; community, 16, 17 18, 142; emancipatory, 34–35, 44; linguistic,

The Thousand and One Nights, 43, 44, 45
trauma, 18, 38, 82, 127, 139; border, 101
translatability, 123, 148, 155–57; cultural, 43
translation: in Benjamin, 71, 77, 155–56;
    cultural, 77, 78, 92, 156; of self, 71,
    87, 92
Trouillot, Michel-Rolph, 55, 57, 161n1
Turkey, history of, 20, 122, 138, 143,
    145–47
Turkish-German literature, 19, 101–2,
    105–6. *See also* Özdamar; Özakin
Turks of Germany (Turkish-Germans),
    100–102
Tyler, Stephen, 132, 154

untranslatability, 13, 144, 148, 157
Uspensky, B.A., and Yurij Lotman. *See* Lot-
    man

Widmann, Arno, 148
Wong, Sau-ling Cynthia: on Kingston's
    Woman Warrior, 73
writing, and memory, 49–50. *See also*
    Gadamer

Zadworna Fjellestad, Danuta, on Eva Hoff-
    man's *Lost in Translation*, 92, 93
Zimmerman, Marc, on Chicano/a literature,
    112, 171n31